Boomer Marketing

Baby boomers (consumers in the 50+ age bracket) are the wealthiest, fastest growing consumer group in the world. Despite this, the vast majority of marketing spend is focused on much younger people.

Recessions always dampen consumer spending, but in the twenty-first century's first recession, the decline in spending among the younger age group has been amplified by excessive borrowing and collapsing house prices. More so than ever before, the current global recession highlights the need for firms to revise their marketing strategies and practices in order to remain competitive. In this book, Ian Chaston uses original case material to propose strategic solutions that take advantage of the moneyed segments of the maturing boomer market. Key topics covered include:

- Marketing errors made by UK banks in the current global crisis
- Market research
- Customer targeting
- Marketing strategies and pricing innovation
- Promotion and distribution

A world first, *Boomer Marketing* is useful for students of marketing and consumer behaviour and is essential reading for practitioners who understand the need for money-oriented marketing.

Ian Chaston is Managing Director of Plymouth University's spin off company and a Research Professor at Centrum Catolica, Peru. He has a wealth of international experience in marketing and has authored 12 books and over 100 journal articles.

Boomer Marketing
Selling to a recession resistant market

Ian Chaston

Routledge
Taylor & Francis Group
LONDON AND NEW YORK

First published 2009
by Routledge
2 Park Square, Milton Park, Abingdon, Oxon OX14 4RN

Simultaneously published in the USA and Canada
by Routledge
270 Madison Ave, New York, NY 10016

Routledge is an imprint of the Taylor & Francis Group, an informa business

© 2009 Ian Chaston

Typeset in Times New Roman by
Swales & Willis Ltd, Exeter, Devon
Printed and bound in Great Britain by
CPI Antony Rowe, Chippenham, Wiltshire

British Library Cataloguing in Publication Data
A catalogue record for this book is available from the British Library

Library of Congress Cataloguing in Publication Data
Chaston, Ian.
    Boomer marketing: selling to a recession resistant market/Ian Chaston.
        p. cm.
    Includes bibliographical references and index.
    1. Market segmentation—United States.   2. Target marketing—United States.
    3. Middle-aged consumers—United States.   4. Baby boom generation—
    United States.   I. Title.
    HF5415.127.C53 2009
    658.8′04—dc22   2008051952

ISBN10: 0–415–48962–8 (hbk)
ISBN10: 0–415–48963–6 (pbk)
ISBN10: 0–203–87639–3 (ebk)

ISBN13: 978–0–415–48962–1 (hbk)
ISBN13: 978–0–415–48963–8 (pbk)
ISBN13: 978–0–203–87639–8 (ebk)

Contents

Figures and tables

Figures

Tables

Preface

Despite the brand wars between companies such as Pepsi-Cola vs. Coca-Cola or McDonald's vs. Burger King, sustained profitability is rarely achieved by entering into prolonged promotional battles to gain a minor increase in market share. The probability of an adverse financial outcome from such activities is even higher in a developed economy exhibiting population ageing where the battlefield is a mature market containing customers in the 18–49 age group. The reason why such activities offer a poor financial return was articulated at a conference by AG Lafley, the chief executive of one of the giants in the world of consumer marketing, the American Procter & Gamble Corporation. In his speech he stated that 'for decades, our industry took for granted that population growth in the developed countries would deliver a substantial part of the sales growth. Few imagined the day would come when we would see zero population growth – let alone decline – in major markets. Yet that is what we are facing today' (Prystay and Ellison 2003).

Mr Lafley went on to explain that although developing countries continue to exhibit population growth, profitability is a major problem because achievable prices for branded consumer goods are typically half that which can be achieved in developed nation economies. In the face of poor sales and profit among Proctor & Gamble's traditional target market of the 18–49 age group, the company is now redirecting marketing efforts towards more affluent older consumers in developed nations through actions such as the launch of a toothpaste formulated for older women, called 'Rejuvenating Effects' and investing in major promotional campaigns in Europe and the USA to exploit the market success being enjoyed by the company's Olay range of anti-ageing products.

Proctor & Gamble is probably one of a minority of branded consumer goods companies which have already begun to shift away from the conventional practice which has lasted for many years of primarily targeting the 18–49 year age group. Those companies which have not recognized the implications of needing to shift their marketing activities towards older financially more attractive consumers now face a even greater problem; namely the impact of a global recession which will probably be the most severe since the Great Depression in the 1930s. Recessions always dampen total consumer spending, but in the twenty-first century's first recession, the decline in spending among the 18–49 year old age group will be much greater than has been experienced in previous economic downturns. This is because the 18–49 year age group is facing the problem of having to repay the huge level of personal borrowings which they accumulated over the previous 10+ years due to the excessively lax lending practices by the financial institutions. In addition, this consumer group, having paid extremely high prices for their homes with the purchase funded in many cases by 100–120 per cent mortgages, now face a massive decline in the value of their homes. This latter, highly adverse situation has further reduced consumer confidence which, in turn, has depressed the level of spending in consumer markets in sectors such as apparel, household appliances and travel.

To succeed in marketing products and services to financially attractive consumers (FACs), there is a requirement to adopt somewhat different marketing practices relative to those which have been in use among the consumer goods companies over the last 50 years to achieve a high brand share among the 18–49 year age group. Hence, the focus of this text is to describe the revisions in marketing theories and practices that are required in order to successfully market products and services to FACs, the most important of whom for the foreseeable future in developed economies are individuals aged 50+. In this text, this 50+ group are referred to as 'maturing boomers'.

Chapter 1 provides an introduction about how changing demographics and consumer wealth are creating new market opportunities. The limited data which exist on how a shift in wealth between age groups can impact buyer behaviour does create certain difficulties when attempting to develop a successful marketing plan. Using case materials, a marketing management process model is presented to demonstrate one approach to developing a strong loyal customer base among FACs. Research techniques described in standard marketing texts and the methodologies often employed by market research firms are usually reliant upon the acquisition and analysis of large, quantitative datasets. Application of these methodologies does create certain problems when researching financially more attractive consumers. This is because these customer groups tend to be constituted of individuals who exhibit extremely heterogeneous buyer behaviours. Hence, marketers need to rely less upon traditional, large scale postal surveys and utilize alternative methodologies to gain insights into the impact of personal financial wealth on consumer consumption patterns. Chapter 2 attempts to achieve this aim by presenting a variety of techniques relevant to researching the FAC.

The destiny of all firms is determined by factors in the external environment over which they have little or no control. Chapter 3 provides a description of how to assess the opportunities and risks associated with the impact of macro-environmental variables on FACs. Only the most extreme of marketing purists still believe customer need is the only variable which should drive all aspects of the marketing process. Available real world evidence indicates success is more probable when firms concurrently focus upon exploiting superior internal competences. Chapter 4 presents the concept of competence assessment and how identified strengths or weaknesses can provide the basis for supporting a successful marketing strategy. As FACs are a more heterogeneous customer group than people aged 18–49, Chapter 5 presents a review of various approaches for identifying the FAC segments. The coverage of segmentation is orientated towards selecting criteria which permit conversion of acquired data into viable targeting and positioning decisions. Chapter 6 examines how firms, by combining their understanding of the external business climate, different consumer segments and internal competencies, can evolve an appropriate marketing strategy for exploiting the spending behaviour of FACs.

Entrance into a new market sector may require changing a firm's current product(s) or internal processes. Chapter 7 examines the identification and implementation of an effective innovation plan that can lead to the creation of a product line appropriate for meeting the needs of the FAC. Building awareness upon entry into a new market or when launching a new product is a critical activity. Chapter 8 examines why promotional campaigns, in order to be effective, must reflect consumer target sensitivities and expectations. The chapter also reviews how the internet can be a mechanism for overcoming the audience size decline and fragmentation which is occurring in terrestrial promotional channels. Many firms assume price competition can provide an effective strategy for building a larger market share. Chapter 9 examines a more sophisticated approach to pricing that can generate a more profitable return to the company. The chapter also reviews the selection and implementation of an optimal distribution strategy.

A feature of the 50+ age group is their demand for services to stay fit, active, and most importantly, to remain young looking. Chapter 10 examines the growing services provision opportunities in the fitness, health and beauty markets. Although academics and marketers are inclined to believe consumer markets are more exciting and sophisticated, significant opportunities also exist in business-to-business (B2B) markets. Chapter 11 reviews how B2B firms can meet the growing demand from their supply chain customers to support strategies for exploiting new market opportunities involving financially attractive consumers. The eventual overall impact of the current global economic crisis cannot yet be forecasted with any degree of accuracy. Nevertheless, there are certain macro-environmental factors which will significantly influence consumer markets for the foreseeable future. Hence, Chapter 12 reviews some of these issues, including how the economic downturn will influence buying behaviour, consumers' ongoing commitment to environmental issues, the implications of rising energy prices and the related issue of global warming.

The standard structure of each chapter is to first present a summary of the key marketing concepts associated with marketing to FACs. This is followed in each chapter by a presentation of relevant managerial concepts. These are complimented by 'real world' case materials to demonstrate the practical validity of how companies can utilize conceptual frameworks to assist in the creation and implementation of marketing management practices to successfully exploit the older FACs, i.e. the maturing boomers. The primary readership target for the text is college students studying for an undergraduate or postgraduate degree, which contains one or more modules which take the student beyond the basic principles of marketing management theory. Individuals participating in executive postgraduate programmes, having gained an understanding of the basic principles of traditional marketing management in an earlier introductory module, will also benefit from using this text to expand their knowledge of the new marketing principles involved in responding to changes in the allocation of wealth across consumer populations. The secondary readership target is company executives and marketing practitioners who wish to be provided with new frameworks that can support more effective exploitation of consumer markets following the instability in consumer spending which has emerged following the banking crisis and global economic downturn.

References

Prystay, C. and Ellison, S. (2003) 'Time for marketers to grow up?', *Wall Street Journal*, 27 February, B1.

1 Financially attractive markets

Generic principles of marketing to financially attractive consumers (FACs)

The coverage of issues in Chapter 1 is designed to illustrate the generic principles of marketing to FACs in relation to:

1 Twenty-first century marketing is concerned with identifying and meeting the needs of consumers with adequate spending power.
2 Mass marketing has become a less appropriate philosophy through which to exploit the opportunities which exist within financially attractive consumer markets.
3 Sustained involvement in mature consumer markets competing on the basis of offering standard products or services will eventually lead to erosion in company profitability.
4 Emerging nation consumer markets are very different from their Western nation equivalents and over the longer term may offer limited, financially viable opportunities to many of the world's existing multinational corporations.
5 Government data can provide an effective, low cost source of data that can be utilized to identify the nature, scale and expenditure trends within financially attractive consumer markets.
6 Compared with the less fortunate members of society, FACs exhibit a much more diverse range of product and service needs.
7 Compared with the less fortunate members of society, FACs place much strong emphasis on product performance, quality and purchase convenience in their selection of product and service suppliers.
8 Financially attractive consumer market needs can change quite significantly in a relatively short space of time. This requires suppliers to exhibit an entrepreneurial, innovative marketing orientation in order to identify and rapidly respond to indications of an emerging trend shift in these market sectors.

Exploiting demand

During the latter stages of the Industrial Revolution, some major companies achieved a leadership position by moving before their competitors to exploit emerging or changing customer needs. In the USA during the nineteenth century, for example, Sears Roebuck created their mail order catalogue business in response to the growing demand for domestic goods from immigrants settling in new lands west of the Mississippi (Moon 2005). Then as the rate of urbanization began to accelerate, the company began to open a chain of department stores which eventually spanned the entire country. A similar proactive strategy of exploiting demand was illustrated by Henry Ford when he recognized the market potential which existed for an affordable automobile. This led to the creation of the mass production manufacturing philosophy used to produce his revolutionary Model T motor car (Raff 1991).

By the end of the Second World War, the accepted managerial philosophy within major corporations, especially those based in the USA, was that the greatest financial rewards from meeting unsatisfied consumer needs would come from exploiting markets characterized by rising customer numbers, increasing *per capita* income and preferably, a relatively low level of competition. Over the 20-year period from 1945 to 1965, the outstanding growth rates achieved in consumer markets around the world by major corporations such as Pepsi-Cola, Proctor & Gamble, Unilever, General Foods and Nestlé all demonstrated the validity of this managerial philosophy. Furthermore, as evidenced by firms such as Polaroid and Apple, these markets offered huge opportunities if a company was able to exploit new technology ahead of competition to achieve market leadership (Hamilton 2003).

A very important influence behind the success of these companies during the period immediately following the Second World War was that consumers in America and Western Europe were beginning to enjoy an unprecedented increase in *per capita* income, falling unemployment levels and a rate of economic growth which permitted Government to fund the provision of free or low cost welfare services across areas such as healthcare and education. Accompanying this period of economic boom was a significant increase in the number of children being born. This population trend led to individuals being born during this period becoming known as 'baby boomers' (Stern *et al.* 1987). Although there is some dispute about exactly which individuals can be considered to be members of the baby boomer generation, most sociologists attribute the label to those persons born between 1946 and 1964.

Academics and marketing practitioners have always been interested in the baby boomers because they were the first generation: (a) where the majority of their parents enjoyed the benefits of secure, well paid, permanent employment and (b) who themselves, were the first ever group in the world to be exposed to television advertising from the day they were born. The massive buying power of households containing baby boomers explains why, even now, many large consumer goods companies still consider their primary target market is the 18–49 year age group (Keller and Kotler 2006).

Sustaining profitability

Once a market moves into maturity, the intensity of competition will often lead to most firms facing declining profitability. The reason for this outcome is that to retain the loyalty of their existing customers in the face of the threat posed by competitors, firms will have to continually increase their level of promotional expenditure. In many cases, this activity is accompanied by either a reduction in unit price or an increase in the level of sales promotion activity. Financial performance is often further weakened because marketers, similar to generals on the Western Front in the First World War, favour the tactic of mounting resource intensive, frontal assaults upon well entrenched competition (Kotler and Singh 1981). The outcome of this strategy is usually a spiralling of promotional expenditure without either party gaining any significant increase in market share. Examples of such events are the brand wars, which regularly break out between firms such as McDonald's vs. Burger King and Pepsi-Cola vs. Coca-Cola.

The bank wars

Case Aims: To illustrate that there are rarely any real financial benefits to be achieved by companies triggering brand wars in mature markets.

In most cases, the usual outcome of brands entering into head-to-head confrontations in a mature market is that there is rarely any fundamental increase in a company's total number of customers, but the cost of the war will be reflected in all parties facing a reduction in operating profits (Thompson 1999). The deregulation of the UK financial services sector in the 1980s was eventually to lead exactly to this depressing outcome. Deregulation caused the UK banks to become much more interested in using mass marketing techniques to attract additional business. By the 1990s, some of Britain's leading High Street banks were engaged in fierce battles to steal each other's retail customers. In the case of NatWest, having triggered a promotional spending spiral by entering into an unsuccessful battle for market leadership with Barclays, the bank's weakened financial position was a contributor to the bank eventually being taken over by the Royal Bank of Scotland in 1999. Instead of learning from the NatWest mistake, another brand war broke out between financial institutions seeking to achieve market leadership in the UK consumer mortgage market. The existing traditional UK consumer mortgage model was based upon lending depositors' money to borrowers who wanted to buy their own home. Essentially, market leadership was based upon being able to attract more consumers to open savings accounts, which in turn then permitted the institution to fund more mortgages than the competition. Then Mr Applegate, then the CEO at Northern Rock, had the apparently brilliant idea of borrowing money in the short-term money markets, where prevailing interest rates were much lower than the rates being paid to savers (Anon 2007). These cheaper funds could then be used to offer mortgages at a lower interest rate than other mortgage lenders in the market. The outcome was that Northern Rock embarked on a battle for market share which saw Mr Applegate being lionised in the financial press for bringing more aggressive, modern thinking into the conservative world of UK banking (Urry 2003). All was going to plan until 2007. Then the sub-prime mortgage disaster in the USA caused banks to become increasingly wary about lending money to each other. Money became scarce and short-term interest rates rose dramatically. This left Northern Rock in the position of being unable to pay off loans that were coming due or to raise additional loans to service the institution's rising cost of the money market debts which had already been incurred. As word spread about the problem, there was a run on Northern Rock as worried UK consumers rushed to remove their savings. The queues that formed outside Northern Rock, the country's fifth-biggest mortgage lender, represented the first bank run in Britain since 1866 (Anon 2007). The chancellor Alistair Darling's attempts to reassure savers seemed to only to lengthen the queues of people outside Northern Rock branches demanding to get their money out of the bank. The run did not stop until Mr Darling gave a taxpayer-backed guarantee that all the existing deposits at Northern Rock were safe. Nevertheless, as the scale of the problem within Northern Rock became known to the UK Treasury and the financial regulators, in the end the only way that the UK Government was able to resolve the situation was to nationalize the bank (Ritson 2007).

The lesson that both senior managers and marketers should learn from such events is that the best response to a brand war is usually to stand back, wait until the dust has settled and then move in to exploit the opportunities created by those firms whose financial position has been weakened. Regretfully it is often the case that the CEOs of one or more of the largest companies perceive a brand war as a personal affront to their reputation and hence seek to become embroiled in the battle. Such was the case with HBOS which was created when Royal Bank of Scotland acquired Halifax, one of the UK's largest mortgage lenders. The HBOS CEO, Mr Andy Hornby, had established a reputation for being extremely aggressive in his response to any threat from competitors. Hence when it was understood that Northern Rock was achieving market share growth by borrowing short-term funds via the money markets, Mr Hornby's reaction was to duplicate the model. As a consequence, this decision sparked off a bank war between most of the mortgage lenders in the UK banking system. In mid-September 2008, after a huge collapse in the value of HBOS shares, the only viable solution was for the UK Government to assist the bank to consider a takeover offer from the more conservatively managed Lloyds TSB. Explaining the demise of HBOS, Mr Hornby was quoted as stating 'we found ourselves impacted by the wholesale market shutting down. We were particularly dependent upon wholesale funding' (Anon 2008). This was not a particularly surprising statement given that HBOS in their fight to retain market domination had by September 2008 created a lending gap of almost £200 billion between the bank's mortgage assets and liabilities.

Eventually in most market sectors, leading firms tend to accept that brand wars are of little benefit and begin to seek alternative ways of sustaining profitability. In most large organizations, the preference of senior managers is to rely on marketing practices which have been important in delivering success in the past (Zajac and Shortell 1989). Thus, when major brands perceive their older, well established markets have entered maturity, many decide to 'follow the money' by attempting to identify new markets exhibiting evidence of higher, future potential consumer spending. The corporate memories of the golden years of mass marketing in Western nation economies caused many large companies to favour markets where there were indications of increasing numbers of middle-class people in the 18–49 age group who are expected to enjoy rising *per capita* incomes over time.

Hence in the 1990s, following the advent of perestroika and demolition of the Berlin Wall, the popular, preferred market option was Russia. Unfortunately, the cultural conditions were not that which Western managers had expected following the collapse of a communist state. They assumed democratization would lead to the emergence of a free market. Instead, organized crime, in many cases working alongside the old communist party bosses, created an environment similar to that which had prevailed in places such as Chicago, USA, during prohibition (O'Connor 1993). The situation further worsened following the election of President Putin because he instigated a Government policy of severely restricting the activities of foreign corporations. In some cases this has led to contracts being arbitrarily cancelled and even assets repossessed. As a result, companies such as BP and brands such as McDonald's have failed to achieve the scale of financial reward in Russia to which they originally aspired.

Russian risks

Case Aims: To illustrate the uncertainty and risks associated with Western firms seeking to achieve ongoing revenue growth by entering the Russian market.

In a review of the lessons learned concerning Russia's response to the entry of foreign firms since the collapse of the Soviet Union at the beginning of the 1990s, Schlevogt (2000) has proposed there are number of sociopolitical factors which can lead to adverse outcomes for foreign investors. He notes that the election of President Putin with his KGB background and the support he has received from the army has resulted in the re-building of a powerful autocratic system that intends to re-assert the nation's sovereignty. One likely outcome is that over the long term, Russians will, where possible, try to avoid having to rely on overseas firms, continuing to operate inside the country. The country's approach to privatization, which in theory was designed to achieve democratization of the Russian economy, has led to a small number of individuals known as the oligarchs who, with their close links to Government officials and politicians, were able to gain control of huge industrial operations at extremely favourable prices. As well as making huge 'paper profits' on their acquisitions, these oligarchs have apparently also been successful in avoiding paying significant amounts of tax on their trading profits. In terms of foreign firms seeking to survive in this environment, Schlevogt points out that:

> Foreign investment regulations often are confusing and contradictory. Government officials at all levels change frequently and are often inexperienced. Property rights remain unclear . . . And law enforcement is highly unreliable. The Mafia often fills this vacuum with its own laws.

[He concludes that:]

> . . . the political situation reminds me very much of the ill-fated Weimar Republic in Germany in the 1920s.

A stark illustration of how an essentially authoritarian regime can determine the fortunes of even large internal corporations is provided by the project to exploit the huge energy deposits on Sakhalin Island on Russia's Pacific sea coast (Lustgarten 2007). In 1996 when Western firms were still optimistic that democratization was creating a free market economy in Russia, and oil was trading at $22 a barrel, Royal Dutch Shell signed a contract that gave the Shell-controlled Sakhalin Energy Investment Corporation the rights to recoup all costs plus achieve a 17.5 per cent rate of return on the investment before Russia would start receiving revenue from oil being pumped from the fields in the region. Unfortunately, Shell does seem to have made some major mistakes in terms of a poor safety record, a failure to meet expectations about infrastructure improvements and damaging the local environment. Shell also encountered technical problems and apparent reversals of opinion by Russia's Natural Resources Ministry which led to a doubling in the estimated costs of bringing the Sakhalin fields on stream. To compound Shell's problems, however, the rapid rise in world oil prices led to a shift in political thinking about permitting foreign ownership of energy reserves in Russia. This meant Shell's days of remaining in control were clearly numbered. Hence, few industry observers were surprised when in 2006, Shell was forced to sell their controlling interest in the Sakhalin project for $20 billion to the huge, state owned, Gazprom organization.

A common outcome of disappointing business performance in Russia was that many multinationals switched their attentions to the consumer markets which are emerging in China and India. Here again, although firms were initially welcomed with open arms, once economic growth has been established, their respective Governments have acted to avoid their economies becoming dominated by foreign investors (Atkinson 2004). Furthermore, in the case of China, it has repeatedly been demonstrated by the behaviour of this country's various authoritarian rulers over the past 300 years, the nation's philosophy is orientated towards the perspective that once their domestic firms have acquired the necessary skills to operate effectively in a specific industrial sector, the ongoing presence of foreign companies will no longer be looked upon with favour.

Seeking to justify the view that China's middle classes are very interested in purchasing Western goods, executives point to the success of fast-food operations such as McDonald's and KFC, or fashion brands such as Gucci and Prada. What appears to be ignored in any conclusions about fast-food products in developing economies is that sales are usually an expression, mainly among younger people, of being seen to be more cosmopolitan (Anon 1996). In relation to premium priced fashion goods, the Chinese are behaving in the same way as people in the rest of the world; namely very wealthy individuals who are enjoying massively high incomes exhibit a purchase behaviour based upon wishing to demonstrate their superior financial position to the rest of society (Anon 2005). What should be of concern to Western executives is the growing evidence that Chinese consumers are actually very loyal to their own domestic suppliers (Wang and Chen 2004). Where examples are identified of international brands being favoured by Chinese consumers, this usually occurs when the overseas company is perceived to be offering significantly superior quality products relative to equivalent offerings from China's domestic suppliers.

Possibly of even greater concern is that executives in some major Western corporations who have expressed huge enthusiasm for investing in China seem unaware of the historical events in terms of the repeated implementation of actions by the Oriental nations to rid themselves of what they perceive is the undesirable influence of Westerners. Very frequently, multinational firms express the view that developing nation economies will always continue to need their expertise and technological capabilities. Expression of such views would appear to indicate how quickly Western businesses have forgotten the outcome of when in the 1980s, Japanese firms, with the overt support of their Government, succeeded in replacing Western firms as the dominant players in specific sectors of the world economy such as cars, consumer electronics, computer games, mainframe computing, laptop computers, machine tools, semi-conductors and robotics.

A Japanese history lesson

Case Aims: To illustrate how a Pacific Rim Government has the motivation and ability to create market conditions and industry systems that will overcome the best of the Western nation multinationals in even high technology industries.

In the 1960s when the Japanese Government department responsible for the country's economic development, MITI, decided that computers represented a strategically important business sector, they imposed tariffs and regulations designed to control the entry of foreign suppliers, especially from America, and incentives to ensure Japanese computer companies could establish a strong domestic market base (Hsieh 1994). Recognizing the potential threat posed by IBM, the Japanese Electronic Computer Company was established. This company purchased Japanese computer systems and rented them to domestic companies at rates far lower than IBM's. Over a 20-year period, the Government also allocated $2 billion in low-interest loans to fund R&D within the Japanese computer industry. Until the 1980s, the US computer firms were able to retain market share through offering superior products by utilizing the dynamic random access memory chips (DRAMs) which were also manufactured in America. Then the Japanese, again assisted by their Government, began to invest heavily in developing their own DRAM manufacturing capacity and by the use of very aggressive, usually price-based, competition, overtook America in this critical area of the computer industry. To further ensure market success, it does seem likely that the Japanese chip manufacturers formed a cartel which permitted them to regulate the volume and price of memory chips being made available to American computer manufacturers. The outcome was that by the beginning of the 1990s, firms such as Fujitsu, NEC and Hitachi had become dominant players in the mainframe computer manufacturing industry. Fortunately for America, entrepreneurs such as Steve Jobs at Apple were provided with vital support from individuals such as Andy Grove at Intel who recognized the importance of retaining leadership in the development of the powerful microprocessors needed to support the creation of the desk top computing industry. Although Japan has not yet managed to emulate Intel's success in continually launching even more powerful new generation microprocessors such as the Pentium generation of products, Japanese firms have become successful in the manufacture of low-cost, reliable, standard microchips. This capability has been critical in the success of companies such as Sony and Toshiba in the world's computer laptop market.

Population ageing

When future historians revisit the twenty-first century, one issue to which they will be attracted is the social and economic impact of population ageing (Johnson 2004). This trend reflects the fact that for some years, in many industrialized nations, the average age is rising and older people are becoming the dominant group in most populations. There are two main causes for population ageing; namely longevity and declining birth rates. The longevity factor is mainly explained by improvements in healthcare provision. Since the Second World War, most Governments have created public sector healthcare systems which offer free or subsidized services. Concurrently major advances in medical technology have abolished many of the illnesses which in previous generations caused people to die at a much younger age (Yakita 2001).

On the issue of declining birth rates, explaining why women are having fewer children is a somewhat more complex issue. One influence has been the intro-duction of improved forms of contraception. Another is that more women wish to enjoy a career and may opt to never have children. Additionally because house prices and energy costs have risen steeply in recent years, some people seeking an adequate standard of living have decided children are now an unaffordable luxury.

Acquiring accurate figures about how population ageing impacts a nation's sociodemographics is complicated by the fact that much of the data collected by many Governments uses the arbitrary classification that only people who are 65 or older are retired. Some people, however, are now retiring in their 50s or early 60s. Hence the precise balance between older people in work and those who are retired will not usually be available from Government statistics. Nevertheless, census data can still provide a reasonable indication of the proportion of retirees within a nation's population.

United Nations data show that in 2005, the 65+ age group in both EU and in the UK constituted over 16 per cent of the population. What is of even greater interest, however, is the United Nation's forecast that although the total population in Europe and in the UK will remain virtually unchanged between now and the year 2050, the number of 65+ individuals will increase by 65 per cent. Governments confronted by such forecasts are concerned about what happens as the number of retired people increases and concurrently, the number of people of working age decreases. This is because unless the shrinking number of people in work are prepared to accept major tax increases, public sector revenues will decline. Concurrently as people are living longer, this will place even further pressure on Governments' abilities to fund state pensions and healthcare provision.

Even before the 2008 banking crisis, observers of population ageing were predicting many Governments will soon be facing a potentially massive fiscal crisis (Jensen *et al.* 1995). On average, the cost of public pensions and healthcare benefits consumes 12 per cent of GDP in developed nation economies. This figure is forecasted to rise to 24 per cent of GDP by 2040. Unless significant changes are made in the way Governments operate their welfare systems, funding of this increase in GDP will require the working population to accept at least a 100 per cent increase in their personal tax burden. The potential scale of the impending crisis varies by country. In Europe and Japan, unless there are fundamental changes in Government policy, the crisis will deepen rapidly because low birth rates mean the size of the working population is declining. The USA will be less affected by population ageing because higher birth rates and a liberal immigration policy will result in a continuing expansion of the number of people in employment (Meeks *et al.* 1999).

Until recently, many managers, having become aware of the fiscal problems associated with population ageing, did not realize that as baby boomers have aged and morphed in being maturing boomers, this group offers an exciting new market opportunity. This lack of interest in older people as potential customers tends to be influenced by the incorrect assumption being made about these individuals' interests and lifestyles (Carrigan and Szmigin 1999). Incorrect perceptions are continually being reinforced by the media presenting tragic stories such as pensioners living below the poverty line in unheated apartments or being put into jail for refusing to pay their property taxes. Additional negative images are created by the film industry's preference to characterize older people as individuals with rapidly declining mental faculties left unsupervised in the lounges of residential care homes.

More recently, sociodemographic data from nations around the world has provided clear evidence that in fact, a significant number of older people are active individuals who enjoy a higher standard of living than their younger generation counterparts (Klaase and Van der Vlist 1990). There are two main reasons for this situation. First, many older people who are still in work have reached the maximum earnings point on their organization's salary scale. Additionally in most cases, their living costs have fallen as their children have finally left home. The second factor is that in the case of retirees, many are in receipt of pensions from both the state and their employers. Additionally, some older people downsize their accommodation upon retirement and this action generates another significant incremental source of funds. Data on older peoples' incomes prompted a spokesperson for the Association of Retired Persons (www.arp050.org.uk) to comment that: 'Now is the golden age of seniors. They have never had it so good. As long as people stay healthy, that seems to be their main criterion for happiness. They only start feeling old when they really feel unwell'.

The important economic implications of older people providing a source of financially attractive consumers are illustrated by the fact that in the USA, individuals age 55+ comprise 35 per cent of the adult population, yet control 70 per cent of the net worth of all household assets. Such a high level of wealth is the reason why older people in America feel able to spend over $1 trillion a year on goods and services. A similar scenario is to be found in the UK. Data from the Office for National Statistics reveals that over the period 1996–2004, retiree annual income, adjusted for inflation, rose by 38 per cent. This rate was well in excess of increases in average earnings of employed persons over the same period. Furthermore, by the beginning of the twenty-first century, the highest median income within the entire UK population has become those individuals in the 60–64 age group, while the over 50s now account for 60 per cent of Britain's savings and 80 per cent of all personal assets.

Exploiting changing wealth patterns

Case Aims: To illustrate that some firms in the home construction industry have responded to the opportunities offered by the shift in wealth from the 18–49 age group to the maturing boomers segment.

Until the recent collapse in the entire home building industry in Western nations, the majority of large construction firms were still primarily concerned with building products for purchase by younger age groups. Nevertheless, in recent years there has been increasing evidence that some firms are already reaping the rewards of refocusing their marketing efforts towards moneyed, older people. Probably some of the earliest successes have been achieved in the USA where, for example, construction companies such as Ginn Corporation and developers such as Avatar International have built massive new housing developments in Florida, specifically designed to meet the needs of retirees wanting to escape cold winters in America's northern states. In the assisted living market, there are also a number of very large players such as American Retirement Corporation and Marriott International. One of the current examples of why reliance upon the traditional 18–49 year age group is an increasingly dangerous marketing strategy is provided by recent events in the US housing market. For some years, rapidly rising house prices have been fuelled by low interest rates and the massive expansion of the sub-prime mortgage market created some lenders being willing to offer loans to even the most high-risk borrowers. Starting in 2006, however, higher interest rates and the rising level of loan defaults in the sub-prime sector have combined to burst this economic bubble leading to a massive decline in house prices. With house prices falling by over 25 per cent between the end of 2006 and late 2007, young families have terminated their traditional behaviour of using rising household incomes to move up the housing ladder. By mid-2007, most homebuilders in America were reporting huge financial losses, with many being forced into bankruptcy. Included in the long list of firms reporting very poor financial results is the country's second largest construction company Pulte Homes Inc. The company's founder Bill Pulte first entered the construction industry in 1950 initially just building homes in the Detroit area. For the balance of the twentieth century, the company expanded by focusing upon building large, suburban homes on massive residential greenfield sites around cities such as Atlanta, Chicago and Washington. To sustain the company's growth over the years, it has entered 54 metro markets across 28 states making a huge investment in both building land and houses under construction. In any contracting market the value of these assets would fall and servicing the company borrowings become increasingly problematic (Kerwin 2005). In 2002, the company appointed Richard

Dugas as the new CEO. Under his leadership, the company has introduced a number of managerial and strategic innovations. Included in these was the recognition of opportunities available in the maturing boomer market. Fortunately, a year prior to Dugas's appointment, the company had acquired a small company, Dell Webb Corporation, which specialized in the construction of retirement properties for blooming boomers. This acquisition was used as the platform to rapidly accelerate Pulte Homes' efforts to recover from having focused for far too long on building homes for the 18–49 year age group. Relying upon the expertise contained with the Dell Webb subsidiary, the company followed their existing strategy of acquiring a large tract of land and then building a complete community. In the case of maturing boomer projects, included in every development were amenities such as a golf course, recreation centre, a social hall and a diverse range of outdoor recreation facilities. By 2006, Dell Webb had opened 42 such communities generating 37 per cent of Pulte's total revenue and very possibly, the majority of the corporation's total profits.

In the UK, McCarthy and Stone was one of the first major construction firms to ignore the conventional industry philosophy of building houses for young families and instead have become a very large national operation by specializing in the construction of self-contained, sheltered accommodation for financially secure, older people. This firm is now diversifying into building intermediate care units where additional support such as basic nursing can be provided to owner-occupiers. The company's demonstration of the opportunities which exist in the UK eventually attracted the attentions of the Scottish entrepreneur Sir Tom Watson. In the summer of 2006, he joined forces with the bank HBOS and venture capitalists, the Reuben Brothers, to make a £1 billion+ take-over bid for the business. This is not Watson's only acquisition in the consumer markets focusing on meeting the needs of older, financially attractive consumers. He purchased the Wyevale Garden Centre chain specifically because gardening is most popular among 50+ individuals. He has also admitted that his team are researching additional deals because they perceive older people as an extremely lucrative market.

Revising corporate attitudes

The conventional large firm model of offering a universal specification, branded product accompanied by heavy promotional spending still remains an appropriate tactic for building market share in those sectors where customers continue to exhibit unchanging needs for a standard product. This approach, known as 'mass marketing', is financially attractive because domination of a large consumer market creates economies of scale that can generate significant profits. These profits then provide large firms with sufficient financial resources to react strongly to any potential threats posed by competitors.

In the case of the financially attractive consumer markets, companies will have to reconsider the validity of adopting a mass marketing philosophy. First, as has been demonstrated by many luxury brands (e.g. Mercedes Benz, Yves St Laurent), customers who have above average wealth tend to exhibit purchase behaviour reflecting a much more diversified set of product needs. Second, many people aged 50+ no longer conform to the traditional stereotype image of becoming white haired couples, sitting in rocking chairs, waiting for their grandchildren to stop by. Instead, many wish to implement a complete change in lifestyle. In some cases this transition can result in becoming much less conventional than their more conservative offspring (Doka 1992).

One illustration of this trend for older people living life to the full is provided by the website of Howard and Marika Stone at www.2young2retire.com. The philosophy of these two individuals, authors of the best selling book *Too Young to Retire* (Penguin 2004), is reflected by the following quote from their website:

> Call it retirement if you insist – although renaissance or renewal are more accurate, as we see it. That's what we're talking about! Our goal is to inspire and motivate you to think differently about so-called retirement planning, to go beyond financial advice and portfolio adjustments (important though they are), and explore what matters to you, what you really, really want to do with the rest of your life – the 20 or more years of an extended lifespan.

The SAGA saga

Case Aims: To illustrate the scale of success enjoyed by an early first mover into the maturing boomer market.

A well established rule of marketing is that the most effective path to achieving and retaining a leadership position is to enter a new market well ahead of competition. In relation to the maturing boomer market, possibly one of the best examples of this rule is provided by UK diversified leisure and financial services company, SAGA Ltd (Aslet 2007). Launched over 50 years ago, Saga's first service market proposition was based upon the provision of holidays specifically designed to meet the needs of older people at a time when other holiday firms were focusing all of their attention of the package holiday market for the 18–49 year age group. The first products offered by the company founder, Sydney de Haan, were low cost coach trips to the seaside. Within only a few years after launch, Saga recognized that an increasing number of older couples, instead of wishing to visit a UK seaside resort or taking a coach tour around England, could afford to travel to more exotic holiday locations. Hence, the firm moved into offering a range of overseas travel packages and, subsequently, also entered the cruise ship market. The company has always been aware of the importance of using appropriate promotional vehicles to establish and sustain effective communication links with their customers. Initially they used products such as direct mailings and free newsletters. To further upgrade the information provision capabilities, in 1984 the firm launched *Saga Magazine*. The publication now has 600,000 paying subscribers and is second only to *Readers Digest* for a paid magazine circulation in the UK. This success has been followed by the introduction of their own website and more recently, the establishment of Saga Radio in Glasgow and the Midlands. Consolidation of a leadership position often depends upon broadening the product line in order to exploit customers' other needs for products or services. Having recognized that older people are seeking a whole range of additional products and services, since the early 1980s, Saga has moved into new market sectors, such as insurance, investments and web-based retailing. In those cases where it lacked the resources and expertise to supply a service, they formed a partnership with an existing major provider (e.g. offering Saga brand savings accounts in partnership with a UK Building Society). Saga's commercial success in exploiting the retiree market led to the venture capital firm Charterhouse Development Capital buying the business for £1.4 billion in 2004. In recent years, Saga has faced increasing competition from other holiday firms who have finally realized the more profitable opportunities which exist by re-directing their marketing efforts away from the 18–49 age group and instead seeking to build market share in the maturing boomer sector. Saga has been able to defend itself against these threats in the vacation market by exploiting the benefits associated with their leadership position, a well established brand name and above-average customer loyalty. Concurrently the company has moved to further expand brand share in the financial services market. Emphasis has been on increasing sales in the insurance market because 50+ individuals own more valuable assets than younger people and can afford to pay higher premiums. The firm is continually being provided by fresh sales leads for financial services products because most new customers to the Saga holidays operation can be persuaded to purchase travel insurance. The firm's latest move has been to acquire the UK Automobile Association (or AA), which at a single stroke has moved Saga into a leadership position by becoming the largest financial intermediary in the UK insurance market (Quinn 2007). This outcome has occurred because the acquisition gives Saga access to the AA's insurance brokerage business. This operation is believed to contain the largest database of 50+ individuals in the UK who are active purchasers of a wide range of insurance products.

Building markets

The Saga scenario provides evidence to support the conclusion that companies successful at identifying and exploiting markets containing financially attractive consumers exhibit certain common organizational characteristics. As summarized in Figure 1.1, these firms understand that successful market exploitation demands recognition that customers exhibit a desire for products or services that are different to those purchased by other, less wealthy members of society. As illustrated by the customer profile of firms in the rapidly expanding ocean cruises market, financially attractive consumers typically wish to demonstrate their wealth, status and lifestyle by consuming products or services that they believe most other, less fortunate consumers would find unaffordable (Coleman *et al.* 2006).

Maturing boomers, having been born into the world's first ever mass consumer society, have developed a strong desire to be provided with information that can assist their purchase decisions. Hence, one aspect of achieving a leadership

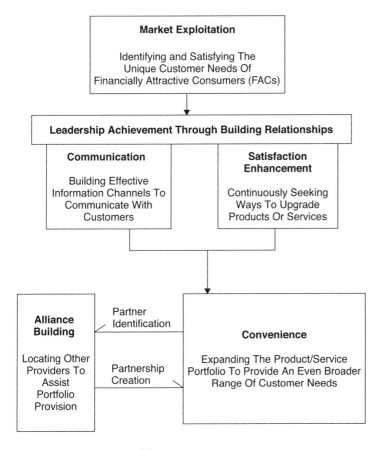

Figure 1.1 The market building process.

position through building a close relationship with this group of customers is to ensure that every opportunity is exploited to create effective customer communication channels. This situation also requires suppliers to carefully monitor consumer behaviour in order to rapidly identify any changes which are emerging in relation to the new channels such as the specific social networking websites that the firm's customer target may begin to utilize.

Financially attractive consumers' experience of purchasing branded goods has sensitized them to the fact that superior quality is usually most likely to be delivered by firms which continually seek to exploit innovation as a pathway for improving the products or services that they make available to markets. Another aspect of financially attractive consumers is their desire to minimize the time taken to acquire products or services. This means that convenience is often perceived as significantly more important than price. Under these circumstances, any action that can broaden a company's product line will be perceived as an advantageous action by their customers because this will reduce the search time associated with making a purchase decision. It is rare that any one company has the breadth of product line to totally satisfy customer needs. Hence, as demonstrated by the success of the online retailer Amazon's affiliate scheme, there is a definite advantage in a company forming alliances with other companies as a route to broadening the range of products or services than can be purchased from a single source.

Market behaviour

Companies operating in branded consumer goods markets such as soaps, detergents and coffee have come to recognize that over time within their primary target group, the 18–49 year age group, there is usually very little shift in consumer needs. This has led these companies to pay only limited attention to consumer attitudes, while concurrently focusing the vast majority of their market research efforts on monitoring the tactical marketing activities of their competitors. Techniques such as store audits are used to assess minor shifts in brand share in relation to actions such as a new advertising campaign or up-weighted spending on in-store promotions (Dube and Manchada 2005).

It is extremely dangerous for these companies to sustain this managerial orientation upon entry into financially attractive older consumer markets. This is because these consumers exhibit a highly experiential approach to life, frequently revising their attitudes, beliefs and purchase decisions as they seek to maximize the satisfaction sought from enjoying their higher incomes and being released from their prior responsibilities associated with bringing up a family. The more perceptive marketers have switched their attention from monitoring competition and instead adopt a much more customer focused orientation in determining appropriate future marketing strategies (Bowden and Corkindale 2005).

Rapid behaviour shifts

Case Aims: To illustrate the rapid purchase behaviour shifts that can occur in markets containing financially attractive consumers.

Ten years ago maturing boomers tended to select somewhat conventional holiday destinations such as Europeans going to Spain and Americans visiting Mexico. These individuals then began to exhibit an interest in more exotic locations, thereby requiring travel companies to rapidly expand the range of destinations to be offered to customers. Most recently, maturing boomers have started to exhibit a desire for greater vacation excitement by purchasing holiday packages offering extreme sports or visiting places well off the beaten track, such as the Amazon rain forest or Tibet (Peterson 2007). In relation to trends in changing consumer needs, American boomers tend to lead consumer trends in terms of exhibiting changing purchase behaviour in relation to purchasing a new home in preparation for, or immediately after, retirement. Only a few years ago in this new-build housing market, maturing boomers primary purchase requirements were sun and security. As a result, many opted to buy new homes inside gated, guarded communities in states such as Florida (Lurz 1998). More recently, however, these individuals seem to have rejected the concept of leading a passive lifestyle involving activities such as playing bridge or painting. In the place of sun and security, the new priority which began to emerge in 2006 was access to active forms of recreation with swimming being rated as the top athletic activity, followed closely by hiking and climbing. These changes have caused the more customer focused developers to build housing communities offering 'must have' facilities such as swimming pools, hiking trails, water sports, biking paths and in more mountainous areas such as Colorado, access to ski runs. Another recent behaviour shift is American boomers not wishing to retire totally, but instead remain involved in some form of work activity. The response to this growing 'work-retirement' trend is that home builders are now including computer and business services centres as standard facilities in their latest retirement community developments.

Recognition of the rapidly shifting nature of consumer demand in maturing boomer markets has led one UK advertising agency which specializes in developing marketing campaigns aimed at the 50+ age group to develop a number of tools to assist their clients to comprehend the diversity of needs which can be exhibited by adult boomers. One technique is based upon working with their clients to classify older customers as having product benefit requirements which fit into one or more of the following three basic types of consumer need:

1 *Physical need*, which is about satisfying the requirements associated with surviving in today's society.
2 *Emotional need*, which is about seeking to achieve mental wellbeing.
3 *Lifestyle need*, which is about attaining a positive attitude towards one's current circumstances.

The agency then uses lists of the type shown in Table 1.1 to stimulate a creative approach to generating problem/solution scenarios to jointly identify with the client how a product or service benefit can best be positioned in terms of fulfilling one or more of the three basic need types. Their experience to-date is that the most successful marketing campaigns are those which communicate benefits that are of appeal to a diverse group of older consumers and, where practical, are perceived as satisfying more than one of the three basic need types.

Table 1.1 Maturing boomer benefit examples

Need types		
Physical	*Emotional*	*Lifestyle*
Accommodation	Accommodation	
Adequate income	Adequate income	
Caring for a partner	Charitable acts	
Communication	Entertainment	Entertainment
Exercise	Exercise	
Family relationships	Family relationships	
Financial services		
Handling death	Handling death	
	Hobbies	Hobbies
In-home care		
In-home mobility	Finding people to trust	
Learning new skills	Learning new skills	Learning new skills
Legal services		
Remaining healthy	Remaining healthy	Remaining healthy
Residential care provision	Residential care provision	Residential care provision
Managing loneliness	Managing loneliness	
Managing tax affairs		
Medical services		
Nutrition	Nostalgia	
Out-of-home mobility		
Property maintenance		
Part-time employment	Part-time employment	
Personal security	Personal security	
Public sector assistance		
Personal hygiene		
	Pets	
Maintaining sight/hearing	Maintaining sight/hearing	
Shopping	Shopping	Shopping
	Vacation	Vacation
	Sustaining friendships	
Transport	Transport	
Utility supplies		

References

Anon (2008) 'Our model was too dependent on wholesale funding, says Hornby', *The Daily Telegraph*, London, 19 September, p. B3.

Anon (2007) 'The Bank that failed – Britain's bank run', *The Economist*, London, 22 September, p. 1.

Anon (2005) 'Selling to China's rich and not so rich', *Strategic Direction*, Vol. 21, No. 6, pp. 5–8.

Anon (1996) 'Keeping tabs on the Chinese consumer', *The China Business Review*, May/Jun, p. 34.

Aslet, C. (2007) 'From small town to global success story', *The Sunday Telegraph*, London, 23 July, p. 11.

Atkinson, W. (2004) 'Doing business in and with China', *Risk Management*, Vol. 51, No. 3, pp. 24–31.

Bowden, J. and Corkindale, D. (2005) 'Identifying the initial target consumer for innovations: an integrative approach', *Marketing Intelligence & Planning*, Vol. 23, No. 6/7, pp. 562–74.

Carrigan, M. and Szmigin, I. (1999) 'In pursuit of youth: what's wrong with the older market', *Marketing Intelligence and Planning*, Vol. 17, No. 5, pp. 222–34.

Coleman, L.J., Hladikova, M. and Savelyeva, J. (2006) 'The baby boomer market', *Journal of Targeting, Measurement and Analysis*, Vol. 14, No. 3, pp. 191–210.

Doka, K.J. (1992) 'When gray is golden in ageing America', *The Futurist*, Vol. 26, No. 4, pp. 16–21.

Dube, J. and Manchada, P. (2005) 'Differences in dynamic brand competition across markets: an empirical analysis', *Marketing Science*, Vol. 24, No. 1, pp. 81–96.

Hamilton, S. (2003) 'The economies and conveniences of modern-day living', *Business History Review*, Vol. 77, No. 1, pp. 33–46.

Hsieh, C. (1994) 'Japan's quest for global leadership in IT: the impact on US computer companies', *Industrial Management & Data Systems*, Vol. 94, No. 2, pp. 23–9.

Jensen, S., Hougaard, E. and Nieksen, S.B. (1995) 'Population ageing, public debt and sustainable fiscal spending', *Fiscal Studies*, Vol. 16, No. 2, pp. 1–20.

Johnson, R. (2004) 'Economic policy implications of world demographic change', *Economic Review Federal Reserve Bank of Kansas City*, Vol. 89, pp. 39–65.

Klaase, L.H. and Van der Vlist, J.A. (1990) 'Senior citizens a burden?', *De Economist*, Vol. 138, No. 3, pp. 302–21.

Keller, K.L. and Kotler, P. (2006) *Marketing Management*, 12th edn., Prentice Hall, New York.

Kerwin, K. (2005) 'BW50 a new blueprint at Pulte Homes', *Business Week*, 3 October, pp. 76–7.

Kotler, P. and Singh, R. (1981) 'Marketing warfare in the 1980s', *Journal of Business Strategy*, Vol. 1, No. 3, pp. 30–42.

Lustgarten, A. (2007) 'Shell shake down', *Fortune*, New York, Vol. 155, No. 2, pp. 92–3.

Lurz, W.H. (1998) 'Second homes: bonanza beginning', *Professional Builder*, Vol. 63, No. 13, pp. 46–51.

Meeks, C.B., Nickols, S.Y. and Sweeney, A.L. (1999) 'Demographic comparisons of ageing in five selected countries', *Journal of Family and Economic Issues*, Vol. 20, No. 3, pp. 223–42.

Moon, S. (2005) 'An analysis of global retail strategies', *Journal of Academy of Business*, Vol. 7, No. 1, pp. 219–25.

O'Connor, R. (1993) 'Risky business', *Journal of European Marketing*, Vol. 4, No. 1, pp. 24–31.

Peterson, M. (2007) 'Effects of income, assets and age on the vacationing behaviour of US consumers', *Journal of Vacation Marketing*, Vol. 13, No. 1, pp. 29–44.

Quinn, J. (2007) 'Saga sees huge cross-selling opening', *The Daily Telegraph*, London, 26 June, p. 3.

Raff, D.M.G. (1991) 'Making cars and making money in the interwar automobile industry', *Business History Review*, Vol. 65, No. 4, pp. 721–54.

Ritson, M. (2007) 'Northern Rock has eroded its equity', *Marketing*, London, 19 September, p. 25.

Schlevogt, K.A. (2000) 'The Russian Federation: time for anticyclical investments', *Thunderbird, International Business Review*, Vol. 42, No. 6, pp. 707–18.

Stern, B., Gould, S. and Barak, B. (1987) 'Baby boom singles: the social seekers', *Journal of Consumer Marketing*, Vol. 4, No. 4, pp. 5–32.

Thompson, S. (1999) 'Takeover stories drive Footsie back above 6,000', *Financial Times*, London, 28 September, p. 54.

Urry, M. (2003) 'Young leader holds on to his dream: mortgage lender's chief executive is happy in his job – but he knows it may not last for ever', *Financial Times*, London, 10 February, p. 22.

Wang, C.L. and Chen, Z.X. (2004) 'Consumer ethnocentrism and willingness to buy domestic products in a developing country setting: testing moderating effects', *Journal of Consumer Marketing*, Vol. 21, No. 6, pp. 391–405.

Yakita, A. (2001) 'Uncertain lifetime, fertility and social security', *Journal of Population Economics*, Vol. 14, No. 4, pp. 635–51.

Zajac, E.J. and Shortell, S.M. (1989) 'Changing generic strategies: likelihood, direction and performance', *Strategic Management Journal*, Vol. 10, No. 5, pp. 413–31.

2 Opportunity research

Generic principles of marketing to financially attractive consumers (FACs)

The coverage of issues in Chapter 2 is designed to illustrate the generic principles of marketing to FACs in relation to:

1 Sustained market success in FAC markets is critically dependent upon firms exhibiting an ongoing commitment to innovation.
2 Innovation management is often a 'fuzzy process' that is rarely assisted by the use of the more conventional approaches to market research such as implementing large scale consumer surveys.
3 Radical innovation will usually involve 'opportunity discovery' in which the entrepreneur is engaged in an intuitive recognition of an idea which can provide the basis for a whole new generation of products or services, or in some cases, the creation of an entirely new sector of industry.
4 Using market knowledge as the basis for identifying emerging need among FACs often requires an organizational ability to read extremely weak signals concerning changing consumer behaviour.
5 Observations of changing lifestyles or the adoption of new life roles by FACs can often assist in the identification of new market opportunities.
6 To progress a 'new to the world' idea for FACs through to market launch often demands that organizations are prepared to forego logical, analytical thinking and instead base their decisions on an 'entrepreneurial leap of faith'.
7 Entrepreneurs often exploit their membership of business networks as a mechanism to assess, validate and acquire assistance in the successful development of a new innovative product or service.
8 The internet has dramatically enhanced the ability of firms to acquire secondary data and also by accessing social networks, gain an early understanding of FACs' dissatisfaction and changing needs.

9 Data from conventional market research can be greatly enhanced by researchers placing greater emphasis on the generation of qualitative information about FACs.
10 Market research can be made more meaningful by developing an interactive relationship with FACs as the basis for gaining greater understanding of their evolving product or service needs.

Opportunity identification

The fundamental tenet of marketing is to fulfil unsatisfied or dissatisfied customer needs through the provision of product or service superior to that available from competitors. This is a valid concept for a company whether or not the organization is already marketing products or services to financially attractive consumers or is attempting, for the first time, to enter this area of market. Success, especially in the case of these latter firms, will usually require an entrepreneurial orientation. Under these circumstances, the identification of an innovation opportunity using conventional market research may not be a viable concept.

Brown (1992) has proposed that market innovation is a process whereby potential customers gradually become favourably disposed to a new idea. He notes that some consumers have a greater propensity to try innovative products than others and the speed with which people begin to adopt a new product or service will vary between items and market sectors. This scenario causes Brown to conclude that market innovation is essentially a 'fuzzy', unpredictable social phenomenon, rather than the outcome from the more conventional practice of the firm undertaking structured, quantitative market research to identify an unsatisfied need. His viewpoint on this issue is based upon real world situations in which, at the time of their initial identification as a potential new idea, no market yet existed for many innovations. Even if a potential market can be identified at the idea generation stage, potential consumers will rarely have sufficient understanding of the innovation to be able to adequately respond to a formal, structured market research survey.

Another issue which should be recognized during the idea generation phase is that the firm should be careful to ignore any biased or uninformed sources. The risks of ignoring this advice is effectively illustrated by Henry Ford's statement that should he have listened to his customers, he would have focused on developing a faster horse. Hence, firms must find ways of 'thinking outside the box'. This will occur where managers or employees are capable entrepreneurs. In those cases where the firm determines there is a requirement for a more creative or far-sighted input, but has limited internal entrepreneurial capability, it will be necessary to turn to external sources. Those that might be exploited include announcements of technological advances in the trade press, reports issued by trade associations, articles in futuristic magazines, or academic publications by researchers within the university sector.

Blumentritt (2004) identified that an important potential barrier to idea generation is that senior managers in non-growth, traditional industries tend to adopt the philosophy that innovation is neither relevant nor productive in their sector of industry. He proposes that these managers need to revise their perspective on this matter and to promote greater innovative thinking and idea generation among all the employees within their organization. In his view, management should initially focus their actions to stimulate new idea generation on those employees who exhibit curiosity, talent and motivation. In relation to the behaviour of managers, Keiningham *et al.* (2006) expressed concerns that another potential barrier to new product success is where the company is led by an excessively optimistic leader who exhibits an autocratic management style and only progresses his own ideas. There is also the risk that some managers may suffer from observing the world through 'rose tinted spectacles'. Such a behavioural trait can cause ideas being progressed which, even from the outset, have no real chance of ever being translated into a successful new product.

Opportunity discovery

The start point in successful innovation occurs when an entrepreneur begins to perceive that an opportunity exists to utilize a new idea that can be evolved into the provision of a different product or service. This point in the innovation process is sometimes described in the literature as 'opportunity discovery' (Sanz-Velasco 2008). The concept of opportunity discovery was originated by the 'Austrian School' of economics. This school of thinking perceives the event as the entrepreneur making an intuitive, instantaneous recognition of opportunity. Subsequently, Shane and Venkatamaran (2000) have posited that the opportunity discovery concept should be widened to also include the entrepreneur having accumulated prior knowledge such that a rational, logical identification of a new idea will occur. These authors have proposed that prior knowledge which can be exploited is contained within one of the following three dimensions:

1   *Market Information* about relationships and needs within a specific supply chain.
2   *Ways to Serve Markets* in terms of how a change such as revision in production process or new source of supply might offer new approaches for delivering customer satisfaction.
3   *Customer Problems* where the solution would offer the market a new benefit proposition.

As noted by authors such as Shaker *et al.* (1995), the highly publicized successes of individuals such as Steve Jobs or Bill Gates tend to cause the marketing literature to primarily focus on the role of new technology as the most critical force driving market innovation. Commercial exploitation of a technological innovation may occur because an individual with either in-depth market knowledge or intuitive insight perceives a scientific advance has potential commercial applications. Another path through which technological innovation is evolved into a market opportunity is where researchers, having recognized the limitations of a product based on existing technology, move to develop an alternative, more powerful technical solution.

One of the risks when seeking to use new technology in the development of superior products is that the organization's R&D team may only focus their attention on what they perceive is the best application for an emerging technology. The potential outcome of an excessively myopic view can be a failure to identify a better application for the technology or alternatively, recognize that another technology would provide a more effective solution (Dew *et al.* 2004). The error in not linking a new technology with the most appropriate market opportunity is known as *exaptation*. A famous example of the concept is provided by Thomas Edison who, having invented the phonograph and identified a number of potential applications, focused his efforts upon building a market for products such as an office dictating machine. After 10 years of limited success in this market sector, he concluded the technology had no real commercial potential. Hence, it was left to other entrepreneurs to develop the market for using phonograph technology to play recorded music.

Another, more recent example of *exaptation* is provided by the laser which was once described by scientists as 'a solution looking for a problem'. The first laser was invented in the early 1950s as a research project to validate a known theoretical scientific principle about amplifying light, which was originally identified in 1916. Again the original developers of the technology were not the individuals who subsequently undertook the *exaptation* needed to evolve the laser into a technology which is now used across a diverse range of commercial applications, such as microsurgery, precision measurements, cutting materials, telecommunications and weapons systems.

Market opportunities

The most likely way to avoid misidentification of the best commercial opportunity for a new technology or a new entrepreneurial idea is to ensure the new product development team is engaged in frequent interactions with individuals who are able to provide insights about markets and customer behaviour. These insights can be based on rational logical analysis of available market data or generated on the basis of an intuitive problem-solving approach. Even within a company exhibiting an interactive entrepreneurial culture, the risk still remains that by focusing upon development of a new technology or progressing an internally generated new product idea, it can lead to a 'push process' managerial philosophy. The possible unwanted outcome is that a firm's employees may ignore evidence of real market need because they perceive change will only occur due to their activities on the supply side of the marketing process (Schewe and Balazs 1992). Given, however, the fundamental aspect of the marketing process being that of identifying an opportunity to fulfil unsatisfied or dissatisfied customer needs, firms must also recognize that innovation can be a 'pull process'. In this latter scenario, opportunity discovery occurs when a new customer purchasing or a consumption behaviour trait is identified that provides the basis for generating an idea that can lead to the development of a new product or service.

Consumer markets are comprised of a group of individuals who share similar needs in relation to an aspect of their day-to-day existence. These needs are reflected through individuals exhibiting the same buyer behaviour. This trait permits opportunity discovery to occur in markets as the result of identifying the first early, usually very weak signals that for some reason purchasing behaviour or consumption patterns habits are beginning to change. Schewe and Balazs (1992) posit that the buying behaviour of consumers is reflective of the differing life or roles of individuals at any point in time. As a consequence, one approach to opportunity discovery in the case of the financially attractive consumer is to examine how roles may change with age. This can provide the basis for identifying how role shift will be accompanied by the emergence of a need for different products or services.

Roles are an overt social activity reflecting the interaction of individuals with others with whom they come in contact. People can transfer between roles (e.g. housewife to employee) and roles change over time (e.g. from child to adult). Humans do not appear to be born with an instinctive understanding of roles. Instead, individuals learn their roles by observing others, seeing how others respond to their behaviour and influences such as the media or actions by members of their peer group.

In terms of role change in later life, Schewe and Balzs have proposed the following will have a significant influence over an individual's social behaviour and consumption patterns:

1   *The Empty Nester Role*, which within the family lifecycle occurs when the children depart the home leaving the parent(s) freer to become involved in activities more orientated towards fulfilling their own personal needs and desires.

2   *The Caregiver Role*, which is becoming increasingly common as people's parents are living longer and because of infirmity, their children need to become the parent. In recent years with young families facing increasing financial stress on earning sufficient money to live, older people are also taking on the caregiver role of continuing to provide economic support to their children. The trend for becoming responsible for one's own parents while also supporting one's children has led to the term the 'sandwich generation'.

3   *The Retirement Role*, where either one or both individuals retire from their career leaving them free to participate in activities totally of their own choice such as pursuing a hobby, returning to education or spending more time playing sport.

4   *The Grandparent Role*, which now that older people are living longer and remaining healthier, means older people are becoming much more actively involved in entertaining their grandchildren and fulfilling the role of being an alternative source of guidance and support.

5   *The Widowhood Role*, which to a certain degree is caused by women having a longer average life expectancy than men. Consequently widows in Western nations outnumber men by approximately 5 to 1 and past the age of 65, approximately 50% of all women are widows. The advent of higher and more frequent divorces when linked with older women 'feeling younger' until much later in life means that there is a trend towards widows being much more socially active.

Lifestyle opportunities

Case Aims: To illustrate how lifestyle classification can be used to define the different opportunities which exist that offer the basis for new ideas that can be evolved in innovative products or services.

In fulfilling new roles at different times in their lives, buying and consumption patterns reflect the lifestyle which individuals have either chosen for themselves, or have been forced to accept as being the most appropriate for a specific period in their lives. In the context of the maturing boomer lifestyle, Pak and Kambil (2006) have proposed that the four key variables influencing lifestyle are: biological, psychological, economic and social. One way of consolidating these variables is to re-define them into two dimensions; namely health and economic state. By applying the simplistic taxonomy of each state being either strong or poor, a firm can then create an opportunity status matrix of the type shown in Figure 2.1. The matrix can be used to determine which of four innovation pathways offer greatest opportunities.

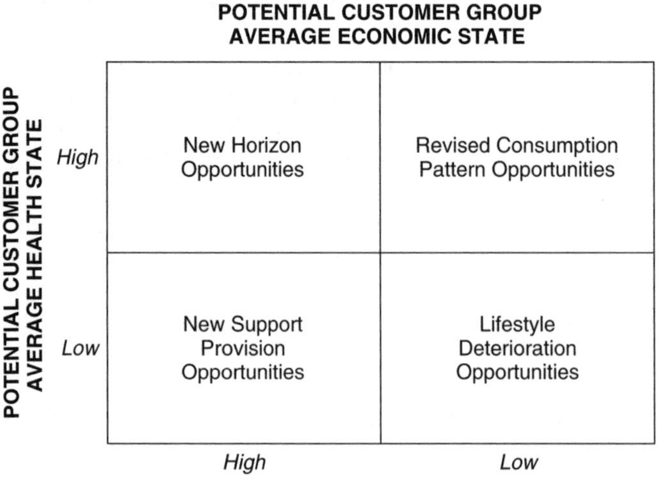

**POTENTIAL CUSTOMER GROUP
AVERAGE ECONOMIC STATE**

		High	Low
POTENTIAL CUSTOMER GROUP AVERAGE HEALTH STATE	*High*	New Horizon Opportunities	Revised Consumption Pattern Opportunities
	Low	New Support Provision Opportunities	Lifestyle Deterioration Opportunities

Figure 2.1 Opportunity assessment options matrix.

Henderson (1998), in his review of why older people offer huge new opportunities for entrepreneurs seeking to create new products or even entirely new industrial sectors, has provided some examples of the types of product which would be suitable for exploiting the four different pathways shown in Figure 2.1. In relation to the New Horizons option, this group of customer has the health and wealth to participate in completely new lifestyle scenarios. This fact has already been recognized by the global travel industry, which has benefited hugely from satisfying the need for unusual, completely different, exotic vacations by offering adventure holidays and African safaris. For those individuals whose health begins to decline, but wealth remains strong, their desire is to continue with a lifestyle of enjoying life while accepting there is a requirement to make use of support services. Thus for example the American insurer USAA has launched a taxi service for older people in Florida called Choice Ride. For an advanced payment in the region of $1,000 older people can take 30 trips in a chauffeured limousine anywhere in a specific area and receive a 90 per cent reduction in their car insurance premiums if they agree not to drive themselves except in the case of an emergency. For older persons who remain healthy but their income in retirement is reduced, their primary need is to be assisted in ways of reducing living costs but concurrently avoiding a deterioration in their lifestyle. Exploitation of this market is exemplified by the activities of both financial service companies and house builders who have created propositions whereby from downsizing, older people can reduce their accommodation costs and have sufficient money left to afford a comfortable lifestyle. The last lifestyle option involves a deterioration in both wealth and health. This sadly is the position faced by many people who earned low incomes during their working lives and have not been able to afford to save for a pension. In terms of meeting this group's needs, this will usually require public sector intervention. New market opportunities for commercial organizations will be somewhat limited. The exception would be, however, if through innovation, a firm can develop a more cost-effective approach which permits the public sector to reduce operational costs by contracting out service provision to the private sector.

Opportunity boundaries

Although the individual inventor may feel free to examine a whole range of different ideas and technologies in the search for a world-beating idea, most organizations usually decide there is a need to define boundaries within which opportunity discovery can be contained. A very common determinant in boundary setting is the scale of opportunity being researched. In an organization where current revenue growth from existing markets remains strong and there are clear prospects of being able to continue to attract new customers, then the revenue requirement from entry into a financially attractive consumer market would probably be set at a relatively low level (e.g. 10–20 per cent of total sales). This scenario would probably result in the management restricting new opportunity identification to ideas which can be evolved by drawing upon the firm's existing output generation expertise and market knowledge.

This situation can be contrasted with an organization which perceives a financially attractive consumer market will become a major source of future sales (e.g. contributing at least 70 per cent of future sales). To achieve this goal, the scale and breadth of the new opportunity search would need to be very significant. Under these circumstances, management would probably place no restrictions on opportunity discovery as they recognize that new ideas will require the development of a new technology or a fundamental change in marketing practices.

Business expansion based upon innovation can be extremely risky. This is demonstrated by reports in various consumer market sectors of 70 per cent of new products failing within 3 years after market launch. Hence, another issue influencing the definition of boundaries for opportunity search is the degree of risk which is acceptable to the organization (MacMillan *et al.* 1985). In relation to assessing risk, the two dimensions which are often critical are markets and organizational capability. Mistakes in relation to either of these two dimensions can lead to errors being made during the innovation development process. The possibility of implementation errors being made will increase as a firm moves from an existing into a totally new market. Similarly adding new internal capability, such as investing in a radically new processing technology, may increase the risk of the emergence of an insurmountable problem.

As summarized in Figure 2.2, risk minimization during opportunity search can be achieved by restricting idea identification to those areas involving no change in market or organizational capability. The increased level of risk from changing a

Figure 2.2 Opportunity options and risk matrix.

single dimension is similar to that for entering a new market or acquiring new internal capabilities. Should changes be implemented across both dimensions, as occurs in a diversified opportunity search programme, this approach would add greatly to the potential risk of the proposed innovation subsequently failing during either development or at the market launch stage.

In determining the degree of risk acceptable to the organization during opportunity search, senior managers must be aware that in most cases a major increase in profitability can only occur if the organization is prepared to take significant risks. Furthermore, different managers, when presented with the same scenario, will often exhibit differing views on the scale of potential risk. This variation in opinion reflects the fact that perceptions of risk are influenced by personal attitude to risk avoidance and a manager's experience of success or failure in relation to previous business decisions (Forlani *et al.* 2002). Characteristically, entrepreneurs who have enjoyed success in the past tend to be less averse to taking new risks. This can be contrasted with managers within more conservative organizations that have a poor track record in the field of innovation management. Such individuals will exhibit a more cautious approach to approving anything they consider is a major departure from the firm's area of expertise or markets being served.

Opportunity validation

The image of the entrepreneur often presented in the media is that of an individual who is so confident about the potential success of a new idea that the product is developed and launched without any attempt to validate market potential. In some cases, this image is not that far from reality. This is because a common trait in entrepreneurially orientated firms is a willingness to believe any innovation will prove successful. This attitude usually exists because senior managers, on the basis of past achievements, have developed a fundamental belief in their own ability to successfully evaluate new ideas. Hence, these individuals feel any market validation research is a completely unnecessary activity (Ogawa and Piller 2006). Unfortunately, due to excessive self confidence, the outcome in some cases is the firm rushes into a new venture without an adequate assessment of either the scale of potential risk or an understanding of the actual complexities that will arise during implementation of the innovation project.

Where an identified innovation concept is a 'totally new idea to the world' proposition, then attempting to validate potential commercial viability can often prove to be virtually impossible. This is because there will be no existing industry expertise that can act as a source of guidance. Furthermore, as the product has never been purchased or used, consumers will be a very unrewarding source of information. In such cases, initiating the new product development programme can be an intuitive leap of faith by the firm's owners or senior managers. This situation can be contrasted with less radical innovation projects because in those instances, as illustrated in Figure 2.3, there exists a well established sequential process which can be used to acquire information to validate the commercial viability for a new idea.

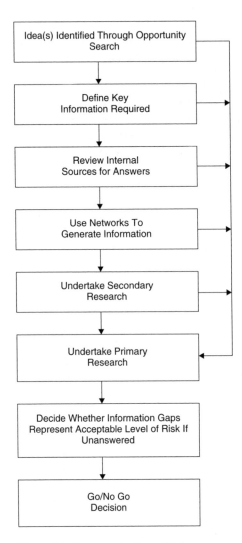

Figure 2.3 The opportunity validation process.

The starting point in the data acquisition process is usually an information search inside the organization. Identified data may come from a number of internal sources. These can include previous market or project evaluation studies, an existing solution which can be re-applied to a new situation or a technology which, with certain modifications, can be used in the production of a new product. A key aim of any opportunity assessment is to minimize costs and maximize benefits. Hence, the process described in Figure 2.3 is specifically designed such that the very early phases of the process will involve minimal expenditure. This means that where an organization acquires all the information needed early into the search process from sources such as those which exist inside the firm, then the more expensive aspects of market research, such as undertaking in-depth interviews, can be avoided.

Business networks

Market research texts recommend that a business exhausts all sources of existing, documented information (or 'secondary data') before expending efforts to generate new data (or 'primary information') by carrying out interviews or implementing a survey. Fortunately many entrepreneurs exhibit the fascinating habit of ignoring the well-intentioned advice of academics. Instead they tend to utilize approaches which they have found to be effective in the real world. As described by the process model in Figure 2.3, such is the case in relation to data acquisition through networking because entrepreneurs will typically exploit this information source before seeking to acquire any secondary data from sources outside the company.

Successful new product development is critically dependent upon access to adequate resources in key areas such as market information, knowledge of new technologies, employee R&D skills, finance and access to specialist equipment. Acquisition of such resources can often be achieved by the firm exploiting their membership of a business network. This membership permits collaboration with other organizations in the identification of new opportunities and in many cases, the subsequent development of the new product (Rogers 2004).

Secondary data

In the last 10 years, the search for market information has been revolutionized by the advent of the internet. Through utilization of search engines operated by organizations such as Google and Yahoo, anybody can now access rich sources of data on a global scale in just a matter of minutes. Usually the richest datasets that emerge early into an online search are those posted by Government agencies, although the researcher needs to be aware that the depth, breadth and quality of data from Government sources does, however, vary by country. One of the best examples of a well constructed site in terms of both quality of data and ease of use is provided by the US Census Bureau (www.census.gov). The site, for example, provides a breakdown of income by age group but also makes available additional detailed information such as expenditure broken down by age group across a wide range of product categories, e.g. food, housing, healthcare, utilities and consumer durables.

During an online search, one will encounter secondary data from a wide range of different organizations. In some cases, all of the required data can be downloaded from one single source (e.g. population data from a Government's national census). The larger trade association websites also usually offer a huge range of free data about topics such as markets, market trends, customer behaviour, supply sources and sector relevant legislation. In contrast, many smaller organizations may be staffed by a part-time volunteer and consequently, their websites only provide somewhat limited, generalized information.

Most markets are covered by sector specific, trade magazines. To retain the interest of their readers, these magazines will contain articles covering a diversity of topics, such as market trends, changing supply sources, new technology and pending Government legislation. Many of these magazines now offer online access to their archives. Additionally some organizations with a specific interest in the older consumer have begun to publish online or terrestrial magazines. These publications contain articles covering both the provision of advice on how to enjoy increased leisure time and guidance on resolving age-related problems such as funding personal healthcare needs. The publishers of these magazines may be charities (e.g. AARP in the USA) or commercial companies interested in attracting business from older people (e.g. the Saga Group in the UK).

Secondary data examples and sources

Case Aims: To illustrate the variety of data that are available from online sources.

Possibly the richest data sources are those available online in America. To illustrate this fact, some useful source examples from the USA, which can be useful in researching the economic and social implication of population ageing, are provided in the following table:

USA Information Source Examples

Economic information	www.conference-org
	www.stat-usa.gov
	www.federalreserve.gov
Industry information	www.asaent.org/gateway
Small business data	www.bizcomps.com
Company data links	www.corptech.com
Franchise information	www.entrepreneur.com
Specific company data	www.dnb.com
500 Top Firms	www.forbes.com
Private company financial data	www.integrainfo.com
State level information	www.llrx.com
Canadian and US manufacturers	www.thomas.register.com
Executive job changes	www.thestandard.com
Design and manufacturing services	www.techsavvy.com
City level company information	www.vaultreports.com

There is an emerging trend across some Government information sites, not merely to provide historic data, but to also forecast future trends. For example, as shown by a sample of materials presented below, the US Government provides population projections from now until the year 2050.

Projected population change in the United States by age: 2000–2050 ('000)

Numerical change   Years

	2000– 2050	2000– 2010	2010– 2020	2020– 2030	2030– 2040	2040– 2050
Total	137,729	26,811	26,869	27,780	28,361	27,908
0–4	8,862	2,208	1,506	1,340	2,027	1,781
5–19	19,736	479	4,146	4,877	4,494	5,740
20–44	26,822	369	4,189	6,115	6,912	9,237
45–64	30,665	18,573	2,641	–1,373	6,331	4,493
65–84	35,050	3,326	13,243	14,487	2,790	1,204
85+	16,594	1,856	1,145	2,334	5,806	5,452

Source: US Census Bureau (2004) 'US Interim Projections by Age', www.census.gov.

In those cases where the researcher is seeking specific market sector information or data on consumer behaviour, this is more likely to be found in publications by commercial organizations such as major market research companies that publish sectoral omnibus studies (e.g. Mintel in the UK) and the leading management consultancy firms.

For example in a downloadable article on maturing boomer trends in *The McKinsey Quarterly* (Court *et al.* 2007), the following data were included:

Total market share of US markets by 50+ households in 2015

Sector	Market share (%)
Food at home	52
Food away from home	50
HbAs	60
Housewares	58
Furniture and appliances	52
Clothing	48
Footwear, other apparel items	44
Consumer electronics	50
Medical services	74
Prescription drugs	83

US net worth and expenditure by age group 2015 (%)

	Net worth	Consumption	Income
Born before 1945	22	11	11
Boomers	57	40	41
Gen X (Born 1965–1981)	20	38	38
Born after 1982	1	11	11

Online communities

Astute marketers have long since recognized that consumer complaints can provide an invaluable source of ideas for both improving existing products or identifying opportunities for new products. The ability to access consumer views has now been revolutionized by the advent of the internet. Quite soon after consumers embraced the new technology, there emerged two phenomena which have proved very useful to organizations wanting to monitor customer opinions; namely blogs and chat rooms (Dwivedi *et al.* 2007).

The term 'blog' is a derivative of the phrase 'web log', which was proposed by Jorn Barger to describe sites that permitted links to other related sites. Blogs are created, mainly by private citizens, to publicize their personal views on a specific issue. The originating author may invite others to post their opinions. Some 'bloggers' have such a high standing within a user community, their views can have greater impact on public opinion than information published by the established media. Popular sites containing criticism of larger companies can provide both the firm and, of course, their competitors, with invaluable insights about user dissatisfaction. This information may then permit identification of new product or service opportunities that could be exploited.

An example of the adverse impact of an influential author is provided by BuzzMachine (www.buzzmachine.com) which is run by a leading American blogger, Jeff Jarvis. When Dell refused to replace his faulty computer, this prompted him to start documenting other peoples' examples of Dell's poor service in his blogs. At first, the company ignored these criticisms in the hope that they would eventually go away. When it became apparent that such optimism was ill-placed, they were forced to use their own corporate blogs in an attempt to defend their reputation.

Chat rooms are created by individuals or organizations as electronic platforms through which interested parties can exchange information and views. Many chat rooms represent a key resource in supporting regular social interactions between users. Some, however, have been created to assist people describe life problems they are facing and to receive suggestions from others about possible solutions. Consumer usage of chat rooms has leapt considerably following the advent of social networking sites such as YouTube and Facebook. This is because these sites permit video streaming and real-time site visitor interaction. Initially many of the more globally popular sites were the preserve of younger people, but increasingly older people have also come to recognize the benefits of becoming members of online communities.

Entrepreneurs who have been monitoring online communication trends have found that older people are more site loyal and, unlike younger people, do not continually switch between sites seeking new social contacts (Richtel 2007). This had led to the emergence of Facebook-type social networking sites such as Eons, Multiply, Boomj and Boomertown specifically aimed at attracting the older consumer. As there are three times more mature boomers than teenagers in most Western nations, the future for these age-specific new sites seems very bright. The breadth of online discussion is extremely wide-ranging across subjects such as healthcare, finance, politics, vacations, dating, product preferences, relationships and resolving family issues. Hence, by monitoring this content, the entrepreneur is very likely to identify an emerging trend long before this becomes apparent by analysing more conventional market research data sources.

Both private and public sector organizations have, for some years, operated large scale terrestrial consumer panels to monitor customer opinions and concerns. Some organizations have now expanded the scale of such initiatives by moving them online and creating company-sponsored, social forums. There is some debate, however, about how effective such networks are in providing a sufficiently broad view of consumer trends and possible shifts in behaviour (Parameswaran and Whinston 2007). This is because panels tend to attract those individuals who are strongly motivated to regularly communicate with a specific organization. Hence, the company runs the risk that panel members are not really indicative of the actual views and opinions of the wider general public.

Primary research decisions

In those cases where data acquired from secondary sources still leave key questions unanswered, the firm will be faced with the necessity of undertaking primary research. The cognitive thinking style of many marketers is biased towards rational, logical analysis as the basis for reaching a conclusion. As a consequence, there is a tendency for many large consumer goods companies to utilize quantitative research methodologies such as large scale consumer surveys to generate a wealth of numeric data. This data format has the appeal of allowing the scale and validity of any identified new market opportunities to be evaluated using statistical techniques.

The effectiveness of quantitative market research as a path through which to identify new opportunities rests, however, upon two very critical assumptions. The first is that the company has sufficient understanding of the market being examined that the researcher can formulate appropriate questions. Second is the requirement that potential customers have sufficient understanding of the features and benefits being offered that they are capable of articulating a viewpoint in relation to an unsatisfied or dissatisfied need. In those cases where one or both of these assumptions prove invalid, then a different approach to opportunity identification will be necessary.

Millier and Palmer (2001) raised the issue of applicability of conventional quantitative market research techniques in relation to problems generating data to support decision-making within the widely accepted linear, 'stage gate' new product process management model. Having simplified the variables within their more complex decision model, as illustrated in Figure 2.4, one can generate three scenarios where alternative opportunity identification research techniques will be required.

In those cases where the customer or intermediaries have an understanding of need, then data can usually be generated by undertaking qualitative research via the medium of focus groups and interviews. Should the customer or intermediary

SUPPLIER UNDERSTANDING OF MARKET NEED

		High	Low
CUSTOMER/INTERMEDIARY UNDERSTANDING OF MARKET NEED	*High*	Conventional quantitative market research approach	Qualitative research approach involving industry experts and customers
	Low	Deductive entrepreneurial approach drawing upon existing data and prior experience	Intuitive entrepreneurial approach drawing upon prior knowledge (or in some cases, involving 'a leap of faith')

Figure 2.4 Research assessment options matrix.

have limited understanding of need, such techniques will be unproductive. In those cases where the firm has an in-depth understanding of the market, then logical rational deductive decisions can be reached by drawing upon existing information and the organization's internal expertise. This approach cannot be utilized, however, where the company has minimal understanding of the market being researched. In this instance an intuitive entrepreneurial decision style will be necessary. In those cases where prior knowledge cannot be used to support an intuitive decision, the firm will have to be prepared to make a leap of faith and rely upon the 'gut feel' of the decision-maker(s).

Research techniques

Techniques associated with primary research include experimentation, observation, interviews and surveys. Selection of the most appropriate approach will be influenced by the nature of the data being sought and the degree to which the managers feel the benefits from expenditure on primary research will exceed costs. Experimentation is intuitively appealing because it appears simple and logical. This is not the case, however, with experiments in consumer markets because the methodology can be adversely impacted by extraneous variables over which the researcher usually has little or no control.

Successful managers, especially those who are also entrepreneurs, have an infinite level of curiosity which causes them to be extremely effective observers of events within their markets. Hence, well planned observation can be an extremely effective tool through which to generate qualitative data on the behaviour of consumers engaged in shopping, leisure or social activities. One-to-one interviews with consumers or knowledgeable intermediaries to acquire an in-depth understanding of unresolved issues are a very effective research technique. During the interview, the direction of the discussions can be altered depending upon the information being provided by the respondent. Furthermore, where the respondent exhibits a detailed understanding of an issue, supplementary questions can be used to probe for additional data. Interviews are a time-intensive activity which means one is only able to implement a small number of interviews in a short period of time. An approach for overcoming this problem is to collect inputs from a group of individuals. Known as 'focus group' research, the approach works best with a group size of not more than 8–10 people.

Where data are required from a very large number of people, it will usually be necessary to undertake a survey. The choices concerning which medium to use to execute the survey include: street intercept, mail, telephone and more recently, the internet. An advantage of the latter technique is the extremely low cost and respondents being able to self-schedule the time of their participation. However, reports about the effectiveness of this approach are somewhat mixed. Some organizations are finding response rates are excellent and for other organizations, response rates are abysmal.

Inviting the customer in

Case Aims: To demonstrate that by developing collaborative partnerships with consumers this can provide companies with new ideas and assist in the identification of future opportunities.

In an attempt to sustain and accelerate innovation in an increasingly competitive world, some organizations, in seeking to overcome the failure of conventional market research to reveal new opportunities, are turning to potential customers as a source of new ideas. Ogawa and Piller (2006) have entitled this process 'implementing collective customer commitment'. The approach offers the benefits of permitting: (a) testing of highly innovative ideas about which minimal consumer experience exists and (b) the development of products across highly heterogeneous consumer segments. The authors note, however, that for organizations to succeed they must be prepared to terminate the practice found in conventional new product development programmes which emphasizes the importance of secrecy and confidentiality. Instead, the organization must demonstrate trust and commitment by providing contributing customers with full disclosure in relation to activities associated with the innovation programme. One example of customer collectives that Ogawa and Piller have identified is a Chicago design company which specializes in hot fashion items such as colourful T-shirts. Instead of relying on market research, the company uses a community of customers including hobbyists and clothing designers. These individuals submit design ideas which are featured on the company website and are then rated by site visitors. The most highly rated designs are put into production and the original creator receives a $1,000 reward, plus their name printed on the T-shirt. A similar practice, but on a much larger scale, is utilized by Muji, a large Japanese retail chain selling apparel and household goods. The company's website is used to gain the response from approximately 100,000 individuals about the company's ideas for new designs. Those items which receive a high rating are progressed through to a final design and website visitors are asked to place pre-orders. Those items for which an adequate level of orders is received are then put into production. In a review of other examples of why Japanese firms, especially in the area of consumer electronics, seem to lead the world in product innovation, Washida (2005) has highlighted the practice in Japan of seeking to exploit the ideas which can be generated by customer feedback early in the development of a new technology. This is achieved by launching a basic proposition, in some cases where the technology has not yet been perfected, and to seek input from customers of what they wish to see improved. For example when Casio launched their first ever very small digital camera in 2002, the product had a 1.24 pixel definition and an MP3 music player function. The first purchasers of such products tended to be 'technology geek' males who were very vocal in generating ideas for improvement. In this case, they had no interest in other functions such as the MP3 player. All they demanded was better picture definition which Casio resolved by immediately moving to launch a higher resolution camera while removing the MP3 player. Further learning occurred as young females began to purchase the improved product. They loved the small size but wanted added functionality such as a zoom facility to be able to take a wider variety of pictures. For this latter group, the product was seen as their 'primary camera', whereas the earlier male customers were using the product as a convenient, small 'secondary device'. Gloor and Cooper (2007) in presenting similar views about utilizing inputs from customers to identify new ideas, refer to the structure and process as 'collaborative innovation networks' (or COINS). One example of a COIN which they provide is the upmarket German car manufacturer, BMW. The company's M Division, which specializes in using advantaged technology to improve vehicle performance, learn from inputs from over 20,000 customers who submit requests for vehicle customization. M Division uses the solutions developed as the basis for new ideas that can subsequently be incorporated in the company's product line. The company also posts engineering challenges on their website for which both employees and customers are invited to develop innovative solutions. To assist the process, the company has created a web-based toolset which consumers can utilize in the development and submission of their ideas about cars of the future. Gloor and Cooper have labelled participative customers as 'swarms' and propose there are three key rules in exploiting customer collaboration in the idea generation process. First, the company must be prepared to give away power by relinquishing this to the swarm in terms of the swarm controlling the direction taken during idea generation. Second, the company must be willing to openly share information with the swarm in order that the potential contributors have a full understanding of the issues and problems which have led to the need for new, innovative solutions. Third, the company should focus not on maximizing near-term profit, but instead put efforts into maximizing the activity of the swarm because in the longer term, the resultant innovation will yield a much higher pay-off.

References

Blumentritt, T. (2004) 'Does small and mature have to mean dull: defying the ho-hum at SMEs', *Journal of Business Strategy*, Vol. 25, No.1, pp. 27–34.

Brown, R. (1992) 'Managing the 'S' curves of innovation', *Journal of Business & Industrial Marketing*, Vol. 7, No. 3, pp. 41–52.

Court, D., Farrell, D. and Forsyth, J.E. (2007) 'Serving ageing baby boomers', *The McKinsey Quarterly*, No. 4, pp. 102–12.

Dew, N., Sarasvathy, S.D. and Ventkataraman, S. (2004) 'The economic implications of exaptation', *Journal of Evolutionary Economics*, Vol. 14, pp. 69–84.

Dwivedi, M., Shibu, T.P. and Venkatesh, U. (2007) 'Social software practices on the Internet: implications for the hotel industry', *International Journal of Contemporary Hospitality Management*, Vol. 19, No. 5, pp. 415–26.

Forlani, D., Mulins, J.W. and Walker, O.C. (2002) 'New product decisions: how chance and size of loss influence what marketing managers see and do', *Psychology & Marketing*, Vol. 19, No. 11, pp. 957–66.

Gloor, P. and Cooper, S. (2007) 'The new principles of swarm business', *Sloan Management Review*, Spring, pp. 81–6.

Henderson, C. (1998) 'Today's affluent oldsters: marketers see gold in grey', *The Futurist*, Vol. 32, No. 8, pp. 19–23.

Keiningham, T.L., Vavra, T.G and Aksoy, L. (2006) 'Managing through rose-colored glasses', *Sloan Management Review*, Vol. 48, No. 1, pp. 15–22.

MacMillan, I., McCaffery, M. and Van Wijk, G. (1985) 'Competitors' response to easily imitated new products – exploring commercial banking product introductions', *Strategic Management Journal*, Vol. 6, pp. 75–86.

Millier, P. and Palmer, P. (2001) 'Turning new products into profits', *Strategic Direction*, Vol. 10, No. 1, pp. 87–98.

Ogawa, S. and Piller, F.T. (2006) 'Reducing the risks of new product development', *Sloan Management Review*, Winter, pp. 65–70.

Pak, C. and Kambil, A. (2006) 'Over 50 and ready to shop: serving the aging customer', *Journal of Business Strategy*, Vol. 27, pp. 18–28.

Parameswaran, M. and Whinston, A.B. (2007) 'Research issues in social computing', *Journal of the Association for Information Systems*, Vol. 8, No. 8, pp. 338–53.

Richtel, M. (2007) 'New social sites cater for people of a certain age', *New York Times*, 12 September, p. 12.

Rogers, M (2004) 'Networks, firm size and innovation', *Small Business Economics*, Vol. 22, No. 2, pp. 141–56.

Sanz-Velasco, S.A. (2008) 'Opportunity development as a learning process for entrepreneurs', *International Journal of Entrepreneurial Behaviour & Research*, Vol. 12, No. 5, pp. 251–60.

Schewe, C.D. and Balazs, A.L. (1992) 'Role transitions in older adults: a marketing opportunity', *Psychology & Marketing*, Vol. 9, No. 2, pp. 85–96.

Shaker, Z., Nash, S. and Bickford, B.J. (1995) 'Transforming technological pioneering into competitive advantage', *Academy of Management Executive*, Vol. 9, No. 1, pp. 17–32.

Shane, S. and Venkatamaran, S. (2000) 'The promise of entrepreneurship as a field of research', *Academy of Management Review*, Vol. 25, No. 1, pp. 217–26.

Washida, Y. (2005) 'Collaborative structure between Japanese high-tech manufacturers and consumers', *Journal of Consumer Marketing*, Vol. 22, No. 1, pp. 25–35.

3 Market assessment

Generic principles of marketing to financially attractive consumers (FACs)

The coverage of issues in Chapter 3 is designed to illustrate the generic principles of marketing to FACs in relation to:

1 Market size assessments should examine behaviour trends of both existing consumers and those FACs who have yet to enter a market sector.
2 Market assessment should extend beyond data on consumer numbers and spending patterns to also examine the influence of macro-environmental variables.
3 The current global economic crisis mandates that a very careful evaluation be made of how changes in the confidence levels among FACs have the potential to alter their future spending patterns.
4 There is a need to assess how the discretionary income of FACs in Western nations will be impacted by probable changes in their respective Governments' future funding and provision of welfare services.
5 The current turmoil in the world's financial markets needs to be assessed in relation to how declining house prices and stock market investments have impacted on FACs.
6 Technological trends often are the most importance source of new products and the creation of entirely new industrial sectors. Unlike young people who can be influenced by needing to be seen to own the latest 'must have' items, FACs usually adopt new products only if they perceive the innovation offers them a clear and superior benefit proposition.
7 Sociodemographic variables can easily be assessed using effective, low-cost software tools which permit detailed analysis of consumer markets

in relation to spending patterns by consumer type and the geographic location of specific financially attractive consumer groups.

8   Culture reflects the attitudes and values of different groups within society and shifts in culture can often provide the opportunity to launch new products or services.

Market size

An important dynamic in determining potential revenue is the expected future size of a market. Large markets are attractive to firms because they usually generate high sales revenue. Additional revenue growth opportunities will exist when the market is forecasted to grow over time. Conversely, markets in late maturity or decline are typically a threat because potential future revenue will probably fall. When examining revenue potential, it is necessary to recognize that markets exist at two levels. The 'actual' market consists of those consumers who are currently actively purchasing the products or services on offer. Within the larger 'potential' market are both consumers who are active purchasers and those who are prospective buyers, but have yet to enter the actual market and make their first purchase.

Most firms' assessments of new market future opportunities tend to focus on the current, actual market size. This is because data are available on how many customers are actively engaged in purchasing goods and services. In terms of determining future opportunities, a firm should also focus upon whether changes in the size of both the potential and actual market can be expected over time. Change can occur because of variation in the number of customers or the average value of purchases per customer. Hence, it is critically important for the marketer when developing market forecasts that any future changes in the circumstances of financially attractive consumers are identified that will influence purchasing patterns. It is also necessary to determine whether consumers are likely to depart or enter the market.

Variations in consumer behaviour reflect an alteration in the need preferences being exhibited by purchasers. In terms of determining whether variation might occur, one approach is to examine demand in relation to the following three types of consumer behaviour:

1   *Economic preference* need which is based upon whether the consumer feels they can afford the potential purchase.
2   *Benefit preference* need which reflects the degree to which the consumer perceives whether a product offers greater purchase satisfaction than alternative expenditure on some other type of goods.
3   *Practicality preference* need which is an indication of the degree to which the consumer decides whether the proposed purchase is a practical proposition at a specific point in time.

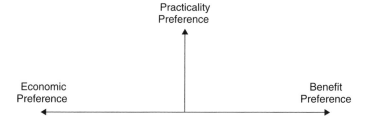

Figure 3.1 The three dynamics of customer need.

As illustrated in Figure 3.1, there can be interaction between need types. For example an older financially attractive consumer seeking to satisfy a desire for exhilarating motoring may decide a sports car is impractical because (a) the vehicle is unaffordable and (b) the need to transport grandchildren.

Applying a consumer needs model

Case Aims: To illustrate the application of a consumer needs model to identify changing opportunities in maturing boomer markets.

In seeking to communicate to companies the necessity of giving more thought to the opportunities offered by older persons becoming the dominant buyer influence in future markets, the accounting practice Deloitte has proposed that as people age they will need to confront four key areas of personal need that may undergo change; namely biological, psychological, economic and social need (Pak and Kambil 2006). The variables can provide the basis for the following need specification model:

1   *Biological needs* that emerge as consumers seek to cope with physio-logical changes in areas such as mobility, flexibility, elasticity, strength, vision and hearing. For example, changes in elasticity affects the skin resulting in a less youthful appearance. To exploit the concerns that older people have about their looks, the health and beauty aids firm Avon developed Anew Line and Wrinkle Corrector which they claim de-ages the skin by enhancing elasticity. Their Cellu-Sculpt Body Treatment is a skin care product designed to maintain current appear-ance and to prevent the build-up of cellulite.

2   *Psychological needs* come about because ageing can be accompanied by changes in areas such as understanding, learning, attitudes and emotions. Companies should pay special attention to these changes in relation to optimising the effectiveness of their communications with customers (e.g. bank employees trained to speak more slowly and listen more carefully).

3   *Economic needs* are those influenced by changes in patterns of saving, consumption and investment. Thus, financial service providers should be orientated towards fulfilling their clients desire to achieve low risk, stable income flows based upon interest bearing products. This aim can be contrasted to the situation of when people were younger and sought higher risk, capital growth opportunities through investing in equities.

4   *Social needs* are a reflection of a person's desires in relation to contact with people such as family, relatives and friends. For example, a couple may desire to re-locate to a warmer climate and will be concerned about building a social network in their new location. Developers can exploit this need by constructing an apartment complex offering facilities to support social networking such as a pool, golf course, tennis courts, club house and a restaurant.

Exploiting understood needs

Case Aims: To illustrate how a small entrepreneurial firm re-directs their marketing strategy to meet the needs of financially attractive consumers.

Bob and Maria Hilliard, who own the property development company Hillback Developments Ltd in Eire, have extensive experience of purchasing older industrial buildings such as mills and converting them into apartments. Confidence in the opportunities offered by the maturing boomer market influenced their decision about selecting the optimal strategy for their new development at Sand Quay Mill in Clonakilty, Cork (Flyn 2004). When marketing the project they stipulated that the over-50s have first refusal on the properties being built. As far as maximizing the appeal of the apartments to potential purchasers, the company recognized that in this sector of the housing market, customers will seek satisfaction in relation to benefit, practicality and economic need. In relation to benefits, they know that many middle- and upper-class retirees, when downsizing to a smaller dwelling, still desire luxury. Hence the development features fitted kitchens, hardwood floors, power showers and wet rooms. Additionally for many older people, security is perceived as a critical benefit requirement. The apartments have videophones to observe visitors and there are electronic locks on both exterior and interior hallway doors. In relation to practicality, many of the apartments are designed with the possible needs that may emerge if residents subsequently become infirm. The ground floor apartments are wheelchair compliant, have wider doorways and hollows beneath the work surfaces. Wardrobes and sinks are accessible from a sitting position. Additionally space on the ground floor of the building has been allocated to the provision of a surgery to be leased or rented by a doctor. As far as economic need, the company has determined that to optimize profitability, they should focus on the sector of the market containing relatively wealthy individuals. This is reflected in the price of the apartments which were offered at an average price of 250,000 euros. The Hilliards accept that few, if any, buyers will come from within the immediate Clonakilty area. This is because most local people have worked in agriculture all their lives and in retirement are living on somewhat limited incomes. Hence, to ensure the apartments are compatible with the economic needs of potential buyers, the company directed their marketing activities at attracting interest from older people living in Dublin and London.

Wider forces

Many marketers take a relatively short-term perspective about future consumer demand. They tend to only be interested in possible changes that might influence the size of the market over the next 12–24 months. To a certain degree this reflects the orientation of many branded consumer goods companies in terms of focusing upon near term financial performance in order to satisfy the demands of major shareholders, such as the major pension funds for year-on-year dividend growth. Success in financially attractive consumer markets, however, will often involve the firm adopting a somewhat longer-term view. This situation requires the acquisition of knowledge concerning important factors likely to influence market size over the medium to long term.

As illustrated in Figure 3.2, there are a number of variables which can influence the size of a market. These variables can have a positive or a negative impact on market growth rates. Fortunately, information on factors influencing at least

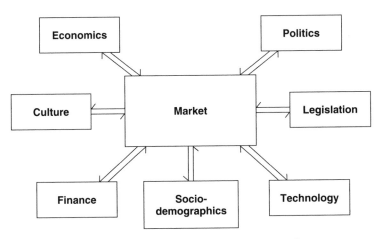

Figure 3.2 Macro-environmental forces influencing market size.

older groups within financially attractive consumer markets are becoming more accessible. This is because growing interest within the academic community about issues such as population ageing and the future role of Governments in funding welfare service provision has increased the number of articles being published containing relevant information. These writings can provide an invaluable source of information about trends in future market size. An excellent example of this type of data is provided in a study by Friedland and Summer (2005) on the US market entitled *Demography is not destiny, revisited*.

Economics

Prevailing economic conditions will strongly influence consumer spending. During a period of economic growth, employment prospects improve, average earnings rise, consumers become more confident and spending levels increase. This is contrasted by a recession during which unemployment grows, earnings fall and a decline in consumer confidence further dampens personal spending levels. Upturns and downturns in the economies of industrial nations occur on a somewhat cyclical basis. Hence, astute marketers will adjust their future business plans to reflect their perceptions of the potential impact of cyclical change on the scale of consumer spending.

Analysis of data on financially attractive consumers indicates that their spending patterns tend to fit the standard model for an entire population; namely that as incomes increase, a greater proportion is spent on leisure activities and socializing (Bahizi 2003). In the past, older people when contrasted with their younger counterparts, have tended to make fewer adjustments to their spending patterns during different phases of an economic cycle (Rubin and Nieswiadomy 1994). This is because those older consumers in receipt of a public or private sector final salary pension scheme, either now or in the near future, have a reasonably clear picture of their future income. In the opinion of Thomas (2006), this is why in America's maturing boomer households, where at least one person has a traditional retirement plan, there exists a higher than average financial confidence about sustaining a comfortable future lifestyle.

A major exception to this observation, however, is now emerging during the meltdown of the world's financial markets in the autumn of 2008 following the collapse of major US financial institutions such as Lehmann Brothers and Washington Mutual. Those maturing boomers who had the majority of their income generating assets invested in equities have been massively affected by the downturn in the world's stock markets. Similarly, those who had assumed their house was their pension have now discovered this was an unwise investment strategy. These types of older financially attractive consumers have become very concerned about a decline in their total income. This will probably cause them to cut back on non-essential spending until they perceive their stock market investments or the value of their homes are beginning to exhibit some signs of recovery. Whether the world's financial crisis will begin to impact those financially attractive boomers who are not so reliant upon a rise in equity or house prices or share prices as yet remains undetermined. It is interesting to note, however, that despite the worsening economic conditions in the Western world, which started in mid-2007, even a year later, many older consumers in the UK did not appear to be revising their social or leisure plans (Morris 2008).

Older people: an economic resource

Case Aims: To illustrate the critical role older people can play in terms of making a major contribution to a local economy.

The overall importance of older people in terms of their contribution to a local economy is demonstrated by the following data on Florida (Destination Florida Commission 2003):

1   Retiree *per capita* income is 25 per cent higher than their 18–49 age group counterparts.
2   Retiree spending generates over 4 million jobs in Florida (i.e. over 50 per cent of the total jobs in the State).
3   Retirees pay almost 100 per cent more *per capita* in sales tax than their younger counterparts.
4   Retirees provide the State with approximately $3 billion of tax revenues, yet only cost the State somewhere in the region of $1.5 billion in terms of health and social services provision.
5   Social security and military pensions paid to Florida residents represent about 55 per cent of Florida's total share of Federal revenues received by the State.

Politics

Politics impact the lives of people as Governments seek to implement the manifesto upon which they were voted into office. Since the Second World War, major parties in democratic nations have received a favourable response to their commitment to provide the electorate with free or subsidized access to public sector services such as education or healthcare. Over time, the cost of these services, and the number of public sector employees engaged in their delivery, has risen dramatically (Lindbeck 1994). With Western nation economies exhibiting minimal growth in GNP over recent years, the funding of public sector services has required increases in personal taxation or Government borrowing. As taxes rise, the concurrent fall in disposable income will impact consumer spending. The implications within this scenario is that total consumer spending will fall in those nations consisting of a declining number of younger people in work and an increasing number of older people living on state pensions (Scruggs 2006).

In 2008, for example, there is evidence to suggest the dramatic rises in energy prices over the last 12 months in the UK have already started to influence buyer behaviour, especially among retirees living on a state pension and in receipt of additional income-related supplementary state benefits. Nevertheless, the Western nation political parties seeking re-election seem to often be more concerned with the impact of their policies on the 18–45 year age group. When attempting to expand their voter franchise, their efforts tend to focus on attracting more first-time voters and seeking wider support among more ethnic minorities (Kaid *et al.* 2007). Increasingly, however, as political parties recognize the need to take more notice that their world is increasingly constituted of ageing populations, new policies can be expected to give greater emphasis to reducing the tax burden of older people.

In America, with the rising number of older people and the tendency of younger people not to bother to vote, political parties are already aware of the need to keep a watching brief on organizations which maturing boomers are now joining, in order for their voice to be heard in Washington (Wessel 2004). One of the largest organizations is the Association of America Retired Persons (www.arp.org). This organization represents the concerns of over 3 million members by undertaking lobbying activities on their behalf. Activities include persuading politicians involved in changing welfare legislation to introduce new laws or change existing laws to improve retiree living standards. The organization also undertakes in-depth research studies to generate data that can be used to substantiate their stance on specific issues. To-date, the AARP has remained apolitical in the sense that it will not support individual politicians, no matter whether they are Democrats or Republicans.

Another American organization is the Gray Panthers who, as their name suggests, is an organization which takes a somewhat more aggressive approach to communicating their demands for change (Anon 1999). In 2001, they organized a protest outside the White House to communicate their concerns about the future costs facing recipients of Medicare and Social Security. They formed the Stop Patient Abuse Now (SPAN) coalition to combat what they felt were unacceptable actions by the Government in relation to healthcare legislation. During 2002, members demonstrated outside a Manhattan courtroom to protest about the pharmaceutical company AstraZeneca receiving what, in their view, were windfall profits from a patent extension for the drug Prilosec.

Legislation

Legislation is a Government's way of defining rules of societal and business behaviour which can be enforced by legal sanctions. New laws are usually invoked when politicians cannot obtain the voluntary co-operation of the general public or commercial organizations. Governments often telegraph their future plans for new legislation through mechanisms such as publishing discussion papers, permitting periods of consultation with interested parties and 'leaks' to the media. Under such circumstances, firms usually have a reasonable length of time during which to determine whether legislation represents an opportunity or a threat to the future market size.

Based upon comments by economists, civil servants and politicians, it is apparent that public sector spending deficits, which are expected to rise dramatically as Governments seek to reduce the depth and breadth of the current recession, will demand the introduction of new legislation specifically aimed at reversing the 'care from cradle to grave' philosophy. Although education is a major area for expenditure, the current wisdom in most countries is that school funding should not be touched because a well-educated workforce is vital for sustaining economic growth. This means it will be in healthcare and pensions where change will have to occur (Taylor-Gooby and Hastie 2003). No political party could expect to be elected on a platform of expenditure cutbacks achieved by reducing the level of the state pension. The focus of politicians will, therefore, be directed at persuading people still in work that they must accept greater responsibility for self-funding their retirement. In the UK, for example, a recent Government White Paper proposed an increase in the retirement age and all people in work being required to enrol in a pension scheme.

Any reduction in healthcare spending for the elderly can also be expected to encounter severe resistance from the electorate. Nevertheless, the ever spiralling costs of healthcare provision will mean Governments of all political persuasions will begin to seek new ways of having older people shoulder a greater share of their medical bills (Aaron 2007). For example, in the USA legislation was introduced in 2005 that offered tax incentives to individuals willing to purchase long-term care insurance. In Germany, there have been revisions to the provision of healthcare services with legislation introduced aimed at persuading people to purchase medical insurance from private companies.

Devil in the detail

Case Aims: To illustrate how an apparently simple legislative change can significantly impact a specific group of consumers within a nation.

Occasionally, Governments decide to rush through new legislation or announce proposed changes to existing regulations without apparently understanding the impact of their actions on commercial organizations or the general public. In March 2006, such an event occurred in the UK in relation to taxing inheritance trusts created by older people (Anon 2006). The trusts in question are legally acceptable entities designed to protect peoples' assets from capital gains tax upon their death. For many years, these trusts had been exempt from most forms of taxation. In the 2006 budget, the chancellor, Gordon Brown, made minor reference to revising the tax status of certain trusts. The Government claimed this would, at most, only impact about 20,000 older people. Within 24 hours, however, the UK financial community realized the potential scale of this unexpected threat. Having read the 'small print' in the proposed legislation, the industry identified a tax implication that could affect over 2.5 million older people. Major firms such as Prudential Insurance were immediately forced to temporarily suspend selling investment trusts. They were unsure about their legal responsibilities concerning the provision of advice to people wishing to create new trusts. This reaction was mirrored by similar advice from the Law Society. For their members, however, a new opportunity also appeared to have been created for lawyers because one implication of the revised legislation was that a large number of older people would need to re-write their existing wills. Eventually the scale of complaints from the financial services industry and coverage of the issues in the media caused the UK Government to reverse their opinion about the proposed change in legislation. In June 2006, the Treasury quietly announced that re-wording of the new legislation would mean that most inheritance trusts would remain exempt for inheritance tax.

Finance

Financial circumstances will always be a focal point of concern for all age groups but is often of especial importance to older financially attractive consumers. This is because, should changes occur in the financial markets, this will impact future and current pension income from sources such as interest on savings, earnings from equity investments, pension fund pay-outs and the size of annuities (Abdel-Ghany and Sharpe 1997). Major downturns on Wall Street and the London Stock Exchange in the late 1990s caused by the bursting of the dotcom investment bubble triggered the decision of Central Banks to hold down interest rates to stimulate economic growth. This action by the Central Banks has been shown to have influenced the scale of spending in the early years of the new millennium (Denton *et al.* 2006). An important additional factor contributing to higher consumer spending over this period was the continued growth in the value of homes. Gains in house prices stimulated many financial institutions to promote equity release as a safe and excellent mechanism through which to increase spending power in retirement (Mahoney 2004). Realization of capital appreciation by individuals who downsized their home as they enter retirement stimulated incrementally higher consumer spending in older financially attractive consumers. This increase in spending was not always associated with the purchase of more expensive products or luxury goods. Analysis of spending by 'empty nesters' in America during the 1990s, for example, revealed that although this group often enjoy higher than average wealth, they continue to seek value for money by shopping in discount outlets (Anon 1995).

Some observers of the financial community's emphasis on equity release programmes began to express concerns that many older people having released capital from their homes were then being persuaded by financial institutions to increase their spending by taking on more credit card debt or taking out additional, low interest bank loans (Hwang 2004). In the USA, these concerns received widespread coverage due to the publication of research studies by Demos, a not-for-profit organization. In one of their studies, for example, Demos concluded that credit card debt among the elderly had increased by 89 per cent between 1992 and 2001. This increasing level of debt stimulated the massive downward slide in house prices since 2007 and the 2008 financial market meltdown means a downturn in older FAC spending must be expected, as these individuals adopt a somewhat more conservative attitude towards their level of spending. In turn, this means firms attempting to forecast market trends should adopt a more pessimistic view about potential growth prospects for most financially attractive consumer markets over the next few years.

Technology

New technology can have a dramatic effect on the fortunes of firms in virtually any market sector. Entrepreneurial organizations who comprehend the potential impact of a new technology and are early market entrants usually enjoy significant financial rewards from their actions. In contrast 'dinosaur firms', who continue to operate as if nothing has changed, may be forced into terminal decline. New technologies are often developed outside of the industries they impact. One example is provided by the advent of the microchip and the resultant devastating impact on the Swiss watch industry, which remains confident that the world would continue to insist on mechanical movements in their watches.

The conventional view in the academic literature is that younger people are much faster in adopting new technologies than any older people. This may have been the case 20 years ago. Now, however, financially attractive consumers, such as maturing boomers who have grown up in the age of consumer electronics and have used computers at work are not slow in adopting the latest advances in electronic products. As illustrated by texting and online social networking, children and teenagers were indeed the first consumer group to adopt these new technologies. Nevertheless, when one examines data on market penetration for technologies such as e-mails and online shopping, it is now apparent that older people have rapidly started to utilize new technologies and products for which they perceive a genuine benefit exists in relation to enhancing their current lifestyle.

Research-based evidence to support the view that older financially attractive consumers should be considered as primary targets in the marketing of new technologies has been provided by a recent study by Niemala-Nyrhinen (2007). This research specifically focused on the issue often mentioned in the literature; namely older people suffer from technology-related anxiety, which causes them to avoid using new technology-based innovations. A large scale survey of Finnish people in the age group 50–64 revealed that the vast majority of respondents did not exhibit any anxiety over using new technologies. Additionally, the results also indicated that as this age group gained experience using products such as the internet or phone texting, this tended to act as a stimulus for people to introduce other technologies into their every day leisure and socializing activities.

Some of the leading consumer electronics and computer firms have recognized the important market opportunities offered by focusing on financially attractive consumers as a primary customer target (Vranica 2002). For example when Microsoft launched their television-based web-surfing device, MSN TV, their television commercials were specifically directed at older people by communicating how the system was effective in building closer links with friends and relatives. Similarly at Christmas 2000, the consumer electronics giant Sony Corporation focused their television advertising campaign on older shoppers by featuring maturing boomers in their television commercials using Sony products such as the Handycam to enhance enjoyment of their leisure time activities.

A very probable reason why some firms have encountered problems penetrating the financially attractive older person market is a failure to recognize that the product proposition which appeals to teenagers often needs modification before being marketed to other consumer groups (McClosky 2006). Young people tend to want electronic products such as mobile phones and digital cameras to offer a multitude of different features. The orientation of older individuals is more towards functionality and value for money. Hence, their preference is not for products which incorporate every aspect of the latest technology. Instead, they tend to opt for reasonably priced goods such as mobile phones which offer effective, easy to use, functional features.

The other critical issue which designers of new products must recognize is that humans' ability to immediately comprehend complex technology can decline with age. Hence, what may seem extremely obvious to a teenager, often becomes much more difficult for a person to understand even at ages as low as just 35. Additionally an early outcome of the ageing process for many consumers is the onset of declining dexterity (Pringle 2005). It was the Japanese mobile phone manufacturers who first recognized the marketing opportunities associated with this fact. Those companies launched mobile phones with larger, clearer keypads and fewer user functions, which achieved immediate success among older Japanese consumers. Retailers of electronic goods in Western nations are also now recognizing that when their staff are engaged in assisting older people select a new product, there is a need to focus on functionality instead of demonstrating how a product offers a huge range of technological features.

In the UK, the mobile telephone operator Vodafone found through market research that even 35–55 year old people would not come into their retail stores because the young staff (1) talked in acronyms consumers could not understand and (2) promoted features about the phones on offer such as cameras and internet browsers in which consumers had no interest. As part of a programme to assist staff to understand the need to modify their selling style to suit the needs of the older customer, the company has started lending their Vodafone Simply product to the parents of their sales staff. By observing the reaction and feedback of their parents, Vodafone are hoping their staff will begin to understand how to be more effective at in-store selling.

Robot butlers and maids?

Case Aims: To illustrate the potential future impact of new technology on one aspect of older peoples' lives.

An example where the technology is still at an early stage and hence potential outcomes are somewhat unpredictable is when, or whether, robots will become part of our daily lives. One emerging impact is the potential of this technology to reduce some aspects of healthcare provision. In leading hospitals in the USA and the UK, clinicians are already experimenting with robots to permit consultations with patients, family members and healthcare staff, not just within a hospital, but also from remote locations (Source: www.intouch-health.com). This technology may also have the potential to resolve the growing healthcare delivery problems associated with a shortage of nurses and the costs of employing nursing staff. Some maturing boomers or their partners will face a decline in health, although not requiring a move into residential care, that is sufficiently serious that in-home assistance with day-to-day chores is necessary. Within a few years, some medical experts are predicting that robots will offer the solution for overcoming the problem of the ever increasing costs of using humans to deliver cost-effective at-home care. Those involved in the development of these domestic service robots face a set of programming problems that are very different from those involved in the creation of industrial robots (Gomi 2003). These latter machines operate on a control programme written for a specific situation in which there is minimal variation in the machine's operating environment. In the case of service robots that are being developed to undertake even the apparently simplest of tasks, such as automated vacuum cleaning, the machines will encounter wide environmental variations such as uneven floors, irregular distribution of dust and irregularly shaped rooms. The robot must also be programmed to automatically stop when encountering any obstacle, including most importantly the presence of a human or animal. The main resultant differences between these two robot types can be summarised as follows:

	Industrial robots	*Service robots*
Usage	Manufacturing	Service, tending humans
Aim	Accuracy, precision	Quality of service
Operation	Repetition	Constant change
Objectives	Definable	Hard to define
Adaptability	Pattern recognition	Evolutionary learning
Co-ordinates	Defined, fixed	Undefined

Unlike the world pictured in science fiction movies, many of the first generation service robot solutions will not involve the creation of an android to live alongside the human race. Instead the technology is being based upon human–computer interfaces where the user will use voice recognition software to issue commands to lights, doors and electronic devices such as televisions and cookers (Coles 2004). By having the people in the house wear a device the size of a wristwatch, these interfaces can also be used to monitor pulse, respiration rate and temperature. Should the data being generated indicate an emerging medical problem, the system can then alert other people, either within the house or the emergency services.

Sociodemographics

Sociodemographics describe the structure of a population in terms of variables such as income, age, employment, education, household size and geographic location. Most industrialized nations undertake a regular census of their inhabitants and make these data freely available to other interested parties. By examining how these data change over time, firms can identify emerging shifts in sociodemographic profiles. It is extremely easy to acquire data from Government agencies on, for example, the forecasted trend in the number of financially attractive consumers living in a specific location. This information can be used to determine whether the trend represents an opportunity or a threat in terms of influencing potential market size. There are also a number of websites where firms can gain further understanding of the impact of sociodemographic change. For example at www.shapingtomorrow.com, the visitor will find articles that provide in-depth analysis and predictions about whether consumer profile shifts are an opportunity or a threat in terms of the impact of changes in the global economy.

Sociodemographic clusters

Case Aims: To illustrate how software tools can be used to develop a deeper understanding of how sociodemographics can be used to generate understanding of variations in consumer buyer behaviour.

There now exists a number of commercially available software tools which marketers can use to gain greater understanding of how interactions between sociodemographic variables such as behaviour, age, income and lifestyle can be used to classify individuals into groups characterized by their purchase behaviour. For example, the website www.demographicsnowuk. com not only provides access to a wide range of data, but the company's proprietary PERSONICX geo-demographic analysis software uses different behaviour patterns to classify individuals into a diverse range of sociodemographic sub-groups. These groups can each be examined as the basis for forecasting trends in population sub-group size. Examples of the characteristics of individuals within two such sub-groups are:

Gourmet travellers

This cluster contains postcodes that have a mixture of life-stage groups. These married couples aged between 55 and 64 live in small towns or rural areas. Their children have left home so they now just have pets sharing their detached house. They generally have at least two cars, sometimes including a convertible and an estate. They also enjoy all the mod cons and the home improvements they have made. They like nothing better than relaxing at home with a whisky or a brandy – Courvoisier, Remy, and Hine being their favourites. Degree educated they have enjoyed professional careers, some running their own businesses. They have probably now retired and enjoy frequent holidays and have travelled all over the world in the last 3 years.

Detached in the city suburbs

This cluster contains postcodes that have a mixture of life-stage groups. These retired couples or widows over 65 years of age have lived in their detached house for over 30 years. They take vitamins and supplements and enjoy lots of relaxation on their cruise holidays. They typically also have private medical cover. Before retirement, they worked in a professional capacity or in senior management and have set up a funeral plan, and invested in Guaranteed Income Bonds, high interest investments, shares and unit trusts. Along with having a newspaper delivered, they also subscribe to *Which?*, *Time* and *National Geographic*.

Culture

Culture is a key element in determining the prevailing attitudes and behaviours of a nation's population. Identifying the early signs of a culture shift is not easy because typically it will only involve a small sub-group within the population. Once recognized, however, these early signs can provide a significant new market opportunity. One example is provided by the smaller firms within the package holiday firms in the travel industry. Some years ago, these firms perceived that older financially attractive consumers were beginning to shift from vacationing in luxury resort hotels to a desire to visit more remote, exotic locations around the world. By moving before their larger national brand competitors and providing new vacation packages that fulfilled these changing consumer needs, these smaller firms managed to capture a significant share of this sector of the travel market.

A firm which does not revise strategy until a culture shift has already influenced the behaviour of a large proportion of the population, risks the possibility that the change has become a threat. For many years, McDonald's was perceived as an iconic brand in the USA, being the eat-out destination for the entire family. Then in the 1980s, a small minority of consumers began to be concerned about green issues and the impact of the American multinationals on the environment (Kramer 2000). This was subsequently followed by consumer concerns about healthier eating with the American fast-food industry being blamed for the nation's rising levels of obesity. McDonald's initially appears to have disregarded these emerging culture shifts. It was not until some years later that the company responded with actions such as introducing recycled packaging materials and subsequently the introduction of new food ranges such as salads and low calorie deserts.

The shift in cultural values within a population can be influenced by a number of different factors. These include the views of parents, personal social experiences, work experiences, religion, political events, economic circumstances and even the views of children. Determining the relative impact of these different variables is extremely difficult. What is researchable, however, is how cultural values change with income and age and may vary between countries. For example Murphy *et al.* (2004) concluded that the top most important cultural values for older Americans in descending order of importance are family security, health/ happiness, accomplishment, self-respect and wisdom. This can be contrasted with the values of 18–25 year old Americans for whom the top five values are health/happiness, love, friendship, an exciting life and family security.

Possibly one the most obvious shifts in the cultural values of financially attractive consumers are the differences which have emerged between themselves and their parents' generation. In Western nations, the values of their parents' generation were moulded by events such as the Great Depression and the Second World War. This caused an entire generation to be very concerned about issues such as achieving financial security, ensuring a secure future for their children and avoiding poverty. In contrast, individuals such as maturing boomers have lived in a world of high employment and material gain. This is reflected in a greater willingness, especially once their children have left home, of being prepared to spend money enjoying themselves through actions such as buying a sports car or taking frequent vacations to exotic locations (Janoff 2000). In fact, this significant shift in the behaviour of financially attractive older consumers in the USA has caused McGuinness (1997) to suggest that their behaviour reflects a reversion to behaviour traits similar to those which these individuals last exhibited when they were still teenagers.

Where to live? (Livette 2006)

***Case Aims: To illustrate how cultural shifts are influencing
housing decisions among maturing boomers.***

A very important emerging culture shift among maturing boomers is their changing attitudes towards selecting where and how they want to live once their children leave home and also upon becoming retired. Until the housing crash of 2007–2008, this culture shift was influenced by factors such as the high re-sale value of the family home and the adverse impact of observing a parent or relative living out their final years in residential care. Higher income couples still in work are tending to buy second homes for use as a weekend retreat or vacation destination. Often their plan upon retirement is to relocate to their second home. There is also evidence in the USA of a strengthening interest in co-housing. This is a trend for people to come together based upon interests or friendships. This concept seems especially appealing to couples with no children, couples with children living some distance away and women made single by death or divorce. The rising cost of houses which has been a boon to older consumers but creating an insurmountable barrier for young people hoping to own their own homes is now showing signs of creating a reversed culture shift in Western nations. Before the Second World War it was the cultural norm in most Western nations that three generations of a single family would live under the same roof. The trend in the latter half of the twentieth century was that as material wealth increased, grandparents lived in one house, their offspring lived in another and their children moved out at the age of 18. Factors including house price inflation in excess of average earnings, longer time spent in college, later marrying ages and the cost of residential care are all combining to create a possible culture shift back towards multigenerational living. In most cases, the greater wealth of the mature boomers will mean that they will be the supplier of accommodation for the older and younger generations in this multigenerational model. Over time, this trend will influence consumer demand in relation to such issues as the nature of services being made available by small businesses in a neighbourhood, new-build house designs and the type of extensions being added to existing houses.

The unmentionable market

Case Aims: To illustrate how the emergence of a change in consumer attitudes about suicide in the face of serious illness or terminal ageing conditions has led some people to accept euthanasia as a morally justifiable act.

In modern Western society, death is not a subject which people openly discuss with each other (Shakespeare 2006). About the only time it becomes a topic of open conversations is when people hear about a death of somebody they knew or after they have recently attended a funeral. Raise the topic of dying with people in their 60s and 70s and it is not unusual for them to admit what they really fear is facing a lingering death in their old age. Typically this conclusion has been reached because they have experienced (1) modern medicine prolonging the life of an extremely ill friend or relative or (2) visiting somebody in residential care who is in an immobile, vegetative state. At the moment the prevailing culture in most Western nations is that most people do not believe it is morally acceptable to commit suicide in order to avoid a prolonged period of suffering. Nevertheless, there are early signs that this widespread belief is undergoing change. In some countries there is already acceptance of the 'living will' which instructs relatives to not permit doctors to resuscitate an individual who is terminally ill. Extrapolating this culture shift leads to the conclusion that actively assisting people to commit suicide is a potentially large market, especially among both spouses and children of retirees. One individual who has already recognized the market implications of this culture shift is the Swiss entrepreneur Ludwig Minelli. Assisted suicide in Switzerland is not illegal and in 1998, Minelli founded Dignitas. This is a clinic for people who wish to terminate their own life. The majority of his clients are people suffering from a terminal illness. Over the longer term, he perceives growing demand not just from more people deciding suicide is acceptable in the face of a long-term illness, but also from people not wishing to spend a prolonged period of time living in a residential home in a completely vegetative state. At Digitas, the patient performs the act of suicide by drinking a lethal dose of a drug such as sodium pentobarbital. The role of Digitas is to make the drug available to the client and to provide a secure location in which the person can commit suicide. Each suicide is video-taped for review by a coroner to prove the act is voluntary. In this way, the clinic avoids being accused of euthanasia, which is where a third party performs the act that causes the person's death. The current fee for the Digitas service is about £2,500. Minelli has plans to expand his operation by opening a chain of clinics across Europe. Attendees will receive information and guidance over the decision to commit suicide. Presumably this move will increase awareness of the Digitas operation and generate an expanding number of clients seeking the firm's suicide assistance service.

Competition

Another potential external influence which may result in revenue change over time is the current or future activities of competitors. In most cases, competitors will be considered as a threat because they can be expected to attempt to steal market share. Occasionally, however, competitors' inability to meet customer needs can result in dissatisfaction being an emerging trend within a market. This can create a new opportunity for another firm. This has occurred in the UK beer market. Major brewers focused on optimizing their costs by offering a standardized, possibly bland, product. This caused a number of entrepreneurs to realize an opportunity existed to sell specialist beers to pubs within a 50–100 mile radius of their small breweries under the generic banner of 'real ale'. Their primary target audience are financially attractive older males who remember the days when beer was not presented as a mass market product.

Consumers, through the impact of advertising and sales promotions, are continually being exposed to brand share battles between major brands. In most cases, these wars, although having some positive influence on sales revenue, are extremely expensive undertakings because they generate a minimal improvement in overall profitability for either of the warring parties. Other firms should learn from these scenarios and in most cases, seek to determine how best to avoid competitive threats that could lead to head-to-head confrontations with others within their market sector. One approach to determining how to avoid costly competitive battles is to map the nature of the propositions being offered by other firms. An effective approach is to assume firms offer products which constitute two benefit dimensions; namely price and product benefit. As illustrated in Figure 3.3, it is suggested that price can range from high to low. In the case of benefits, it is proposed that potential strategic choice can extend across offering a broad range of benefits (e.g. extensive product choice, pre- and post-purchase service, extend warranties, etc.) through to a limited range of benefits (e.g. single product, no warranty). Combining these two dimensions generates four different product propositions that can be offered to the market.

Two of the propositions use low price as the important attribute of the product. The differentiator between these two price positions is that 'economy' involves offering a limited range of benefits, whereas 'high value' is made available at a similar price but also promises a much broader range of benefits. Providing a broad range of benefits at a high price is the basis for a 'high performance' proposition. The 'constrained' offering is based upon a limited benefit proposition, where either there is a need to charge a high price because of high operating costs, or because demand exceeds supply and the firm can hold the market to ransom. The

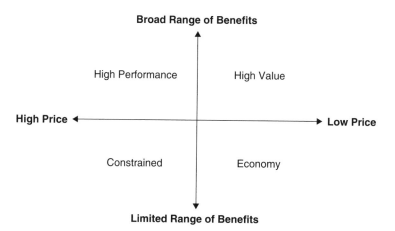

Figure 3.3 A product positioning map.

nomenclature of 'constrained' not only reflects these two scenarios, but also suggests that there will be much less opportunity for revenue growth in this sector of the market.

By observing other firms in the market sector, marketers can identify the position of these organizations. Where market sector mapping reveals a large number of other firms clustered into a single sector, competition will tend to be intense and the ability to achieve an adequate level of profitability will be limited. Hence any firm wishing to avoid an intense level of competition would be well advised to select a different area of the market in which to operate. The suggestion assumes, however, that moving to another sector of the market is a viable proposition for the company.

References

Aaron, H.J. (2007) 'Budget crisis, entitlement crisis, health care financing crisis – which is it?', *Health Affairs*, Vol. 26, No. 6, pp. 1622–44.

Abdel-Ghany, M. and Sharpe, D.L. (1997) 'Consumption patterns among the young-old and old-old', *Journal of Consumer Affairs*, Vol. 31, No. 1, pp. 90–113.

Anon (2006) 'Private client/family: dating game', *The Lawyer*, London, 4 September, p. 33.

Anon (1999) 'Gray Panther renaissance', *Wall Street Journal*, New York, 7 June, p. 5.

Anon (1995) 'Empty nesters bring affluence to discount retailers', *Discount Store News*, Vol. 34, No. 7, p. 29.

Bahizi, P. (2003) 'Retirement expenditures for whites, blacks, and persons of Hispanic origin', *Monthly Labour Review*, Vol. 126, No. 6, pp. 20–7.

Coles, C. (2004) 'Robots and sensors make seniors mobile', *The Futurist*, Vol. 38, No. 3, pp. 12–15.

Denton, F.T., Dean C. and Spencer, M. (2006) 'Age retirement and expenditure patterns: an econometric study of older households', *Atlantic Economic Journal*, Vol. 34, No. 1, pp. 421–33.

Destination Florida Commission (2003) 'Florida as a destination for retirees: the economic benefits', www.ccfj.net/DestFlaFinRep

Flyn, D. (2004) 'Only the over-50s need apply', *Sunday Times*, London, 5 September, p. 14.

Friedland, D. and Summer, P. (2005) 'Demography is not destiny, revisited', Georgetown: Centre for Ageing Studies, University of Georgetown, www.cmwf.org

Gomi, T. (2003) 'New AI and service robots', *Industrial Robot*, Vol. 30, No. 2, pp. 123–39.

Hwang, S.L. (2004) 'Personal finance – family finance: more seniors are piling up debt', *Wall Street Journal*, New York, 18 February, p. D2.

Janoff, B. (2000) 'The aging of Aquarius', *Progressive Grocer*, New York, Vol. 79, No. 8, pp. 79–83.

Kaid, L.L., McKinney, M.S. and Tedesco, J.C. (2007) 'Introduction: political information efficacy and young voters', *The American Behavioural Scientist*, Vol. 50, No. 9, pp. 1093–1113.

Kramer, G. (2000) 'McDomination', *Harvard International Review*, Vol. 22, No. 2, pp. 12–14.

Lindbeck, A. (1994) 'Overshooting, reform and retreat of the welfare state', *De Economist*, Vol. 142, No. 1, pp. 1–19.

Livette, M. (2006) 'Retirement housing for sale and differences in the decision to purchase that are determined by gender or marital status', *Property Management*, Vol. 24, No. 1, pp. 7–20.

Mahoney, J. (2004) 'Reverse mortgages can drive deposits and strengthen relationships', *Community Banker*, Vol. 13, No. 5, pp. 50–2.

McClosky, D.W. (2006) 'The importance of ease of use, usefulness and trust to online customers: an examination of the technology acceptance model with older consumers', *Journal of Organizational and End User Computing*, Vol. 18, No. 3, pp. 47–66.

McGuinness, K. (1997) 'Baby boomers at "middle youth"', *The Futurist*, Vol. 31, No. 3, p. 9

Morris, H. (2008) 'Global tourism defies slowing economic trends', *Financial Times*, London, 5 July, p. 2.

Murphy, E.F., Gordon, J.D. and Anderson, T.L. (2004) 'Cross-cultural, cross-cultural age and cross-cultural generational difference in values between the United States and Japan', *Journal of Applied Management and Entrepreneurship*, Vol. 9, No. 1, pp. 21– 49.

Niemala-Nyrhinen, J. (2007) 'Baby boom consumers and technology: shooting down stereotypes', *Journal of Consumer Marketing*, Vol. 24, No. 5, pp. 305–14.

Pak, C. and Kambil, A. (2006) 'Wealth with wisdom: serving the needs of aging consumers', *Deloitte Research Report*, www.deloitte/com/research

Pringle, D. (2005) 'Softer cell: in mobile phones, older users say more is less, all the features just confuse', *Wall Street Journal*, New York, 15 August, p. A1.

Rubin, R.M. and Nieswiadomy, M. (1994) 'Expenditure patterns of retired and non-retired persons', *Monthly Labour Review*, Vol. 117, No 4, pp. 10–22.

Scruggs, L. (2006) 'The generosity of social insurance, 1971–2002', *Oxford Review of Economic Policy*, Vol. 22, No. 3, pp. 349–60.

Shakespeare, J. (2006) 'A date with death', Sunday Times Colour Supplement, *Sunday Times*, London, 16 April, pp. 28–32.

Taylor-Gooby, P. and Hastie, C. (2003) 'Paying for world class services: a British dilemma', *Journal of Social Policy*, Vol. 32, No. 2, pp. 27–45.

Thomas, T. (2006) 'Hidden doubts cluster behind consumers' retirement confidence', *National Underwriter, Life & Health*, Vol. 110, No. 18, pp. 13–15.

Vranica, S. (2002) 'Firms woo older holiday shoppers', *Wall Street Journal*, New York, 12 November, p. B7.

Wessel, D. (2004) 'The economy: keeping pension promises poses challenge', *Wall Street Journal*, New York, 16 September, p. A2.

4 Internal capability

Generic principles of marketing to financially attractive consumers (FACs)

The coverage of issues in Chapter 4 is designed to illustrate the generic principles of marketing to FACs in relation to:

1 Achieving and sustaining a successful market position is critically influenced by the internal capabilities (or competences) of the organization.
2 A critical need is the capability of being able to read weak market signals that provide the basis for developing an effective strategy which focuses on innovation to fulfil the product or service benefits being sought by FACs.
3 Long-term market success of firms is usually associated with the presence of an entrepreneurial leader capable of establishing a culture of innovation across the entire organization.
4 Minimal price sensitivity and the importance FACs place on being provided with the best possible products or services means innovative organizations will enjoy higher profitability than suppliers which exhibit a lower level capability for sustained innovation.
5 Success based on innovation still requires the organization to exhibit a high level of employee productivity in order to maximize profitability.
6 Above average employee skills are mandatory in the case of successfully meeting the needs of FACs. This is because these customers in determining their preferred choice of supplier place great importance on the expertise and commitment exhibited by an organization's staff.
7 Delivering superior service quality in FAC markets requires that the organization has the capability to rapidly identify the degree to which customer needs are changing and can evaluate the diversity of expectations which exist in these types of market.

8   The importance which FACs place on being supplied with error free products or services means that successful firms need to create internal information systems that can rapidly identify and diagnose any problems which may occur during the customer need fulfilment process.

Business failure

The history of business is littered with examples of companies which were born, achieved a high market share and then went into decline. Sometimes the final outcome was that of the firm disappearing completely (e.g. the US airline Pan Am). In other cases, some form of intervention permitted the business to survive but as a radically different trading entity (e.g. the once mighty, global UK motorbike brand Norton, which now only exists as a niche manufacturer of specialist machines).

Some marketing texts tend to indicate that many major corporate downturns are the result of a completely new, innovative product entering the market (e.g. Kodak impacted by the arrival of the digital camera). However, a more common reason for a major firm losing their leadership position is another company stealing market share by introducing an improved version of the existing product or service. A recent example of this scenario is provided by the two originators of the global car industry, Ford and GM. Over the last 10 years, these two companies have permitted competitors such as Toyota and Honda to introduce superior products and thereby overtake them in world markets.

In an attempt to gain further understanding of why some very successful firms go into decline or lose significant market share to competition, Miller and Friesen (1978) undertook an extensive analysis of published case studies of over 80 large corporations. This led them to conclude that failing firms can be classified in the following four archetypes:

1   *The Impulsive Firm.* This is an organization run by an extremely powerful, risk-taking CEO who in the past has succeeded using a strategy based upon boldly entering new markets, launching new products or by acquiring subsidiaries. Unfortunately, the latest bold move underestimates the scale of the challenge because the firm is put in the position of facing an extremely hostile market environment and also may lack the capabilities to deliver products that can defeat some extremely strong competitors.
2   *The Stagnant Bureaucracy.* This is an organization which has become used to operating in a benign, unchanging market. Consequently, the firm has been lulled into a false sense of security. When there is a sudden change in the external environment such as the entry of an extremely aggressive new competitor, the firm's structure and internal culture all create insurmountable barriers in relation to the firm being able to implement an effective response.

3   *The Headless Giant.* This is an organization which lacks a strong or unified leadership and exhibits a very conservative internal culture towards responding to any external threats. As a result, the company drifts along without any real sense of strategy or direction. Eventually a more aggressive company recognizes the leaderless nature of the firm and executes a successful attack resulting in a major loss in market share.

4   *The Upstream Swimmer.* This is an organization which, having enjoyed some success, due to poor leadership fails to consolidate this achievement by actions such as investing in the acquisition of resources needed to sustain business growth. In an attempt the resolve the problem, a new CEO is appointed who unfortunately also lacks the leadership skills necessary to reverse the firm's market decline.

The lemming

Case Aims: To illustrate another potential cause of business failure; namely duplicating a flawed strategy that is already being used by other larger companies.

On the basis of what has occurred during the 2008 meltdown of financial markets, there would appear to be another failure archetype which could be added to Miller and Friesen's list, namely *The Lemming*. This is an organization whose CEO thinks other larger companies in the same market sector have identified a new, more successful strategic concept which the individual decides to duplicate. Unfortunately, because the firm is a late market entrant, the decision is made to implement an even riskier version of the same strategy in order to achieve rapid business growth. An example of this scenario is provided by the UK bank Bradford & Bingley. Not only did the CEO, Christopher Richardson, copy the disastrous Northern Rock/ HBOS banking strategy of borrowing short-term funds to be support lending on long-term mortgages, he then decided to enter the buy-to-let market offering mortgages to consumers whose survival was totally dependent on house prices continuing to rise (Wallop 2008). The bank also decided to attract more business by entering the self-certification mortgage market where self-employed persons just had to fill in a form declaring their earnings as the basis for being assessed as suitable individuals to whom a loan would be granted. Further growth was achieved by the acquisition of the Mortgage Express which specialized in finding mortgages for the self-employed, people buying second homes and consumers entering the buy-to-let market. When the UK Government was forced to intervene in September 2008, arranging the sale of the savings and branch operation to the Spanish bank Santander and nationalizing the remainder of the bank's operations, Bradford & Bingley had £22 million of saving deposits and £41 billion liabilities in issued mortgages.

The resource-based view

Many of the case studies about how large firms have lost market share to competition usually reveal that customer needs have not undergone any real, fundamental change. Instead, the leading incumbent firm has not placed sufficient focus upon continually seeking ways of launching new superior products or using innovation to develop improved organizational processes in areas such as productivity or quality. This failure to invest in retaining superiority over other firms provides a competitor with the opportunity to develop the necessary internal capabilities through which to deliver greater customer satisfaction.

The managerial philosophy concerning market success based upon exploiting superior internal capability is known as the 'resource-based view of the firm' (or 'RBV') (Hamal and Prahalad 1996). It offers two types of strategic opportunity. First, a company may develop the capability to develop and launch improved existing products (e.g. Honda's excellence in engineering capability used to support their entry into the marine outboard engine market). Alternatively a firm may be able to initiate price-based competition by passing onto the customer savings achieved through the exploitation of superior operational technologies and processes. This latter approach is exemplified by the way major supermarket chains in the USA lost market share to Wal-Mart. This upstart retailer exploited superior capabilities in the areas of procurement and logistics as the basis for offering much lower prices to the American consumer.

Observing changes in the fortunes of well known companies should cause all firms to recognize the vital importance of how inadequate internal capabilities can impact market performance. The important lesson to be learned is that firms of any size can use internal strengths as the basis for achieving competitive advantage. Concurrently however, the firm must ensure any internal weaknesses are neutralized in order to protect firms from attacks by competition.

Assembling the skills

Case Aims: To illustrate how firms can assemble the necessary skills to create a successful new business focusing upon meeting the needs of maturing boomers.

Some new innovative businesses are launched because the founder is able to draw upon knowledge and expertise acquired while working for a larger corporation. These individuals also need, however, the entrepreneurial ability to recognize where they will need to compliment these capabilities by drawing upon the skills of others. Prior to his retirement, Sam Farber was the Chief Executive Officer of successful houseware company. He noticed his wife Betsey, who suffered from arthritis, had difficulties gripping ordinary kitchen implements. As he lacked skills in product design, he hired a company called Smart Design. He already understood how to use market research to acquire information about customers. Interviews were undertaken with various people including consumers, chefs and retailers. As he lacked an understanding of the special needs of older people, Sam hired a well-known gerontologist, Patricia Moore, to provide this capability. The outcome in 1990 was the founding of a new company Oxo. Under the brand name of 'Good Grip', Sam introduced a product range of 15 kitchen tools. Since then the company has gained an international reputation as a design icon and the expanded the product line now includes over 500 items. Sam sold the business in 1995. It was acquired by World Kitchens Inc., a houseware company based in Virginia. Oxo was subsequently purchased by Helen of Troy Ltd (www.oxo.com).

The advent of online retailing has greatly increased the feasibility of launching new electronic outlets which focus upon the needs of a specific customer segment. The founders of SeniorS SuperStoreS in South Carolina defined their strategy as drawing upon the expertise of individuals with a broad understanding of the maturing boomer market as the basis for delivering a wide range of products to enhance comfort, lifestyle, health and leisure. To deliver this strategy, as well as assembling a workforce with the appropriate skills to operate an online operation (e.g. website design, procurement, accounting, logistics, etc.) they brought together a group of individuals with extensive experience of delivering various services to older consumers. The group included physicians, therapists, pharmacists, nurses, financial planners, accountants and attorneys. These experts provide guidance on product line selection and contribute to the website's Community Room where maturing boomers can gain access to free information about health, safety and finance. The company has also established www.E-Seniors-Village.com to create an online fun location where older consumers can meet in a chat room and obtain information on topics such as weather and travel (www.seniorsuperstores.com).

Core capabilities

Although a specific superior internal core capability is often fundamental in terms of determining the strategic market position that will be adopted by the firm, research on entrepreneurship demonstrates that other internal capabilities are also critical in terms of achieving sustained business growth. One example of research undertaken to identify other critical capabilities necessary to support entrepreneurial performance was undertaken by Chaston and Mangles (1997). Data selected from a review of published studies were used to evolve and then quantitatively validate the internal capability model shown in Figure 4.1. The model proposes that there is a requirement for three key core capabilities types; namely leadership, identifying effective strategies and the existence of an integrated five component operational system.

The entry point into the model is the assessment of strategic competence. This includes the capability of the firm to monitor the external environment and to

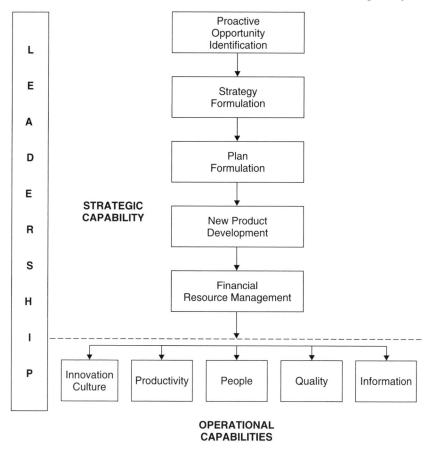

Figure 4.1 Internal capability factors contributing to market success.

identify new opportunities. Day and Schoemaker (2005) have suggested that fundamental to the exploitation of this competence is the ability to identify weak signals in the external environment. In commenting on weak signal identification, MacKay and McKiernan (2004) posit that conventional business planning and market research tools are somewhat ineffective in fulfilling this critical task. Furthermore, they feel that individuals who exhibit this skill seem to exhibit an unusually highly developed, intuitive ability to identify such signals and evolve entrepreneurial responses well ahead of their competitors.

Exploiting newly identified opportunities demands the company is capable of specifying an appropriate and effective strategy. This involves developing a concept to service new identified market opportunities in a way which is superior to offerings from competitors. The model shown in Figure 4.1 also indicates the need for involvement in some form of planning activity to assist the company to assess the validity of the proposed strategy and to define the actions required to successfully exploit identified opportunities. This conclusion is supported by a number of research studies on managing innovative business strategies. For example, in a study of manufacturing firms in Texas, USA, Khan and Manopichetwattan (1989) found that non-innovative firms exhibited a limited understanding of strategy, had poor planning skills and lacked the ability to implement an integrated response to changing market environments.

It may be the case that the firm's existing products are not the most effective way of satisfying financially attractive consumer needs. Under such circumstances, success will only occur if the entrepreneurial firm has the capability to develop and launch one or more new products (Martin and Staines 1994). Quite frequently, new product development projects can encounter cost overruns or fail to achieve the forecasted level of revenue. Therefore it is critical that the firm has sufficient financial resources to survive a new product development delay or a project failure. Should a new product project start to drain the business of large amounts of cash, the project may have to be terminated. In most extreme circumstances, the project may have the potential to totally destroy ongoing business viability. Hence the firm must have the capability to access the funds required to successfully implement a strategy founded upon the development and launch of new products. These funds may be sourced from retained profits, cash inflows from trading, external borrowing or from the issuance of new equity (Hogarty 1993).

Entrepreneurial leadership

The influence of individuals such as Jack Welch at GE, Lord King at British Airways, Lou Gerstner at IBM and Stuart Rose at M&S in the large firm sector is strong evidence to support the view that possibly the most critical internal capability in any successful organization is the presence of an effective leader. Some of the earliest writings on entrepreneurial leaders attempted to draw upon trait theory to identify behavioural patterns shared by successful entrepreneurs. Not surprisingly, as is graphically illustrated by seeking to identify any similarities between the personalities of Bill Gates of Microsoft and Steve Jobs of Apple, this approach was soon abandoned by academics as being unproductive.

One of the earliest quantitative studies on vital areas of organizational competence within entrepreneurial firms was undertaken by Stoner (1987). His research concluded that the most critical internal capability is the knowledge/ experience/skills of the company leader. The study concluded that only a very limited number of a very diverse group of small businesses located in Illinois, USA understood that to succeed, the company leader needs to create a 'distinctive competence' for the business. He posited that distinctive competence is critical in providing the basis for a competitive advantage that can provide the foundations upon which to base business growth. A similar theme has emerged in many subsequent studies in both Europe and the USA in terms of identifying the critical importance of leaders having the skills to direct the operation into evolving into a larger, highly successful business. O'Regan *et al.* (2005), for example, concluded from a study of 194 small manufacturing firms that strong leadership led to much better market performance than organizations where senior managers exhibited an uncertain or weak leadership style. Stoner (1987) also concluded that in the case of entrepreneurial service businesses, the commonest distinctive competence was the leadership that can ensure the firm is differentiated from competition through the delivery of superior service quality.

Identifying certain aspects of the leadership role often requires the use of qualitative research techniques. In seeking to understand the role of the entrepreneurial leader in high-tech firms as these organizations move from the start-up into the business growth phase, Swiercz and Lydon (2002) adopted a qualitative approach involving in-depth interviews with 40+ successful entrepreneurs. They concluded that all the entrepreneurs interviewed recognized the need to have acquired 'functional competencies' across areas such as marketing, finance, HRM and business operations. Furthermore, their depth of knowledge in these areas needed to develop further over time in order that the firm could successfully implement a growth strategy. These researchers also posited that entrepreneurs exhibit less tangible, non-functional competencies that are also necessary in order to be an effective leader capable of creating and then building a sustainable business proposition. Labelled by the researchers as 'self competencies', these included:

1   Exhibiting intellectual integrity in terms of understanding their own personal strengths and weaknesses, hiring people to complement their own weaknesses and being focused on continuing to learn from both formal and informal sources.
2   Moving over time from a 'me' to a 'we' attitude in terms of describing the firm to outsiders once business growth commences and being able to successful change from being a director of operational activities to the new role of being a coach and mentor.
3   Creating a sustainable business by becoming a strategic thinker. This involves focusing on longer-term issues while delegating day-to-day matters to others. There is a concurrent need to identify what exactly they, as the business founder, can contribute to the ongoing successful future management of the firm.

In seeking to gain further understanding of entrepreneurial leadership Fernald *et al.* (2005) adopted a somewhat different research approach. These researchers used a diversity of published information and case materials to determine whether there are characteristics which are common to both successful business leaders and successful entrepreneurial leaders.

Gifford Pinchot (1994), who coined the phrase 'intrapreneurs' to describe highly innovative individuals working inside large companies, feels that entrepreneurial leaders exhibit the following characteristics:

1   Ability to identify a vision which meets the criteria of creating value for all stakeholders, adds value to the business, represents moderate levels of risk and reflects the individual's personal values.

Table 4.1 Summaries of the identified shared characteristics

Characteristic	Entrepreneurial leaders	Business leaders
Ability to motivate others	X	X
Achievement driven	X	X
Creative	X	X
Flexible	X	X
Not adverse to taking risks	X	X
Patient	X	X
Persistent	X	X
Visionary	X	X

2   Has a stubborn persistence, but is flexible, listens carefully, never rejects help and is responsive to feedback from others.

3   Never abandons the goal of innovation, is extremely practical, accepts that false starts or blind alleys will arise, but after every setback starts looking for a new solution.

4   Recognizes the benefits of a team-based approach to implementing innovation and recognizes that multidisciplinary teams are more likely to overcome unforeseen problems than individuals working in isolation.

5   Shares rewards and positive acknowledgement of success with the team, but accepts total responsibility for any major errors during the project implementation phase.

Leader–customer values convergence

Case Aims: To demonstrate (a) how personal goals and the life experience of a business leader will influence idea identification and (b) can continue to determine the ongoing management strategy as an entrepreneurial business grows from a small firm into a global brand.

The majority of successful consumer goods companies tend to be run by CEOs about whom the general public knows very little. In those cases, however, where the company founder is still directing operations it may be beneficial for the marketing department to use this individual as a person with whom consumers can identify. Thus, for example, the Virgin Corporation has frequently exploited the eccentric behaviour of the founder Richard Branson as the basis for publicizing the launch of a new venture. The closeness with which consumers identify with a company CEO is directly influenced by the degree to which people feel this individual shares their values (Fernald *et al.* 2005). In terms of financially attractive female consumers, preferences which are often important to them in the owners or leaders of businesses to which they are loyal include the business being run by a successful woman who is hard working, articulate, can overcome any obstacles and demonstrate a strong belief in green issues. An individual who met these criteria and thereby achieved rapid market acceptance for her new, innovative business was Anita Roddick, the founder of the globally successful retail chain The Body Shop (Oates 1988). While employed by the United Nations, Anita visited various countries and was fascinated to discover how local people in countries such as Sri Lanka used vegetables and fruits as skin care products. Upon returning to the UK she married and, with her husband, opened a restaurant. He then developed a wander lust and went off on a horse-back ride from South America to New York that would take him 2 years. Anita did not feel she could manage the restaurant on her own, so she decided to open a shop. Anita's eco-orientation caused her to believe that women wanted products made from natural, organic ingredients and that none of the products while being developed should ever be tested on animals. She opened the first Body Shop store with a bank loan of £4,000. In the early years, although committed to her idea of eco-friendly cosmetics and skin care products, her primary business aim was survival in what was a very undercapitalized business. Gordon Roddick's horse died, so he returned to assist in managing the administrative side of the operation. Having proved there was a growing demand from eco-orientated women, the Roddicks persuaded a friend to invest in their business expansion plans. Even with this injection of capital, the company lacked the financial resources to rely on opening their own new retail outlets as the way to grow the business. So the decision was made to offer people the opportunity to buy a Body Shop franchise. This proved an exceptionally effective mechanism through which to build the business not just in the UK, but in numerous other countries around the world. In many cases, the franchise holder was another woman who saw The Body Shop as a way of proving their own entrepreneurial capabilities. During the development of a global business, Anita placed emphasis on ensuring The Body Shop remained loyal to her personal values of seeking to assist less advantaged people. To fulfil this aim she travelled tirelessly finding new sources of products in developing nations. Where necessary, The Body Shop provided financial assistance to local people in these countries to support the expanded production of ingredients and the manufacture of skin care products. Eventually the need for further capital to support business growth led the Roddicks to float the business on the UK stock market in 1984. The injection of additional cash sustained the further expansion of the business and by 1988, The Body Shop had 1,200 stores spread across the world, of which 90 per cent were franchise operations. By going public, Anita Roddick was exposed to pressure from major shareholders such as pension funds to make what in their eyes was a more conservative, properly run, professionally managed business (Davidson 1996). These investors attempted to apply pressure for a change in business philosophy, especially during periods when sales were affected by economic downturns in key markets such as

America and the UK. Anita's reaction was to remain unaffected by such demands. She continued to travel the world seeking new ways of helping people in developing nations and assisting in the creation of community support programmes for the unemployed. The activities and her decision to become a corporate member of environmental protest organizations such as Greenpeace and Friends of the Earth made the financial community extremely nervous. By the mid-1990s, it was apparent that Anita Roddick was increasingly frustrated by the constraints and criticisms of major investors which had the potential to block her desire to ensure the core values upon which The Body Shop business philosophy had been built remained unchanged. Although she stayed involved in developing new product ideas and overseas production sources, her level of participation in the day-to-day management of the business declined. She began to commit more of her time to social issues such as promoting ideas concerned with new ways of delivering education and the development of the UK's next generation of effective managers. Then in 2006, the last business surprise she sprang on the world was to sell The Body Shop to the French cosmetics firm L'Oréal for £100 million. Her supporters in the environmental movement accused her of selling out to a large multinational which was involved in animal testing and exhibited no environmental responsibility. Anita Roddick defended her actions, pointing out that she negotiated a deal in which L'Oréal had undertaken to become more environmentally aware and to cease participation in testing new products on animals. Only time, however, will tell whether these promises prove to be correct and that the new owners exhibit the values which are so important to The Body Shop's customers.

An innovative culture

As consumers, we all have experience of major brands advertising the introduction of their 'new, improved product'. The degree to which innovation has improved product performance can range from marginal (e.g. Parazone bleach being sold in a new, spill-proof bottle) to significant (e.g. Nike's launch of a new design of football boot to coincide with the 2006 World Cup). The scale of change and the frequency with which it is necessary to launch new products varies between industries and market sectors. In mature, low technology consumer goods markets such as soaps or detergents, change may be quite minimal and new products may only appear every 2–3 years. This can be contrasted with rapidly growing, high technology markets such as telecommunications and electronics (Montoya-Weiss and Calantone 1994). Here product innovation tends to result in major upgrades with new improved versions of the product appearing every few months (e.g. mobile telephones). In these markets, any delay in product launch will have a dramatic impact on revenue. This is because consumers tend not to wait for the postponed market introduction. Instead they switch to another supplier. This was the scenario faced by the Sony Corporation following their failure to launch their latest generation PlayStation product in time for the key 2005 Christmas market. The outcome of this failure was their potential customers switched their purchase loyalty to Sony's main competitor, Microsoft Corporation.

Chaganti and Chaganti (1983) determined that the highest level of profitability in manufacturing firms is to be found among those organizations which exhibit an innovative culture. This culture permits these organizations to successfully offer a broad range of products, use innovation to frequently up-date their product line and to be able to respond positively to market demands for product customization. They noted, however, that an innovative organizational culture has an equally important role in the implementation of process changes improvements within the organization. The usual focus of internal process enhancement will be to achieve one or more of the three key aims of reducing costs, improving quality and saving time. Although an entrepreneurial senior manager will probably act as project leader, ultimately success in process innovation is usually critically dependant upon the involvement of the entire workforce.

Productivity

The primary role of any firm is to convert inputs into a product or service that can be sold for a profit. Survival can only be achieved when the product or service can be marketed at a price that exceeds total operating costs. The difference between price and costs can be described in terms of the profit generated. This profit describes the 'added value' achieved by the workforce. Productivity is a measurement of added value. The importance of productivity is reflected by many Governments considering data on the productivity of firms in their respective countries being a key indicator of the competitive capabilities of their national economies.

The effectiveness of a company can be assessed by comparing productivity with that achieved by other firms in the same industrial sector. To permit comparisons between firms, productivity is usually expressed in terms of added value per employee. This figure is calculated by dividing annual profit by the number of employees. Although smaller entrepreneurial firms are considered to be more responsive, flexible and able to react more rapidly to new opportunities, in most countries smaller entrepreneurial firms are less productive than larger companies (Taymaz 2005). This reflects the influence of factors such as large firms being able to exploit economies of scale, having the buying power to procure raw materials at much lower cost and an ability to afford to hire highly trained staff.

In many low technology consumer goods firms, labour costs are often the highest single item of expenditure. For these firms to achieve higher productivity there are a number of capability enhancement options available which can save time or reduce direct costs. Gunasekaran *et al.* (2000) have proposed that in many cases, firms can make cost-effective gains in productivity by focusing upon improving internal work flows. Typically, this will involve simple actions such as improving procurement practices, identifying and removing bottlenecks on the production line, introducing a more structured approach to switching between items being manufactured and investing in upgrading workforce skills. The researchers also reviewed the alternative solution of replacing employees with machines. Their conclusion is that the approach should only be considered where the combined costs of purchase and operation of the new machines greatly exceeds the costs of continuing to use employees to undertake the task. Aris *et al.* (2000) however, reached a different conclusion about investing in advanced manufacturing technology. In their view, this should be considered as a priority strategy when considering ways to improve productivity. These authors did note, however, that obstacles such as lack of awareness of the latest technology, an inability to select the best solution or inadequate workforce skills can lead to the return on such investments being much lower than had been previously forecast when originally making the decision to invest in new equipment.

People

Many firms frequently claim their employees are the company's most valuable asset. The statement is extremely valid in relation to service sector situations. This is because where there are minimal differences between the services offered by providers, employees are often the only way to ensure customers receive an experience superior to that available from a competitor. An example of this achievement is provided by the ongoing success of the US speciality retailer Nordstrom. For over 100 years, this retailer has focused on the importance of staff using their merchandise expertise and personal commitment to deliver outstanding service as the basis for building strong relationships with customers (La Vere and Kleiner 1997).

Firms considering entry or expansion of existing operations in a financially attractive consumer market which involves employees interfacing directly with customers will need to examine whether their existing workforce has the appropriate skills for building strong relationships with customers. Available evidence would suggest that maturing boomers, for example, prefer communicating with older rather than younger service staff. This is because older staff are more likely to share similar values and exhibit greater respect for customers than younger employees (Peterson 2007). Hence, firms operating in financially attractive consumer markets are likely to be more successful where the workforce contains some appropriately skilled older employees. When the firm's workforce lacks this capability it is advisable to close this identified skills gap by hiring new staff.

Although there has only been a limited amount of research to generate a greater understanding of the benefits of hiring and retaining older staff, firms who have been trading for 10+ years usually find those staff who have been with the company for many years are often the most productive and effective employees. These individuals are typically highly popular with the firm's regular customers. Additionally they are respected by younger employees as the person(s) to turn to for advice or guidance on solving an operational problem (Paul and Townsend 1993).

Case materials about the effectiveness of older people in the workplace are supportive of the concept that older people can be classified into the four categories of age-impaired, age-enhanced, age-neutral and age-counteracted (Warr 1994). Age-impaired activities are those for which older people are not suited because they demand basic skills such as rapid analysis of high volumes of data or strenuous physical labour. Both of these skills are ones which tend to decline with age. Conversely, age-enhanced activities are those where employees' capability improves with experience. Examples of where this scenario exists in terms of fulfilling work roles are sales people and supervisory staff. In the case of age-neutral activities, the work is fairly routine and performance does not vary with age. This can be contrasted with age-counteracted activities where older people find tasks increasingly difficult. However, such problems can usually be overcome by re-designing the work environment, modifying the work task or providing further training.

Capability and loyalty

Case Aims: To illustrate the benefits of hiring and retaining older employees.

Rachel's is a major producer of organic dairy products in Wales that has employees ranging in age from 17 to 63. Their older employees are considered critical in terms of reinforcing company values, especially in terms of emphasis given to customer sovereignty, and helping teams develop mature and responsible attitudes. Similarly, another Welsh firm, Classic Canine Cuts, has staff ranging from their 20s to their late 50s. The older staff are perceived as critical to the firm's success in areas such as building strong relationships with customers and having in-depth experience of working with animals (Hilpern 2004). The idea of retaining older people, or giving preference to older people when hiring, is in conflict with conventional managerial thinking that has prevailed in the past. This is because many senior managers hold the opinion that older people are less productive, are paid higher wages and can lead the company into facing increased healthcare insurance premiums. Growing evidence of reality conflicting with perception, however, is being provided by those more enlightened firms whose response to labour shortages caused by population ageing has been to actively seek to hire older people. These companies report that compared with younger employees, older people are often more productive, committed and loyal (Albrecht 2001). Older employees exhibiting a high level of performance has also been the experience of a medium size Oregon firm, Poorman-Douglas Corporation. This company specializes in high speed cheque, invoice and other mailing services and through its legal division, legal noticing and claims processing. About 10 per cent of the permanent workforce is over 65 and many of them have been with the company all of their working lives. There are times when the volume of work exceeds workforce capacity, thereby necessitating recruitment of more employees on a short-term contract. The firm has found that older people are the best source of hard working, highly flexible, temporary staff.

Quality

During the 1970s, many Western manufacturers, fighting to sustain profitability in the face of both inflation and a refusal by militant unions to permit revisions in working practices, passively allowed the topic of quality to disappear from their organizational radar screens. Countries such as Japan, quick to realize the vulnerability that this situation created, moved into world markets offering high quality, reliable products at reasonable prices. It was only after inflation began to decline and unions began to adopt a more co-operative attitude that European and American firms became able to introduce Japanese inspired concepts such as Total Quality Management (TQM) to re-inject quality back into their operating philosophy (Anderson and Sohal 1999).

As the service sector became the dominant contributor to GNP in the Western World in the 1980s, the initial reaction of many organizations was to adopt the mass marketing techniques originated by the fast moving consumer goods firms (FMCGs), such as Unilever and Nestlé. They soon discovered, however, that heavy expenditure on television advertising or offering sales promotions (e.g. open a bank account and receive a cuddly toy) was not a cost-effective philosophy. The more perceptive firms realized that market success is dependent upon delivering a service experience which exceeds customer expectations.

A key reason for relying on quality as the basis for competitive advantage, especially among entrepreneurial organizations, is the ever present threat of the market leader offering services at much lower prices. For example, in both the retailing and catering sectors, smaller firms usually face a cost disadvantage in relation to the market leader (Kaynak *et al.* 1987). This is primarily due to the financial advantages which leading firms enjoy through being able to bulk buy or being of a size that permits exploitation of economies of scale. Entrepreneurs have long realized that smaller companies should focus on creating a highly flexible workforce because this permits their firms to be more responsive to customers demanding higher quality products and services. To achieve this goal, however, does require strong internal capabilities in areas such as measuring customer perceptions, identifying causes of customer dissatisfaction, diagnosing the cause of quality failures and implementing appropriate changes in organizational processes (Upton *et al.* 2001).

The other benefit in focusing on a quality-based market position in the case of the financially attractive consumer markets is that these customers usually exhibit a preference for higher quality goods. They also tend to be more loyal than more price-orientated consumers. The higher price sensitivity in this latter group means they can be more easily persuaded to switch brands by being offered sales promotions such as price pack or money off coupons (Moschis *et al.* 2004). The probable reason for lower price sensitivity among financially attractive consumers is that these individuals enjoy a higher average *per capita* income. In cases such as purchasing apparel they can afford to ignore the issue of affordability and hence can purchase named brands or the latest fashion goods. These consumers also exhibit a preference for shopping in upmarket department stores or speciality retailers. This behaviour can be contrasted with less financially secure consumers who have to make purchases for an entire family and therefore tend to shop in large supermarkets or discount outlets.

The key aim in delivering consumer satisfaction is to ensure that the perceptions of the customer which are formed by their actual purchase experience are equal or exceed their expectations about the service received. This concept is now widely understood in both manufacturing and service sector organizations. In terms of ensuring that perceptions equal or exceed expectations, organizations can use the Services Gap model (Zeithmal and Bitner 1996) which proposes that there are five potential problem areas which can arise in their service quality management activities. The nature of each of these gaps is as follows:

- *Gap 1* occurs because the organization has not acquired accurate information about what customers expect in terms of service delivery.
- *Gap 2* occurs because the organization has failed to set quality standards that can be used by management and employees to monitor the service delivery process.
- *Gap 3* occurs because the organization lacks the internal capabilities to deliver the required standard of service.
- *Gap 4* occurs because of incorrect information being communicated to the market.
- *Gap 5* represents the overall combined impact of the problems created by the existence of Gaps 1–4.

Over the last decade, both Governments and trade bodies within Western nations have focused on communicating the importance of exceeding customer expectations for firms wishing to achieve business success in increasingly competitive global markets. As a result, many firms have upgraded their operations in order to qualify for being awarded an international recognized quality standard such as ISO9000. The alternative has been to create their own company-specific, service quality management system. The outcome of either solution is that fewer organizations are now adversely impacted by the occurrence of one or more gaps in their service operations.

A possible exception to this generalization about the low occurrence of service gaps may exist within relation to meeting the needs of the more financially attractive consumers. This can arise because some organizations have yet to recognize that (1) the market needs of financially attractive consumers can be extremely heterogeneous and (2) the expectations among this type of consumer change rapidly over time due to their own purchase experience or the influence of inputs from others who are members of their social networks. The failure to recognize these two trends may result in firms, although able to create an effective system through which to ensure delivery of consumer expectations in mass markets, lack the capability to fulfil the service quality expectations of financially attractive consumers. The potential consequences, as summarized in Figure 4.2, are the emergence of the following service gaps:

- *Gap 1a* which occurs because the organization has not acquired accurate information about what different segments within the financially attractive consumer market expect in terms of service delivery.
- *Gap 1b* which occurs because the organization has not acquired up-to-date information about what expectation changes are emerging in relation to expectations within the financially attractive consumer market.
- *Gap 2a* which occurs because the organization fails to set quality standards reflecting expectation variation among different financially attractive consumer segments.
- *Gap 2b* which occurs because the organization is slow in updating the quality standards to accurately reflect the current quality expectation in a financially attractive consumer market.

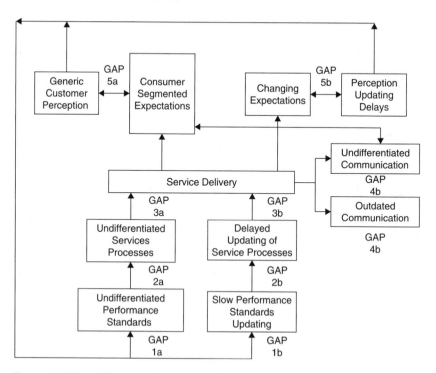

Figure 4.2 Financially attractive consumer (FAC) market service gap model.

- *Gap 3a* which occurs because the organization fails to develop the internal capabilities required to deliver differentiated standards of service across the various consumer segments which constitute their financially attractive consumer market.
- *Gap 3b* which occurs because the organization is slow in updating the internal capabilities required to deliver ongoing changes in expectations within their financially attractive consumer market.
- *Gap 4*a which occurs because of the same company information being communicated to the different consumer segments which constitute the financially attractive consumer market.
- *Gap 4*b which occurs because outdated company information is being communicated to financially attractive consumers.
- *Gap 5a* which represents the overall combined impact of the problems created by the existence of Gaps 1a–4a.
- *Gap 5b* which represents the overall combined impact of the problems created by the existence of Gaps 1b–4b.

Same consumers, different needs

Case Aims: To illustrate how the needs of the consumer in relation to tourism products may change as they move from the baby boomer into the mature boomer phase.

Due to both rising incomes and the declining costs of air travel, the baby boomers were the first generation in which most of whom could afford to take overseas vacations. They have retained this enthusiasm for international travel as they have grown older. In many cases, a nostalgia influence often causes them to return to locations where they holidayed previously with their children (Chirivella and Hart 1996). On the earlier trips when still young, their location and accommodation decision was usually based upon wishing to fulfil two needs: (1) sun and (2) prices sufficiently low to be able to take the whole family. On the basis of available research by organizations such as the World Tourist Organization, it is apparent that as boomers mature, their vacation needs change significantly. This situation even applies when nostalgia prompts a return to a location previously visited when younger. Sun and low prices are now rarely important issues. Instead the maturing boomer is much more interested in the accommodation and the surrounding amenities in relation to the following issues:

1   Ensuring their visit will be safe in relation to issues such as fire prevention regulations, local crime and terrorism.
2   Avoiding the risk of illness by ensuring the accommodation and other local facilities are sufficiently hygienic in terms of meeting food safety standards in the preparation, storage and serving of meals.

3   Extremely high levels of personal service being achieved by the hotels setting and achieving high standards for guest comfort, courtesy and speed of service.

4   Transparency over all aspects of the proposition being offered at the time of booking such as no 'hidden costs', genuine description of the true physical state of the accommodation and realistic descriptions in relation to ease of access to all local facilities.

5   Authenticity in terms of the services and facilities reflective of local culture and values, and hotels not having distorted their operational ambience in order to create a 'home away from home' environment for overseas visitors.

Those hotels and locations in the international travel market that recognized early market signals of the ageing of boomers being accompanied by a change in the product and service needs among this consumer group have had sufficient time to begin the process of repositioning their operations. Strategic changes have involved actions such as upgrading accommodation, expanding the portfolio of services and re-training staff. The outcome has been to sustain sales revenues the maturing boomer market sector. In contrast, their competitors who ignored these trends and retained an economy positioning are now often finding difficulty in surviving in what is an increasingly competitive global market. The ability of this latter group to survive will probably decline even further because early indications of one of the outcomes of the 2007–2008 financial crisis is that their other important customer group, younger, more price sensitive consumers with families, now feel unable to afford an overseas holiday.

Information

Data stored in a person's mind is known as tacit information. Ensuring others can access tacit knowledge usually requires a 1:1 interaction between individuals. This contrasts with explicit information which is stored in an accessible form, such as a written report or a computer file. The complexities associated with managing large organizations have long caused these entities to recognize the critical importance of maximizing the volume of information that can exist in an explicit form. Hence, these organizations have focused on creating systems for the acquisition and storage of data in a form that can be readily accessed by others. Successful consumer goods firms also understand that the most critical information for assessing potential opportunities and threats are the data that permit employees to gain insights into all the factors influencing potential shifts in consumer behaviour (Chaston 2004). Sources of explicit data which can assist employees make more informed decisions include secondary data on generic consumer trends, the firm's own financial records, the firm's operational control systems for activities such as monitoring service quality and market research studies undertaken to generate primary data about a specific market situation.

Generalized secondary information on issues such as *per capita* income, expenditure patterns, savings patterns, leisure pursuits, social activities and political opinions can all provide useful indicators of potential future changes in the generic consumption patterns within financially attractive consumer markets. These types of data can often be acquired from sources such as Government expenditure surveys and commercial market research omnibus studies undertaken by companies such as the Gallup Organization.

In utilizing these data to gain both an understanding of consumer buyer behaviour trends and early indicators of emerging changes in lifestyle, there is a need to be aware that the definition of the 'older consumer' used in published research studies can vary greatly (Tongren 1988). For example some studies may encompass all persons aged 50+, whereas others may only focus on individuals of a 'pensionable age'. In this latter case, the information generated is only applicable to consumer behaviour patterns of individuals aged 65+. Even where the report contains a clear definition of the age of consumers covered by their research, another problem affecting the validity of data is the highly heterogeneous nature of the behaviour traits exhibited by financially attractive consumers. This wide variability is a reflection of differences in needs, interests and lifestyles. These are not strongly influenced by a person's specific age, but instead by the much more important key factors of health and income. In commenting on the potential data bias caused by researchers only using age as a classifier in their analysis, Sherman and Cooper (1988) have proposed that it would be preferable for such studies to also attempt to measure respondents' degree of 'life satisfaction'. They posit that this approach would then permit a much clearer understanding of the degree to which respondents are content with their lifestyle. This is because lifestyle satisfaction has a very strong influence over decisions concerning choices in relation to physical activity, consumption, leisure and social activities.

Although market research studies are rarely much use during the opportunity search phase associated with developing totally new product or service ideas, following market launch primary data generated through customer research can become an invaluable resource for providing early warnings of potential problems and new opportunities. Regrettably there is a tendency among entrepreneurs to continue to rely on intuition in the diagnosis of business situations even after a market for the new product has been successfully established. As a consequence, these individuals tend not to create any form of Marketing Information System (or MIS) within their company which could be used to exploit available information as the basis for building new forms of competitive advantage. The more enlightened entrepreneurs, however, accept that these systems can be invaluable in the acquisition, storage and dissemination of explicit information to employees. The recognized benefit of these systems is that they are extremely useful in assisting employees make more informed decisions about actions designed to ensure the organization can continue to outperform competition (Tanabe and Watanabe 2005).

Historically, the creation of MIS structures to provide access to up-to-date, detailed market information often relied on the construction of an extremely expensive, organizationally specific, computer system. The advent of low-cost computer systems in business and the existence of extremely sophisticated 'off-the-shelf' database management software has made a significant impact on dramatically reducing the costs of creating company knowledge systems which bring together diverse sources of information from across the entire organization (Kotzab *et al.* 2006). As a consequence, entrepreneurs can no longer make the excuse of being forced to continue to rely on intuitive decision-making. This is because the advent of low-cost computer-based systems means virtually any company can now afford to create and operate a sophisticated, computer-based MIS operation.

The ability to exploit market data is further enhanced in the cases of firms selling products via the internet. This is because the firm is receiving real-time data on customer purchasing patterns which, through the use of data mining software, can rapidly identify new opportunities. One of the early exponents of this technique was Amazon.com. The company has developed software which upon placement of an order by a customer, uses knowledge of generic buyer behaviour patterns to recommend other products which might also be of strong appeal to the visitor to the company website.

Probably the world's airlines were the first major industry which moved to exploit online buyer behaviour data to create highly targeted marketing programmes (Garrow *et al.* 2007). The critical issue for any airline is maximizing the number of occupied seats on every departing aircraft. Even prior to the advent of the internet, those airlines which rewarded customer loyalty by offering redeemable points for each flight had a wealth of data on the business and leisure travel patterns of both individuals and specific sociodemographic groups. Once an airline created an online selling operation, it became possible to monitor in real-time seat occupancy levels for a specific flight. In those cases where occupancy levels remained low, the airline could then use their knowledge of passenger travel patterns to instantly create a price-based promotional offer to attract additional customers. In many cases the prime target for these offers are older financially attractive consumers. This is because the group when compared with younger people (1) can make additional trips without having to be too concerned about affordability, (2) have minimal family ties so can travel at almost a moment's notice and (3) tend to be interested in visiting a very wide variety of destinations.

References

Albrecht, D.G. (2001) 'Getting ready for older workers', *Workforce*, Vol. 80, No. 2, pp. 56–61.

Anderson, M. and Sohal, A.S. (1999) 'A study of the relationship between quality management practices and performance in small business', *International Journal of Quality & Reliability Management*, Vol. 16, No 9, pp. 859–72.

Aris, S.S., Raghunathan, T.S. and Kunnather, A. (2000) 'Factors affecting the adoption of advanced manufacturing technology in small firms', *S.A.M., Advanced Management Journal*, Vol. 65, No. 2, pp. 14–23.

Chaganti, R. and Chaganti, R. (1983) 'A profile of profitable and not-so-profitable small businesses', *Journal of Small Business Management*, Vol. 21, No. 3, pp. 43–51.

Chaston, I. (2004) *Knowledge-based Marketing*, London: Sage.

Chaston, I. and Mangles, T. (1997) 'Competencies for growth in SME sector manufacturing firms', *Journal of Small Business Management*, Vol. 35, No. 1, pp. 23–35.

Chirivella, C.M. and Hart, M. (1996) 'Market dynamics: three "S" tourism and the maturing single lady', *International Journal of Contemporary Hospitality*, Vol. 8, No. 2, pp. 10–18.

Day, G.S. and Schoemaker, P.J.H. (2005) 'Scanning the periphery', *Harvard Business Review*, October/November, pp. 135–46.

Davidson, A. (1996) 'The Davidson interview: Anita Roddick', *Management Today*, London, March, pp. 42–6.

Fernald, L.W., Solomon, G.T. and Tarabishy, A. (2005) 'Entrepreneurial leadership', *Southern Business Review*, Vol. 30, No. 2, pp. 1–10.

Garrow, L.A., Jones, S.P. and Parker, R.A. (2007) 'How much airline customers are willing to pay: an analysis of price sensitivity in online distribution channels', *Journal of Revenue and Pricing Management*, Vol. 5, No. 4, pp. 271–91.

Gunasekaran, A., Forker, L. and Kobu, B. (2000) 'Improving operations performance in a small company: a case study', *International Journal of Operations & Production Management*, Vol. 20, No. 3, pp. 316–35.

Hamal, G. and Prahalad, C. (1996) *Competing For the Future*, Harvard, MA: Harvard Business School Press.

Hilpern, K. (2004) 'Diversity at work', *The Guardian*, London, 21 June, Special Supplement, p. 4.

Hogarty, D.B. (1993) 'Beating the odds: avoid these mistakes at all costs', *Management Review*, Vol. 82, No. 1, pp. 16–22.

Kaynak, E., Ghauri, P.N. and Olofsson-Bredenlow, T. (1987) 'Export behaviour of small Swedish markets', *Journal of Small Business Management*, Vol. 25, No. 2, pp. 26–33.

Khan, A.M. and Manopichetwattan, V. (1989) 'Innovative and non-innovative small firms and characteristics', *Management Science*, Vol. 35, No. 5, pp. 597–606.

Kotzab, H., Grant, D.B. and Friis, A. (2006) 'Supply chain management implementation and priority strategies in Danish organizations', *Journal of Business Logistics*, Vol. 27, No. 2, pp. 273–300.

La Vere, S. and Kleiner, B.H. (1997) 'Practices of excellent companies in the retail industry', *Managing Service Quality*, Vol. 7, No. 1, pp. 34–9.

MacKay, R.B. and McKiernan, P. (2004) 'Exploring strategy context with foresight', *European Management Review*, Vol. 1, No. 1, pp. 69–78.

Martin, G. and Staines, D. (1994) 'Managerial competences in small firms', *Journal of Management Development*, Vol. 13, No. 7, pp. 23–34.

Miller, D. and Friesen, P.H. (1978) 'Archetypes of strategy formulation', *Management Science*, Vol. 24, No. 9, pp. 921–33.

Montoya-Weiss, M.M. and Calantone, R.G. (1994) 'Determinants of new product performance: a review and a meta-analysis', *Journal of Product Innovation Management*, Vol. 11, No. 5, pp. 397–417.

Moschis, G., Curasi, C. and Bellenger, D. (2004) 'Patronage motives of mature consumers in the selection of food and grocery stores', *Journal of Consumer Behaviour*, Vol. 21, No.1/2, pp. 123–33.

Oates, D. (1988) 'Keeping body and soul together', *Director*, Vol. 42, No. 12, pp. 64–8.

O'Regan, N., Ghobadian, A. and Sims D. (2005) 'The link between leadership, strategy and performance in manufacturing SMEs', *Journal of Small Business Strategy*, Vol. 15, No. 2, pp. 45–58.

Paul, R.J. and Townsend, J.B. (1993) 'Managing the older worker – don't just rinse away the gray', *The Academy of Management Executive*, Vol. 7, No. 3, pp. 67–75.

Peterson, R.T. (2007) 'Small retailer employment of older workers: an assessment', *Journal of Business Strategies*, Vol. 24, No. 2, pp. 123–41.

Pinchot, G. (1994) 'Entrepreneurial leadership', *Executive Excellence*, Vol. 11, No. 11, pp. 15–19.

Sherman, E. and Cooper, P. (1988) 'Life satisfaction: the missing factor in marketing to seniors', *Journal of Health Care Marketing*, Vol. 8, No 1, pp. 69–71.

Stoner, C.R. (1987) 'Distinctive competence and competitive advantage', *Journal of Small Business Research,* Vol. 25, No. 2, pp. 33–9.

Swiercz, P.M. and Lydon, S.R. (2002) 'Entrepreneurial leadership in high-tech firms: a field study', *Leadership & Organizational Development Journal*, Vol. 23, No. 7, pp. 380–9.

Tanabe, K. and Watanabe, G. (2005) 'Sources of small and medium enterprises excellent business in a service orientated economy', *Journal of Service Research,* Vol. 5, No. 1, pp. 5–21.

Taymaz, E. (2005) 'Are small firms really less productive?', *Small Business Economics*, Vol. 25, pp. 429–45.

Tongren, H.N. (1988) 'Determinant behaviour characteristics of older consumers', *Journal of Consumer Behaviour*, Vol. 22, No. 1, pp. 136–57.

Upton, N., Teal, E.J. and Felan, J.T. (2001) 'Strategic and business planning practices of fast growth family firms', *Journal of Small Business Management*, Vol. 39, No. 1, pp. 60–73.

Wallop, H. (2008) 'Where did it all go wrong? The rise and fall of B&B', *The Daily Telegraph*, London, 29 September, p. 4.

Warr, P. (1994) 'Age and job performance', in J. Snel and R. Cremer (eds) *Work and Ageing: A European Perspective*, London: Taylor and Francis.

Zeithmal, V.A. and Bitner, M.J. (1996) *Services Marketing*, New York: McGraw-Hill.

5 Customer identification

Generic principles of marketing to financially attractive consumers (FACs)

The coverage of issues in Chapter 5 is designed to illustrate the generic principles of marketing to FACs in relation to:

1 As personal incomes have risen and lifestyles become more diversified, the philosophy of mass marketing involving the provision of a standard product to all consumers has become a less effective business strategy.
2 Market segmentation is an effective technique through which to respond to the increased diversity in buyer behaviour which accompanies the emergence of FAC groups.
3 Successful exploitation of different financially attractive consumer segments requires that these segments fulfil the criteria of measurability, accessibility and viability.
4 Simple segmentation based on a factor such as age lacks the accuracy required to permit accurate targeting of different FAC groups.
5 Sociodemographic segmentation involving a combination of factors such as income, age and social class permits a more accurate identification of FAC segments.
6 Enhanced accuracy in identifying FAC segments can also be achieved by using geodemographics which is the technique that links sociodemographics with a location variable such as a country's post-code system.
7 The change in spending patterns during the different phases of peoples' lives means life-stage segmentation can provide an effective tool through which to relate the spending patterns of FAC groups to their current position on the consumer lifecycle curve.
8 Targeting accuracy for older FACs can be made more precise by using gerontodemographics. This is a technique that bases segmentation on a

> group of variables relevant to older persons such as age, health and level
> social interactions with others.
> 9   Moving from transactional to a relationship marketing philosophy is an
>   extremely effective strategy in terms of enhancing customer satisfaction
>   within FAC groups.
> 10 Customer relationship management (CRM) is an even more appropriate
>   tool for managing FACs because the technique exploits customer
>   purchase data to permit even more precise targeting of products and
>   services aimed at maximising customer satisfaction.

The phases of marketing

The Harvard academic, Professor Richard Tedlow (1990), posits that the evolution
of the marketing concept can be divided into three distinct phases. Phase I, or
'fragmentation', that exists because transportation and communications barriers
cause markets to be constituted as local or regional entities. Phase II, or 'unifica-
tion', is facilitated by the development of a national transportation and communications structure. Within the manufacturing sector this phase is accompanied
by some companies constructing large factories to minimize production costs. At
this juncture, some firms exploit improvements in transportation infrastructure by
expanding their distribution base and thereby benefiting from the economies of
scale of becoming a national business. To consolidate their market position and to
achieve market leadership, these national firms use the profits generated from
economies of scale within their operations to fund the selling of large volumes of
a standard product at very competitive prices.

An important aspect of the evolutionary processes underpinning Phase II of the
marketing concept was the influence on the manufacturing sector of Henry Ford's
vision to build a car which the average person could afford. This he achieved by
creating the world's first mass production manufacturing operation. He and other
American corporations, by linking together the philosophy of mass production and
the sale of a competitively priced standard product, then evolved the managerial
philosophy which has subsequently become known as 'mass marketing'. Tedlow
has proposed the following generic guidelines concerning the strategies appropriate for establishing successful mass market brands:

- *Guideline 1* is the requirement that the firm is able to exploit the economies
  of scale associated with mass production to sell huge volumes of low margin
  goods which generate a high level of absolute profits.
- *Guideline 2* is the requirement that the high level of absolute profits generated
  are re-invested in funding a high level of promotional activity as a mechanism
  through which to shape market demand.
- *Guideline 3* is the requirement that the firm, in seeking to create a high level
  of stability in the external environment, should create vertical supply chains

through which raw materials are sourced, production operations are managed and products delivered to the final consumer.

- *Guideline 4* requires that having achieved mass market dominance through being the first entrant into a major market sector, this action is followed by the creation of economies of scale barriers to ward off attacks from competition.

A critical requirement for successful mass marketing is that the majority of the population can afford to purchase the product. During the last half of the nineteenth century and the first half of the twentieth century a large proportion of the population in Western nations still lived at or below the poverty line. Consequently the few mass market brands which emerged during this period tended to be those which were either staple goods or perceived as affordable luxuries. Early examples of UK companies which have subsequently evolved into well-known global brands are the chocolate producer Cadbury and the Dove soap brand marketed by Unilever. Equivalent operations in the USA are Proctor & Gamble's Ivory soap brand and the Hershey's chocolate bar.

Following the end of the Second World War, consumers in the USA, subsequently followed by other Western nations, enjoyed an unprecedented growth in income and employment. Their purchasing power was further enhanced by the advent of the welfare state providing free or subsidized education, healthcare, pensions and unemployment benefits. The consequence was that in the early 1950s, many firms were able to achieve massive national and international growth through exploitation of the mass marketing concept to meet the needs of the world's first 'consumer society'.

Segmentation

The final phase in the Tedlow evolutionary model is Phase III, or 'segmentation'. This occurs because suppliers recognize that customers are beginning to exhibit variation in the benefits they are seeking from products. At the stage where it appears there are an adequate number of customers exhibiting different specific benefit requirements, suppliers are able to divide the markets into segments into which more specialized, targeted goods can be sold. An associated benefit of segmentation is that the supplier is often able to shift from prices being defined by the intensity of prevailing market competition for standard goods to achieving higher prices based upon the level of added value which is perceived by consumers to be provided by the more targeted products.

Once the opportunities for segmentation emerge in a market sector, a mass marketing firm can consider switching from offering a standard product to making available a range of products each targeted at meeting consumer needs within different market segments. The majority of consumer goods companies only began to perceive the potential for segmentation in their market sectors in the early 1960s. The emergence of this opportunity occurred because as *per capita* income continued to grow, consumers began to exhibit a desire to purchase a much greater variety of goods (Kotler 1989).

Segmentation is only feasible if the criteria of measurability, accessibility and viability can be met (Keller and Kotler 2006). Measurability requires that a segment's parameters can be measured using variables such as customer need, the number of customers and their location. Accessibility is concerned with being able to make contact with the customer in order to deliver the product and associated promotional messages. Viability is the issue of whether the revenue from the segment can exceed operating costs, thereby generating an adequate level of profit.

In the early years of moving from mass to segmentation marketing, many large firms were unable to provide products or services at a unit cost lower than achievable price. In the manufacturing sector this obstacle has since been removed through advances in technology (e.g. using robots on the production line) and by the adoption of more flexible production processes. Another important cost reduction catalyst has been the ongoing advances in computer technology. These have increased data processing power and lowered data storage costs. The outcome is that data storage, re-accessing data and analysing large volumes of customer information have become economically feasible. Further cost reductions have been generated in the large scale acquisition of data as a side-effect of consumers using electronic transmission channels such as credit cards and the internet (Pitta 1998).

The degree to which firms are able to implement a market segmentation strategy to assist sales revenue growth varies by both country and industrial sector. Virtually every Western nation firm should be aware, however, that the available research evidence indicates that the financially attractive consumers represent a much greater opportunity for market segmentation than the marketers' perennial favourite customer target: households within 18–49 year age group. This is because financially attractive consumers have greater spending power and are a much more heterogeneous group in terms of the diversity of their product needs and purchase behaviour.

Judgement segmentation can be misleading

Case Aims: To illustrate that marketing based upon assumptions about consumer segments can be misleading and may cause incorrect promotional decisions to be implemented.

Service marketing only began to be recognized as a specific and very different managerial concept in the 1980s. Adoption of a scientific approach to service market segmentation studies has lagged behind the tangible consumer goods industry. As a consequence, it is sometimes the case that segmentation decisions are based upon erroneous assumptions and judgements made by companies or Government agencies. This situation can lead to incorrect decisions being made over the focus of marketing strategies aimed at specific consumer groups. An example of this problem is provided by Prideaux and Crosswell's (2006) study of tourism marketing being undertaken in relation to Norfolk Island, a self-governing Australian territory in the South Pacific. For many years the Island has relied on tourism as the most important source of export revenue. When the researchers sought to understand the factors influencing consumers' decision to visit the Island, they were informed by local tourism representatives that their market segmentation strategy is based upon the following assumptions:

1   Visitors were mostly elderly and predominantly pensioners.
2   Most visitors were repeats.
3   Most visitors were retired couples.
4   Most visitors were low income earners.
5   Visitors were attracted by the environment of Norfolk Island.
6   Shopping was a major attraction.
7   Visitors were attracted by the Island's heritage reputation.

The researchers decided that there was a need to assess the validity of these assumptions and implemented a survey of visitors to the Island. This survey revealed a number of differences between the data generated and the assumptions being used by the Island's tourist representatives. In Australia, the age definition for pensioners is 65+. What the survey revealed was that although the Islands are popular with pensioners, the far greatest number of visitors are maturing boomers in the age group 50–64. In relation to the assumption about the high level of repeat visitors, the survey revealed that 72 per cent of respondents were visiting the Island for the first time. The assumption about most visitors being retired couples also proved incorrect because this group only constituted 32 per cent of the people surveyed. Not surprisingly the low proportion of retirees in the visitor mix also meant that the assumption about most visitors being on low incomes was also found to be invalid. This error was confirmed by the fact that 47 per cent of all visitors enjoyed an above average income in the country where they are domiciled. In relation to why visitors are attracted to the Island, heritage proved the most important factor followed by the natural environment. For the majority of visitors, shopping was seen as a very unimportant activity. Not surprisingly, the results caused the researchers to reach the conclusion that 'the use of unsubstantiated perceptions or personal assumptions may have serious consequences particularly if those tasked with marketing and planning are not aware of the entire spectrum of visitors. Segments that should be identified, and for whom new products should be created, may not be identified and, importantly, changes in long term patterns may be missed'.

Simple segmentation

The evolution of simple segmentation variables was dependant upon the ease with which customer data could be acquired. Gender of an individual is easy to determine. It is, however, a somewhat crude measure. To gain any benefit from this knowledge usually requires a second variable to be added such as age or income. Age has been a basic segmentation variable for many years. This is because although obtaining data on any individual's precise age can be difficult, observation does permit a reasonably accurate sub-division of customers into groups such as children, teenagers, young people, middle-aged people and retirees (McCrohan and Finkleman 1981). Different age groups tend to exhibit variation in their requirements for products and services. Thus, for example, a restaurant chain might focus on targeting teenagers/young people in some locations and middle-aged/older people in others. In relation to financially attractive consumers, however, age can be a somewhat misleading variable. This is because purchase behaviour can be dramatically altered by factors such as health or mobility. Thus, for example, maturing boomers approaching retirement but suffering from arthritis may not be in the market for golf club membership; whereas there are a significant number of healthy 85+ individuals who will be found on the golf course several times a week. Another popular single segmentation variable is discretionary income because this can be easily correlated with certain types of purchase behaviour. Again, however, the accuracy of this approach to segmentation is heavily influenced by health and mobility.

Age is a blunt instrument

Case Aims: To illustrate why a single variable such as age is of minimal benefit in seeking to segment markets as the basis for improving the effectiveness of promotional campaigns aimed at older people.

Legalized gambling is a huge and growing industry in many countries. As the intensity of competition has risen between providers of gambling services and between nations, companies within the industry have begun to turn to techniques such as market segmentation to gain a better understanding of consumer gambling behaviour. One such study was undertaken on behalf of the American Gambling Association (AGA) involving gaining understanding of the purchase behaviour of older consumers deciding to visit gambling resorts in the Midwest (Moufakkir 2006). The focus of the survey was upon issues such as a preference for day trips versus staying overnight; a preference for visiting gambling resorts on weekdays versus weekends; being a single individual or travelling in a group; the amount budgeted for gambling plus other spending; and sources of information used to select a gambling destination. It would appear from Moufakkir's article that the only segmentation variable used in the study was the age of the respondents. The results of the study revealed that:

1   The behaviour of elderly versus younger gamblers appears to be very similar.
2   Elderly people are more likely to travel by charter bus to the resort.
3   The majority of elderly and younger gamblers both engage in social recreational gambling, with level of expenditure being positively correlated with income.
4   Most elderly and younger people tend to visit resorts in a group.
5   Elderly people, especially those who are retired, tend to prefer to visit casinos during the week, whereas people in work prefer to visit casinos at the weekend.

It is apparent that by only using the very blunt single variable of age by which to segment consumers, the results of this research provided very little new knowledge. Furthermore it seems extremely probable that the same data could have been acquired more rapidly and at a lower cost by merely asking the views of the staff who worked in the casinos. Certainly in terms of assisting casinos develop more effectively targeted marketing campaigns, the only useful knowledge generated by the study is that any promotional incentives aimed at older people should probably focus on special offers orientated around weekday visits.

Geographic location, especially in the retail sector, is another simple, practical segmentation tool. Most shoppers are only prepared to travel a certain distance to purchase goods. As the value of an item rises, willingness to travel a greater distance will increase. One approach for gaining understanding of travel patterns is to enter customer addresses onto a map. This permits the retailer to develop a 'retail footprint' describing the maximum distance travelled by customers and also the variations in density of customer addresses within a defined area around the outlet. This knowledge can then be utilized in the design of cost-effective promotional activities such as targeted mail shots to specific geographic areas within travelling distance of the retail outlet.

The power of geographic location as a segmentation tool has been increased by Governments collecting population census data and by postal authorities creating postal (or Zip) code systems that group a small number of addresses into a unique alphanumeric or numeric code (Andreasen 1966). This information is in the public domain and thereby has allowed market research companies at very low cost to create data files on entire populations. These files contain names, addresses and the number of people living in a geographic area. The availability of such data means that even a small firm can undertake customized promotional activity by purchasing a list of names and addresses selected on the basis of specified postal codes.

Sociodemographic data

Developed originally to assist in the planning of public sector provision of services such as healthcare, education and housing, sociodemographic data cover a range of variables. Factors covered include age, income, occupation and social class. The latter measure is especially useful because it can be used as a surrogate to identify consumer lifestyles. The assumption which marketers make when using social class as a classifier is that consumers in higher social groups have a propensity to allocate a greater proportion of income to future satisfaction (e.g. insurance and pensions). This is contrasted with people lower down the social scale who, it is assumed, tend to spend more of their income on immediate satisfaction (e.g. beer).

Sociodemographic data that contain a specification of social class have permitted companies to use this information to classify markets into segments (e.g. insurance policies matched to different social classes). Researchers have noted, however, that within any social class there can be significant differences between the purchase behaviour of individuals. Concern about the possible errors which may develop using sociodemographic information has led to the development of geodemographic data as a more accurate way of classifying consumer groups (Pearce 1997).

A leading innovator in geodemographics has been the UK market research company, CACI Ltd (www.caci.co.uk). This firm used statistical analysis of population census data; a classification of residential neighbourhoods; Government expenditure surveys; and data on consumer behaviour generated by proprietary research, to create the ACORN classification system. Their latest version of ACORN classifies the UK population into five primary groups (Wealthy Achievers, Urban Prosperity, Comfortably Off, Moderate Means and Hard-Pressed). Each group is further sub-divided into groups from A–U, thereby yielding a total of 18 sub-groups. Each sub-group is then further sub-divided in relation to neighbourhoods exhibiting specific, common characteristics. For example within Group 1, Wealthy Achievers are broken down into Group A: Wealthy Executives, Group B: Affluent Greys and Group C: Flourishing Families. Then, within Wealthy Executives there are four further sub-divisions (e.g. sub-division 1: 'wealthy mature professionals located in high status urban areas living in large detached houses').

Postal codes and sociodemographic information is now available in a number of countries which means market research firms are able to supply geo-demographic data for most nations across the Western world. Some limitations in the application of the technique exist due to population variability within neighbourhoods and differences in buying patterns for products by households in the same area. As long as the user is aware of this potential drawback, however, systems such as ACORN remain an extremely cost-effective tool through which to define customer segments.

Acquiring geodemographic understanding

Case Aims: To demonstrate how geodemographic data can be utilized in the more targeted marketing of services to maturing boomers.

Geodemographics can be an extremely powerful marketing tool as long as the marketer has been able to determine a match between consumer types and purchasers of the product or service. A marketing consultancy company, Conclusive Strategies, based in Austin, Texas, confronted this specific dilemma when seeking to assist a private clinic develop a more effective marketing strategy for laser eye surgery (LASIK) some years before wider adoption of the technique permitted even national chains of opticians to offer this service (Barber *et al.* 2001). In an era where the major health insurers are putting pressure on the medical profession to control or even reduce the costs of healthcare, as demonstrated by the number of extremely wealthy plastic surgeons living in Los Angeles, elective surgery is an extremely attractive market for private clinics. This is because this type of surgery is rarely covered by healthcare insurance and hence the doctor is more able to self-define service prices. Additionally, as elective surgery is often undertaken for purely cosmetic reasons, the patient tends to be wealthier, with appearance being a much more important purchase issue factor than service affordability. The problem facing Conclusive Strategies was that although it is known that maturing boomers are the primary consumer group to whom elective surgery marketing should be directed, there is a lack of precise data about which segments in this market sector any promotional campaigns should be targeted. Further complications emerged because the consultants soon discovered that although the healthcare industry generates huge quantities of data, these are often scattered across numerous non-compatible computer files and these data frequently omit critical information such as the patient's income. To overcome this problem, the company undertook a two-stage research process. The first stage was to develop a customer profile describing variables such as age, income, size of household and the type of geographic areas where people lived. This was achieved by using the client's own records on 1,200 prospective patients interested in the LASIK procedure, but who did not have the surgery and 700 individuals who actually underwent surgery. The second stage involved a random mailing using a commercial database of US consumers supplied by the Experian Corporation to 1,000 consumers using the Zip (i.e. postal) codes which predominated in the clinic's patient records. Data from this survey were analysed using Experian's consumer lifestyle software product. This revealed that certain specific lifestyle groups exhibited a much higher probability of being potential purchasers of the client's LASIK service. This knowledge could then be utilized to develop a much more closely targeted marketing campaign which was significantly more cost-effective than the clinic's earlier marketing efforts.

Other approaches

Over the years, academics and market research firms have expressed concerns that standard classification systems such as ACORN do not identify segments which accurately reflect customer needs or purchase behaviour. To improve customer identification, a number of techniques have been tried in an effort to achieve greater segment identification accuracy. One of the earliest approaches was based upon product usage. By identifying sociodemographic differences between, for example, heavy users, average users and light users, it proved possible to develop customized promotional campaigns that could be targeted at these different user groups.

Firms in the mail order industry have long relied on usage patterns as the basis for segmenting markets. Segmentation is an effective approach for mail order firms because they are able to capture accurate, detailed customer data from sources such as requests for catalogues and orders placed by customers. The major source of profit for these firms is from loyal customers making regular repeat purchases. It is a relatively simple process to analyse customer records in relation to recency (the date of the most recent purchase), frequency (number of purchases) and money (total level of spending). This analysis will permit segmentation of the customer database into heavy, average and low purchase levels. Using this classification scheme, decisions can be made on increasing the frequency of promotional or catalogue mailing to heavy users or experimenting with different promotional approaches to stimulate increased purchase activity by customers currently classified as low purchasers (Schmidt 1992).

Another classic approach for segmenting customers is to exploit identified differences in the benefits sought from a product category (Haley 1968). Financial investment products, such as certificates of deposit, money market accounts, stocks, annuities, mutual funds, US savings bonds and corporate bonds are characterized by different combinations of three benefits: stability, growth and liquidity. Hence financial services companies can use this knowledge to determine which investor groups are more likely to be attracted by the benefits provided by their type of products (Chang and Chen 1995). Benefit segmentation is also a very important tool for banks. As alternative investment providers proliferated in the 1980s in the USA, in order to retain market share, banks started to offer mutual fund investment opportunities to individual investors and thus broadened their product offerings. The banks had a distinctive advantage over many investment firms; namely being locally recognized by investors who felt more secure when investing with a local financial service provider. Additionally, the bank's product portfolio includes savings accounts, checking accounts, money market accounts, certificate of deposit, annuities and mutual funds. Consequently, they are able to offer a one-stop proposition but concurrently use benefit segmentation as the basis for targeting products of appeal to specific customer groups.

Life-stage segmentation

The problems with poor accuracy of the single variable approach to define a consumer segment has caused researchers to conclude that the greater the variety of information acquired on consumers, the simpler it becomes to create an accurate description of the market segments which they occupy. This has led researchers to favour composite datasets. A popular approach is to use age, marital status and family size as the basis of classifying people into segments based upon their position on the family lifecycle curve. Support for the concept that life-stage status provides a more accurate basis for segmentation is provided, for example, by a study comparing the purchase behaviour of retired and working mature female boomers of a similar age (Widgery *et al.* 1997). Although both groups sought to optimize the value of their purchase, working women were most interested in issues such as manufacturer rebates, loan interest rates and monthly repayment levels. These variables were of little interest to retirees. Instead they were much more concerned about warranties, dealer reputation for integrity and developing a trust in the sales person.

In the case of life-stage models in relation to older people, this has generated classification systems such as: *Empty Nest I* (older couples, no children at home), *Empty Nest II* (older couple, retired, no children at home), *Working Survivor* (older person, partner has died or departed) and *Retired Survivor* (partner has died or departed) (Green and Welniak 1991). This type of classification system provides the basis for making available different products to meet the needs of specific segments. Thus, a travel company may promote different package holidays to two types of empty nesters. Using the assumption that Nest I couples have high incomes, the company would focus on offering customers in this segment a choice of distant, exotic locations. In contrast, Empty Nest II couples tend to have a lower fixed income and will probably be more interested in low-cost holiday packages in locations not far from home.

Hopkins *et al.* (2006) posit that the accuracy of any life-stage segmentation technique can be enhanced by incorporating the influence of two additional variables, namely role and coping theories. Roles are highly central to peoples' self definition about the lives which they lead. A role can be perceived as 'positive' when causing an individual to undertake activities associated with achieving lifestyle satisfaction such as purchasing the latest fashion goods or refurnishing their home. Conversely a 'negative' role is an adverse activity. An example is provided by the death of a partner causing an individual to withdraw from the world and refuse to accept attempts by friends and relatives to help the person through the grieving process.

Role transitions can evoke powerful emotions and coping theory is concerned with how people adapt and handle the stress associated with the major challenges which they will encounter throughout their lives. Individuals who are able to cope are those who find the strength to overcome the initial impact of an adverse life challenge and implement appropriate solutions. People who fail to cope often face periods of prolonged stress or, in some cases, develop stress-related illnesses such as high blood pressure or strokes.

To demonstrate the interaction of role and coping theories in terms of influencing the nature of consumer segments, Hopkins *et al.* (2006) researched the nature of lifestyle traits across areas such as income, purchasing behaviour and appraisal of personal circumstances of individuals who had recently retired. Cluster analysis revealed the following consumer segments:

1   *New start posture*, which are individuals who perceived retirement as the beginning of a completely new stage in their lives.
2   *Continuation posture*, which is exhibited by individuals who were not totally dedicated to their careers and, even before retirement, had developed activities outside of work which they intend to sustain during their retirement.
3   *Disruption posture*, which is exhibited by individuals who were deeply committed to their work, had made no plans for the future and find retirement a totally negative and frustrating experience.
4   *Old age posture*, which is exhibited by individuals who perceive retirement as the final phase in their life and hence become reflective, introspective and unwilling to consider participating in any new forms of activity.

The researchers propose that by classifying individuals into one of these four types, this can provide marketers with indications of probable purchase behaviour and response to a specific product or service proposition. For example individuals within the new start or disruption posture groups can be expected to be prepared to increase their level of spending and will respond positively to experiential or activity-orientated propositions. In contrast, those within the continuation or old age posture groups are likely to exhibit a more conservative spending pattern and probably opt to purchase product categories which are non-experiential or supportive of a more passive, inward orientation.

Gerontographics

In the 1970s, in an attempt to use personality measurements in market segmentation, advertising agencies in the USA and Europe began to pioneer the idea of using consumer lifestyles to identify different customer groups. The concept underlying lifestyle classification is to group consumers on the basis of common activities (e.g. leisure, work, shopping), interaction with others (e.g. role perception as a teenager, adult, parent) and opinions (e.g. politics, social issues). To develop a lifestyle classification system requires a large scale survey to obtain respondents' degrees of agreement with questions concerning activities, interaction and opinions. Statistical tools are then used to classify respondents into specific groups based on the data acquired.

In an extensive review of the research techniques that have been utilized to develop lifestyle segmentation systems relevant to older financially attractive consumers, Bone (1991) concluded that the key classification variables should include discretionary income, health, activity level, discretionary time and response to others. In her view, discretionary income is significantly more important than total income because the former provides a much better indicator of the degree to which financially attractive consumers can afford purchases such as luxury goods, products associated with an active life and leisure services. Health is clearly a critical variable because ageing is often accompanied by a decline in physical and mental faculties which will have a very significant impact on consumption patterns. A variable which is related to health is activity level. This reflects the fact that some individuals will opt to remain at work. Those who do retire may remain active by becoming involved in a range of endeavours including helping in the community, taking up new hobbies or becoming involved in some form of sport. There will also be some people who, upon retirement, withdraw from society and become very inactive. Discretionary time reflects the level of freedom and choice that individuals have over how they spend their time. The level of discretionary time can in some cases be limited because the individual is caring for ageing parents or possibly looking after the offspring of the children while these latter individuals are out at work. Response to other people reflects the degree to which individuals engage in social activities, re-align their social networks or withdraw from society. Behaviour in relation to this latter variable will be influenced by whether individuals are 'other-directed', which means they are concerned about others, or 'inner-directed' persons who tend to focus on being concerned about just their own wants and needs.

Another application of lifestyle classification to gain further understanding of the older consumer has been developed by Professor Moschis at the Centre of Mature Consumer Studies at the University of Georgia (www.robinson.gsu.edu/marketing/Centers/CMC). Moschis (1992) utilized gerontographics to determine whether older people could be classified into distinct groupings that can provide the basis for more accurately targeted marketing programmes. Based on a large scale survey of retirees covering 136 measures of exhibited characteristics, such as biophysical, psychological and ageing, Moschis used statistical analysis to group respondents into four basic types: *Healthy Indulgers* (focus is on enjoying life), *Healthy Hermits* (healthy but socially withdrawn), *Ailing Outgoers* (still active despite declining health) and *Frail Recluses* (chronically ill, often living in isolation).

The UK advertising agency Millennium (www.millenniumdirect.co.uk), which specializes in developing marketing campaigns aimed at older people by using their 'Grey Power' database, has developed a similar, proprietary four segment classification system. Dr Ken Dychtwald (2005), an American who has made a lifelong career out of advising large corporations about lifestyle marketing, has also undertaken research that permits retirees to be classified into distinct customer segments. In a study which he undertook for AIG SunAmerica, he concluded that retirees could be divided into four segments. The *Ageless Explorers*, who make up 27 per cent of retirees, have carefully planned their retirement permitting them to be active, productive and independent in retirement. The *Comfortably Contents*, who constitute 19 per cent of retirees, who have also planned for retirement but lead a more relaxed life with emphasis on travel and recreation. The *Live For To-days*, 22 per cent of retirees, who are financially unprepared and although aspire to be Ageless Explorers, lack the financial resources required to support such a lifestyle. Finally, the *Sick & Tireds*, who constitute 32 per cent of retirees, are often widowed or in poor health, causing them to be resigned to a somewhat unfulfilled and less than satisfying lifestyle. A later study by Dywchtwald in 2006, on behalf of Ameriprise Financial (www.ameriprise.com) again concluded that retirees could be segmented into four groups. The names allocated to the groups were different from those used in the 2002 study but again revealed that older financially attractive consumers were individuals who had carefully planned their retirement and hence were able to enjoy life in a way that is virtually impossible for older people with limited financial resources, in poor health or living alone.

Targeting maturing boomer segments

Case Aims: To illustrate the application of gerontographics in the development of product propositions that can be directed at specific market segments.

If a firm is able to find a way of classifying potential customers into segments by applying techniques such as gerontographics, this knowledge can be used to develop products or services specifically targeted at different customer types. *Ailing Outgoers* may have health problems which require that they pay special attention to their diet. They are also likely to have limited disposable income. As part of a programme aimed at attracting more *Ailing Outgoers*, the International King's Table regional restaurant chain in Eugene, Oregon offers a healthy menu that changes daily and provides a range of entrées, hot vegetables, salads and desserts. As an added incentive, the chain offers discounts to these retirees by giving out money off coupons. *Healthy Indulgers* tend to enjoy a high income, downsize into a smaller luxury dwelling such as a town house upon retirement and spend heavily on new furniture and other possessions. These individuals, therefore, make an important target group for companies selling home security systems and high-technology electronic, home entertainment goods. *Healthy Hermits* on the other hand tend to want to remain in the family home, are not very social, tending to spend their days doing DIY projects. In recognition of the purchase behaviour of such individuals, the US hardware chain Home Depot makes a point of addressing this target group by hiring older employees who can better relate to assisting older customers (Moschis 1996).

Relationship marketing

In the 1980s, when service industries first began to dominate Western nation economies, the success of fast-food chains such as McDonald's and Kentucky Fried Chicken were seen as evidence that service sector firms could exploit conventional tangible goods mass marketing strategies to build market share. Some of the first people to challenge the relevance of mass marketing techniques in service markets were academics from the Nordic Universities such as Professors Gronroos (2004) and Gummesson (1999). These individuals suggested that mass marketing placed too great an emphasis on making the next sale, whereas the aim of service firms should be to build closer relationships with their customers. In their view, the key elements of relationship marketing involves moving to a two-way communication process between customer and supplier, using this interaction to determine how to maximize customer value and to align the resources of the firm to ensure that customers receive real value from the purchased proposition.

As these observations about the need to focus on building closer relationships were being made, ongoing improvements in computer software systems were permitting service firms to reduce marketing costs by mining their databases to segment customers into high, average and low prospect opportunities. The concept of using databases to segment markets was widely adopted by large service sector firms and provided a golden era for consulting companies who specialized in database software system design and installation. Concurrently, academics such as Reichheld (2003) were recommending that companies needed to move from a transaction orientation and focus on building lifelong loyalty among their customers.

By the 1990s, the concept of relationship marketing had been refined and evolved into a new business philosophy known as 'customer relationship management' (CRM). An important catalyst in generating widescale acceptance of CRM, especially in the USA, were advances in database marketing software and the advent of data distribution using mainframe computers networked with desk-top PCs to undertake very rapid analysis of customer records. Companies marketing CRM products initially selected American banks as a priority target. This was because banks had the most detailed customer records of any of the service sector providers. Their records provided data on factors such as age, location, employer, income, banking services utilized and, via customers' usage of credit cards, information on expenditure levels and products purchased. By entering these records into a statistical analysis package and applying what is known as 'cluster analysis', bankers obtained definitions of customer segments reflecting different types of bank service usage behaviour. Having defined segments based upon customer characteristics and purchase behaviour, it was then a simple task to classify an individual in terms of which segment to which they belong (Perrien *et al.*1992).

The usual approach when assessing actual bank service usage is to use the classifiers of affinity, frequency, recency and transaction scale. Affinity is about prior product purchases because it is easier to sell people new products similar to those about which they already have an understanding. Frequency is important because the greater use a customer makes of a bank, the higher is the probability that they will be receptive to the idea of purchasing additional services. Recency refers to the fact that response to a promotional message is greater if delivered very near to the date of the customer's last transaction. Transaction scale reflects the fact that the larger the sums of money passing through an account, the greater is the probability the customer will be receptive to the idea of purchasing additional services from the bank. Using these classifiers and identifying where an individual is found not to be using a service usually associated with a specific segment (e.g. 55+ individuals investing in a personal pension scheme), the bank can undertake cross-selling to persuade the customer of the benefits of purchasing the additional service proposition. By tracking customer behaviour over time, it is also possible to assess the actual effectiveness of a specific marketing message or channel through which the message is delivered (e.g. television advertising, radio drive time commercials, direct mail, etc.) (Anon 2002).

It was not long before some academics began to question whether the power of classifying customers purely on the basis of prior service utilization records was the best way to classify customers into segments which would be responsive to bank marketing campaigns. Initially such discussions centred upon how to enhance the effectiveness of campaigns directed at existing customers. This was soon followed by consideration of whether by refining cluster analysis techniques, CRM could be used as the basis for attracting new customers. An identified solution was to link the customer records with additional information about customer perceptions of service product benefits, attitudes, beliefs, values and lifestyle. To generate knowledge about these issues, the banks funded large scale surveys of their customers seeking their opinions about a wide range of different issues. Survey results were merged with customer records and another cluster analysis implemented. It is claimed that the resultant profiles provide a more accurate specification of customer needs by segment. These data then permit the development of very tightly targeted customized marketing campaigns aimed at both existing and new potential customers (Dibbs 2001).

As marketers became aware of the potential of CRM to enhance the effectiveness of promotional activities, this led to service firms in other sectors such as retailers, insurance companies and the airlines to increase their commitment to using CRM as the basis for managing markets (Cuthbertson and Laine 2004). In 2003, for example, the UK holiday firm Saga which markets services to 50+ individuals, announced the appointment of a predictive software supplier DataDistilleries to exploit the firm's 6.5 million strong customer database. Saga hoped to reduce the cost of direct mailing activities, increase new customer acquisition, improve customer retention rates and expand cross-selling between holiday products and other items in their portfolio, such as insurance and investment products (Anon 2003).

One of the criticisms of CRM is that the firm may be using static, historic information as the basis for analysing markets. The advent of e-commerce has vitiated this criticism because a company website can provide a wealth of real-time data concerning customer behaviour. Initially the software required to analyse online customer behaviour was both expensive and difficult to install. As with most software development patterns, the cost of these analysis tools has declined, installation has become simpler and the sophistication of the analysis techniques has increased immensely (Shah and Murtaza 2005).

Most large firms have tended to host and manage their own websites from the outset. They also had the financial resources and in-house IT skills to create effective customer analysis systems. This permitted them to move into online CRM more rapidly than many smaller firms (Lin *et al.* 2006). However, as major internet service providers (ISPs) have sought to identify ways, other than lower price, to retain clients for whom they provide website management and operation services, many have now expanded their activities to provide data analysis and CRM services. This has permitted even small, entrepreneurial firms to exploit online CRM as an effective tool through which to more fully understand customer behaviour.

Initially the majority of companies engaged in web-based marketing focused on the utilization of online CRM to expand sales among teenagers and people in the 18–49 age group. Although this was probably an appropriate strategy in the very early days of the internet, within a relatively short period of time, the level of older consumers' online shopping activities soon approached that of younger people (Whitney 2008). Initially, having recognized the growing importance of online purchasing among older consumers, the usual assumption was that buying behaviour was similar to that of young people. Hence, there was a tendency for firms to continue to use marketing campaigns which had previously proved success-ful with younger customers. By utilizing CRM tools, however, firms now realize that in many cases, older customers' behaviour is very different. The consequence has been that companies' online marketing strategies have been revised and customized to meet the needs of different market segments (Sorce *et al.* 2005).

Banks and closer boomer relationships

Case Aim: To illustrate the marketing strategies used by smaller regional banks in the USA were used to build closer relationships with the maturing boomer customers.

In the 1980s, as the major US banks began to embrace the concept of ser-vices marketing, their tendency was to adopt a mass marketing philosophy based upon the assumption that their consumer market was homogeneous and all consumers would be satisfied with being offered highly standardized packages (Thomas 1994). As part of this philosophy many of these larger banks made their account packages 'ageless'. This meant that if customers who were 40 years old and had $40,000 deposited with the bank, they should be rewarded with the same benefits that previously had been restricted to customers age 55+ who also made use of the bank's other financial services. This behaviour pattern among the larger banks was recognized by the smaller, more local banks as an opportunity to increase their market share by introducing entrepreneurial service programmes specifically aimed at building closer relationships with their maturing boomer customers. Their decisions were based upon the realization that in the consumer banking industry, the opportunities for growth in profitability do not come from attracting more savings deposits, but from the fee income that can be generated by capturing more of the maturing boomers' investment business. One example of the relationship building activities by the smaller banks is provided by Santa Barbara Bank in California. Under the guidance of the bank's public relations manager, the bank launched a programme aimed at maturing boomers known as 'Our Gang'. The incentive for customers to join the programme is that as members, if they undertake to keep a minimum balance in either their current or savings account, they receive free cheques, no monthly service fees, bank-by-mail with postage paid, no fees on traveller's cheques, a monthly Newsletter and free financial consultations. The programme focuses on having a strong community identity. Hence, Santa Barbara Bank & Trust provides financial seminars, flu shots, lawn bowling and health fair sponsorships. Some of the programme is delivered in association with other commercial organizations and is aimed at stimulating the creation of both higher customer loyalty and expanding members' social networks. A joint travel programme, for example, offers trips lasting 1–3 days, or cruises and tours of North America and Europe. A similar concept known as Premium Partners has been created by Premier Bank in Baton Rouge. Participants have to be aged 50+ and maintain at least $2,500 in their account. In return, Premier offers no charge for processing cheques, 24-hour live customer service, no charges for traveller's cheques, money orders or cashier's cheques. Members are also provided with free financial and trust management services and reduced commission fees when the bank undertakes stock transactions on behalf of the customer. In addition to these financial services, the bank provides Premier Partners with various non-financial services, including eye wear discounts, $100,000 common carrier insurance, accidental death insurance and a travel programme. The Key Corporation Bank in Cleveland has created the Prime Advantage Programme. To participate, customers must be at least 50 years old and must maintain at least $10,000 in one or more of the following accounts: regular or money market checking, passbook/ statement savings, money market accounts or certificates of deposit. The services provided by the programme include no service charge on current accounts and customized cheque books supplied free. Additionally, no service fees are charged on a range of other services such as credit cards, money orders or cashier's cheques. Participants receive a special discount on services such as certificates of deposit, direct depositing of Social Security cheques and notarizing personal documents. A range of non-financial services include single- and multiple-day tours escorted by Prime Advantage Bankers, special national and international travel programmes at reduced rates, special discounts at over 1,300 hotels nationwide, a quarterly Investment Newsletter and regular financial seminars.

References

Andreasen, A. (1966) 'Geographic mobility and market segmentation', *Journal of Marketing Research*, Vol. 3, No. 4, pp. 341–9.

Anon (2003) 'Saga holidays build insights through behaviour analysis', *Precision Marketing*, London, 15 August, p. 8.

Anon (2002) 'The four faces of retirement', *Journal of Financial Planning*, September, pp. 29–30.

Barber, F.A., Thomas, R.K. and Huang, M. (2001) 'Developing a profile of LASIK surgery customers', *Marketing Health Services*, Vol. 21, No. 2, pp. 32–7.

Bone, P.F. (1991) 'Identifying mature segments', *Journal of Services Marketing*, Vol. 5, No. 1, pp. 47–60.

Chang, T. and Chen, S. (1995) 'Benefit segmentation: a useful tool for financial investment services', *Journal of Professional Services Marketing*, Vol. 12, No. 2, pp. 69–81.

Cuthbertson, R. and Laine, A. (2004) 'The role of CRM within retail loyalty marketing', *Journal of Targeting, Measurement and Analysis for Marketing*, Vol. 12, No. 3, pp. 290–305.

Dibbs, S. (2001) 'Banks, customer relationship management and barriers to the segment of one', *Journal of Financial Services Marketing*, Vol. 6, No. 1, pp. 10–24.

Dychtwald, K, (2005) 'Ageless ageing: the next era of retirement', *The Futurist*, Vol. 39, No. 4, pp. 16–22.

Green, G. and Welniak, E. (1991) 'The nine household markets', *American Demographics*, Vol. 13, No. 10, pp. 36–42.

Gronroos, C. (2004) 'The relationship marketing process: communication, interaction, dialogue, value', *Journal of Business & Industrial Marketing*, Vol. 19, No. 2, pp. 99–113.

Gummesson, E. (1999) *Total Relationship Marketing: Rethinking Marketing Management From 4Ps to 30Rs*, London: Butterworth-Heinemann.

Haley, T. (1968) 'Benefit segmentation: a decision-orientated research tool', *Journal of Marketing*, Vol. 32, No. 3, pp. 30–6.

Hopkins, C.D., Roster, C.A. and Wood, C.M. (2006) 'Making the transition to retirement: appraisals, post transition lifestyle and changes in consumption patterns', *Journal of Consumer Marketing*, Vol. 23, No. 2, pp. 89–101.

Keller, K.L. and Kotler, P. (2006) *Marketing Management*, 12 edn., New York: Prentice Hall.

Kotler, P. (1989) 'From mass marketing to mass customization', *Planning Review*, Vol. 17, No. 5, pp. 10–15.

Lin, C., Lin. K, Huang, Y. and Kuo, W. (2006) 'Evaluation of electronic customer relationships management: the critical success factors', *The Business Review*, Vol. 6, No. 2, pp. 206–13.

McCrohan, K.F. and Finkleman, J.M. (1981) 'Social character and the new automobile industry', *California Management Review*, Vol. 24, No. 1, pp. 58–69.

Moschis, G.P. (1996) 'Life stages in the mature market', *American Demographics*, Vol. 8, No. 9, pp. 44–9.

Moschis, G.P. (1992) 'Gerontographics: a scientific approach to analysing and targeting the mature market', *Journal of Services Marketing*, Vol. 6, No. 3, pp. 17–27.

Moufakkir, O. (2006) 'An analysis of elderly gamers: trip characteristics and gambling behaviour: comparing the elderly with their younger counterparts', *UNLV Gaming Research & Review Journal*, Vol. 10, No. 2, pp. 63–75.

Pearce, M.R. (1997) 'Succeeding with micromarketing', *Ivey Business Quarterly*, Vol. 62, No. 1, pp. 69–76.

Perrien, J., Filitraut, P. and Line, R. (1992) 'Relationship marketing and commercial banking: a critical analysis', *International Journal of Bank Marketing*, Vol. 10, No. 7, pp. 25–35.

Pitta, D. (1998) 'Marketing one-to-one and its dependence on knowledge discovery in databases', *Journal of Consumer Marketing*, Vol. 15, No. 5, pp. 468–79.

Prideaux, B. and Crosswell, M. (2006) 'The value of visitor surveys: the case of Norfolk Island', *Journal of Vacation Marketing*, Vol. 12, No. 4, pp. 359–79.

Reichheld, F.F. (2003) 'The one number you need to grow', *Harvard Business Review*, Vol. 81, No. 12, pp. 46–54.

Schmidt, J. (1992) 'Growth and profit strategies', *Direct Marketing*, Vol. 55, No. 8, pp. 39–42.

Shah, J.R. and Murtaza, M.B. (2005) 'Effective customer relationship management through Web services', *Journal of Computer Information Systems*, Vol. 46, No. 1, pp. 98–110.

Sorce, P., Perotti, V. and Widrick, S. (2005) 'Attitude and age differences in online buying', *International Journal of Retail and Distribution Management*, Vol. 33, No. 2/3, pp. 122–33.

Tedlow, R.S. (1990) *New and Improved: The Story of Mass Marketing in America*, New York: Basic Books.

Thomas, V. (1994) 'Banking on the mature market: an update', *Bank Marketing*, Vol. 26, No. 9, pp. 15–21.

Whitney, D. (2008) 'Booming buying power', *Television Week*, Chicago, 18 February, p. 23.

Widgery, R., Angur, M. and Nataraajan, R. (1997) 'The impact of status on married women's perceptions', *Journal of Advertising Research*, Vol. 37, No. 1, pp. 54–63.

6 Strategy

Generic principles of marketing to financially attractive consumers (FACs)

The coverage of issues in Chapter 6 is designed to illustrate the generic principles of marketing to FACs in relation to:

1   In sectors where major companies are still involved in mass marketing using tools such as sales promotion and pricing to steal share from competition, this environment leaves the more entrepreneurial firms free to exploit opportunities offered to focus on satisfying the needs of FAC groups.

2   Given the preference of FACs for products or services offering superior performance, any firms operating in this sector of a market would be advised to utilize differentiation as the basis for achieving competitive advantage.

3   Cost-based competitive advantage should be avoided because in many cases, the firm will eventually be replaced in the market by another organization capable of offering even lower prices.

4   The income and lifestyle of many FACs is such that their orientation is towards purchasing products and services that offer the benefit of some form of life satisfaction enhancement.

5   FACs have usually reached the point where functionality is less important when selecting a product or service. Instead the purchase decision is often based upon an emotional, intellectual or altruistic reason.

6   Customer focused strategies are of greatest appeal to FACs where the benefit proposition is that of offering superior quality and value.

7   The move from mass to customized marketing is usually accompanied by higher operational costs. As FACs are more able to pay a premium price, this means these consumers offer the best target market option when seeking to establish a profitable customized marketing operation.

8   Companies exploiting customization to build market share among
     FACs rarely need to be concerned about large mass marketing com-
     panies becoming a competitive threat. This is because these latter
     organizations usually lack the flexibility in areas such as production,
     logistics and distribution that would permit them to effectively meet the
     needs of consumers seeking a more personalized product or service.

Conventional wisdom

Most new management theories usually emerge because research on real world
management practices identifies an operational philosophy which has proved
beneficial to a number of organizations. In the case of marketing management
strategies, early theoretical foundations were based upon studies of major
consumer goods companies such as Proctor & Gamble and Unilever in the decades
following the Second World War. The success of these firms was attributed to their
adoption of a mass marketing philosophy involving the supply of a standard
product to satisfy consumer needs linked to exploit economies of scale to generate
the profits required to support high levels of promotional spending. The low
technology manufacturing processes for consumer goods such as detergents,
soaps, coffee and frozen food does mean it is virtually impossible to create
products which are technically different from those offered by competitors. Under
these circumstances, the issue of the level of promotional activity is usually
critical. This is because achieving and retaining market leadership in many cases
is often determined by the ability to fund a higher level of promotion than the
competition (Strasser 1989).

The success of large branded goods over the years provides a strong justification
for the merits of adopting a mass marketing strategy. Consequently, the concept is
still widely practiced by major multinational companies in many markets across
the globe. Some academics have expressed the view that mass marketing is no
longer a viable marketing philosophy in today's consumer markets. Based upon
real world scenarios, however, it is clear that the concept still remains a commercially successful strategic option. This is especially true in those cases where
the consumer is still seeking standard goods at a competitive price or there are very
limited opportunities to permit the introduction of radically different product
propositions by the company (Kotler 1989).

A mass marketing strategy reliant upon heavy promotional expenditure is most
effective while large numbers of new customers are continuing to enter the market.
Eventually, however, the market will move into the maturity phase because all the
potential customers have become purchasers. At this point, the only source of
incremental revenue growth is to persuade consumers to switch brands. The need
to stimulate brand switching behaviour in consumer goods markets has been an
important influence in the evolution of the concept of basing a company marketing

strategy upon a Unique Selling Proposition (or 'USP') (Fraser 1983). As there are minimal actual variations in the performance characteristics of many branded goods, the identified USP will usually have to be based on some form of perceived difference. This difference is usually established in the mind of the consumer through the medium of advertising. For example in the UK lager industry, Foster's advertising is based on the platform of a product drunk by Australians. This can be contrasted with Carlsberg Export's promotional message of being 'so good, Danes hate to see it leave'.

A criticism of firms myopically focusing all their efforts on stealing brand share from the existing competition is that this can lead to fulfilment of consumer need becoming a somewhat secondary marketing objective. Should this situation develop, this can create an opportunity for a new, more consumer orientated firm to enter the market. A recent example of this scenario is provided by the eco-logically friendly Ecover brand from Holland which has entered the UK liquid detergent and washing powder markets. The brand has successfully challenged the incumbent multinational company brands because these latter organizations have apparently failed to recognize and then respond to a growing demand from consumers for more environmentally friendly household products.

Examples across a number of consumer markets of the success enjoyed by a new firm challenging existing brands have led to the emergence of alternative theory about how to achieve strategic success. This alternative perspective suggests firms should base their strategy around exploiting a key internal capability (or 'core competence'). This concept usually known as an RBV-based strategy is posited as providing the firm with the basis for delivering a superior proposition (Hamal and Prahalad 1996). An example of the RBV concept is provided by the ability of the Japanese company Toyota to identify new tech-nological solutions, which when linked to exploiting new materials and engineering excellence, provided the basis for achieving market leadership in the eco-sensitive California market through the launch of the Toyota Prius.

Breaking conventions

Case Aims: To illustrate that an alternative perspective on market trends can provide the basis of a successful market entry by an entrepreneur.

The essence of any entrepreneurial success is the originator of the business idea who has identified a way of breaking with convention as a path through which to deliver greater customer satisfaction (Connolly 2006). An example of this philosophy is provided by Angelika Deliga. In her opinion, the German retailers' focus on younger people as their primary target market is somewhat myopic. This is because German demographic data clearly indicate that in excess of 25 per cent of the population will soon be aged over 60 and that retirees enjoy a higher level of disposable income than many younger people still in work. She decided that the time has come, therefore, to ignore conventional thinking and to establish a department store specifically aimed at meeting the needs of retired people. To understand potential customer demand she undertook research with retired couples and people living in residential care homes. From these data she recognized the requirement to select products which reflect the differences between the product needs of old versus young people. Potential goods to be stocked include computers with enlarged keyboards, telephones with large buttons, speaking clocks, magnifying rulers and support stockings. She also appreciated that potential customers would like to purchase without any embarrassment, products specifically applicable to certain health problems associated with ageing such as incontinence pads and underwear. Her perspective about the importance of creating the most appropriate in-store environment influences the design and layout of her new store. Changing rooms are big enough for two people, aisles are wide, signs are written in large letters and there are no steps or stairs. The range of clothing sizes is much broader. There is also a booth containing a 3-D machine that can measure an individual shopper as the basis for making available customized clothing. Her perspective is that for older people, shopping should not be a chore but instead the basis for several hours of social interaction. This led to the installation of a schnapps bar, a coffee shop and facilities to mount daily fashion shows. Her first store, 'Seniorenmarkt' is located in Grossraschen. The store's unofficial motto that is communicated to customers is 'why go hungry for the sake of your heirs?' This message is aimed at convincing retirees, who have a higher disposable income than any other group in Germany, to enjoy life by spending money on themselves. Early indications suggest Angelika's ideas are having a major impact among her target customer group. This has caused her to create a Seniorenmarkt franchise with the aim of rapidly opening 10 more stores across the country.

Strategic advantage

Whether one favours the mass marketer's strategic preference for offering a standard product or service backed by heavy promotional spending or the RBV view that strategy is driven by exploiting a core competence, the aim common to both philosophies is that of outperforming the competition. Determining how to achieve this performance objective usually requires the firm to decide which strategic positioning would be the most appropriate option for the organization. Conventional wisdom on selecting a strategic position draws heavily upon the model originally proposed by Professor Michael Porter (1985a). He posited that the two key variables influencing the positioning decision are market coverage and how to achieve a competitive advantage over other firms. As summarized in Figure 6.1, this theory posits that there are four basic options facing the firm:

1   A broad marketing position based upon exploiting a cost advantage over competition. This is typically reflected by the company attempting to build market share by offering a lower price proposition to the majority of the market.
2   A broad position based upon exploiting a performance advantage over competition. This typically is achieved by the company building market share by offering a superior product at a premium price to the majority of the market.
3   A focused market position based upon exploiting a cost advantage over competition. Typically the company will attempt to build market share by offering a lower price to a specific geographic or customer market segment.
4   A focused position based upon exploiting a performance advantage over competition. This is usually reflected by the company seeking to build market share by offering a superior product at a premium price to a specific geographic or customer market segment.

As most large firms seek to maximize their absolute profits, this type of organization will usually opt for broad market coverage in order to make their offering available to as many potential consumers as possible. Smaller firms usually attempt to avoid becoming embroiled in market confrontations with larger companies. This aim can be achieved by identifying a market niche in which a 'focused' strategy can be adopted aimed at serving the needs of a subset of customers within a market sector.

The other decision is should the firm use a cost advantage or superior performance as the basis for defeating competition. The academic literature tends to favour utilization of a superior performance, or 'differentiation strategy'. This viewpoint is based on available evidence which suggests differentiation is more

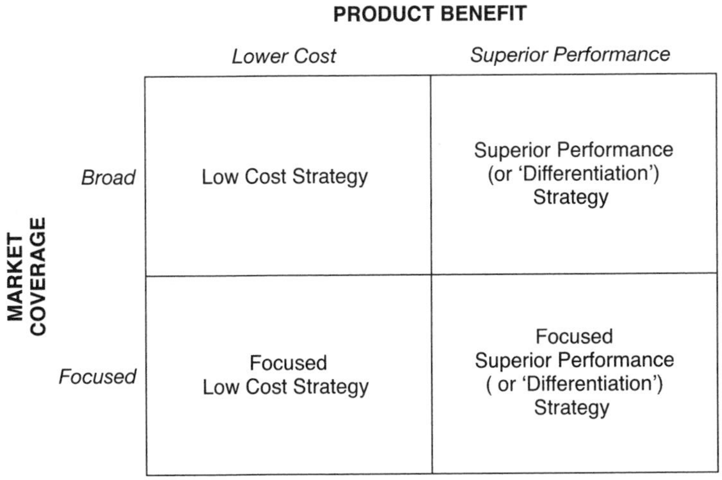

PRODUCT BENEFIT

	Lower Cost	Superior Performance
Broad	Low Cost Strategy	Superior Performance (or 'Differentiation') Strategy
Focused	Focused Low Cost Strategy	Focused Superior Performance (or 'Differentiation') Strategy

MARKET COVERAGE

Figure 6.1 Alternative competitive advantage options.

likely to increase the probability of long-term survival and higher profitability than the alternative proposition of competing on the basis of low price. This is because there is a major risk with price-based competition; namely the firm may only be able to support this strategy for a limited period of time. In many cases the firm will eventually lose the ability to compete on the basis of lower operating costs because an alternative, more cost-effective provider will enter the market (Porter 1985b). For example some UK specialist organic food producers who successfully built a customer base among older financially attractive consumers in the 1990s subsequently lost market share to imports from countries such as Poland. The UK firms could not recover their higher wage and other operational costs because in most cases, consumers could not be persuaded that there were benefits in continuing to pay a significantly higher price relative to those charged for organic food from overseas producers.

Among Western firms the option of a cost or a performance-based strategy being mutually exclusive strategies is based upon a fundamental key assumption that consumers will not believe the claims of a brand which offers a superior product at a below average price. This is because consumers have long since decided that in the context of purchasing a product from many Western companies, 'one gets what one pays for'. The implicit perception underlying this adage is that lower prices will be accompanied by lower quality. In the 1990s, however, the Japanese confounded marketing theorists because Western consumers were prepared to purchase high performance goods such as cars (e.g. the Toyota Lexus range) or electronic goods (e.g. Toshiba laptops) at a price significantly lower than the Western nation equivalent. Consequently, in addition to the four strategic positions described in Figure 6.1, one should add the two further strategic options; namely mass or focused concurrent value and superior performance propositions.

Having determined the basis of the firm's proposed strategic position, the next issue is to determine how this can be evolved into a practical reality that can fulfil the identified needs of the customer. As summarized in Figure 6.2, this aim will require identification of the nature of the purchase satisfaction being sought by the consumer and the degree to which the consumer desires a customized product or service solution.

Marketing a brand experience

Case Aims: To illustrate that to appeal to financially attractive consumers such as maturing boomers, an effective marketing strategy is often that of offering an exclusive, personalized brand experience.

A significant proportion of maturing boomers are now enjoying the financial fruits of successful careers. This causes them to be more orientated towards making emotional purchase decisions instead of the sensible logical buying patterns previously exhibited when they were still fulfilling a parental role. One route through to satisfying emotional needs is to spend their money on upmarket products and services. Suppliers of such goods are aware of this trend among maturing boomers. Hence they utilize a marketing strategy based upon ensuring these consumers feel they are part of an exclusive consumption experience. One company which excels at implementing this strategy is the apparel and high fashion goods company Hugo Boss (Eastwood 2007). In the case of their range of products for women, instead of the conventional promotional approach of featuring the latest Hollywood starlet as a product user, Hugo Boss prefers to leverage elite, focused events. For example in Canada the company has introduced 'personal shopping nights', where an individual or company hosts a private viewing of the latest Hugo Boss collections. Toronto hair stylist Paul King, for example, recently invited 60 of his clients to a cocktail reception in the Hugo Boss showroom. Some of these clients were previously unaware that the company supplied the female high fashion market. The company also seeks to be perceived as the 'man's man' of elite clothing industry. To support this strategy, since the 1980s, Hugo Boss has been involved in sponsoring upmarket sports such as golf, cricket, tennis and car racing. The other aspect of the company operations is to focus upon the provision of highly individualized service. Store employees keep detailed notes on their customers' preferences and strive to bring the latest fashions onto the shop floor as soon as possible. This is because moneyed customers such as the female maturing boomer are early adopters who upon observing a fashion shift, want immediately to be seen wearing the latest trend in apparel or accessories.

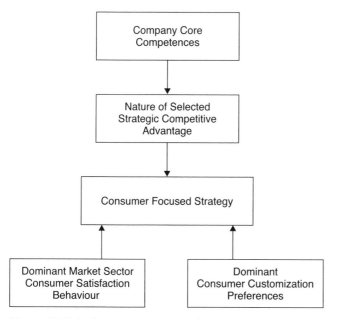

Figure 6.2 Selecting a customer focused strategy.

Consumer satisfaction

When one examines the mass marketing and RBV-based concept of strategy as outlined in many marketing texts, the focus is reflective and reliant upon Professor Porter's perception that outperforming competition should be the primary force driving strategic decisions. In the case of products or services marketed to the conventional target of the 18–49 age group households, this is possibly a valid concept. This is because the majority of purchase decisions within this consumer group are orientated towards making the best selection relative to those products and services that are available for meeting the consumption needs of the family.

When one examines the motivation of financially attractive consumers and case materials about consumer purchase decisions in relation to luxury brands, it is apparent that this group's behaviour often differs from that exhibited among the average consumers who constitute the standard 18–49 age group customer target of interest to the mass marketing brands. Two key reasons for this difference in behaviour is that the financially attractive consumer (a) has a higher than average income, thereby permitting the purchase of more expensive goods and (b) in the case of older individuals within this category, they are usually no longer responsible for supporting children and hence are able to focus on satisfying their own personal consumption needs. This orientation has been described by Cooper and Mialoulis (1998) as consumption based upon 'life satisfaction'. In their view, the key characteristics of life satisfaction are: (1) taking pleasure in daily activities, (2) considering life meaningful, (3) holding a positive self-image, (4) having a happy and optimistic outlook and (5) feeling successful in achieving the objectives of enjoying life. In their view, marketing strategies designed to assist the financially attractive consumer such as the maturing boomer to achieve life satisfaction are now critical to any firm seeking to achieve success in these sectors of the market.

Wolfe and Sisodia (2003) in their analysis of the purchase behaviour shifts of consumers over time point to the work of the psychologist Carl Jung. He posited that as people become older they wish to achieve a state of personal authenticity. This causes them to dissolve their earlier persona of achieving social integration and success. They dispense with the perceived need to fulfil society's demands to behave as responsible adults focused upon appearing to be effective, responsible parents. Instead older individuals place greater emphasis on actions to enhance satisfaction within themselves as individuals. A similar concept has been presented by Maslow (1964) in his hierarchy of needs model. This model posits that humans exhibit five different needs. The most basic needs to be satisfied are physiological and safety, which relate to issues such as the acquisition of food, drink and housing. Once these basic needs are met, the individual is free to implement actions related to the mid-level hierarchical needs of social and personal esteem. The ultimate level of need is that of self-actualization which involves actions related to the satisfaction of total self.

The behaviour shift associated with a move by the older financially attractive consumer to being more self-orientated will be reflected by their purchase decisions being made in terms of moving away from 'functional' goods towards a preference for 'cerebral' items. Functional goods are those which are selected on essentially practical grounds as being the best for fulfilling a specific task or purpose (e.g. the selection of the best mode of transport for optimizing the costs of commuting to work). These can be contrasted with cerebral goods where practical, logical reasons are far less important to the consumer. This is because these latter goods are selected for intellectual or emotional reasons. As illustrated in Figure 6.3, when one combines the two variables of purchase purpose and the primary beneficiary of a purchase, this generates four different strategic purchase decision options that are available to the financially attractive consumer.

The usual strategic option for households in the 18–49 year age group is the purchase of goods for functional purposes to satisfy the needs of the family. Hence, in this situation, the motivation of the purchaser is usually that of 'necessity satisfaction'. This can be contrasted with an individual such as an older financially attractive consumer making a functional purchase based entirely on meeting their own benefit needs. In this latter case, the purchaser is engaged in 'self gratification satisfaction'. In the period following the departure of the children, empty nesters often embark on this type of spending. Examples include fathers who purchase their first ever luxury car such as a Mercedes Benz or mothers who can now focus on their own personal appearance and begin to buy top of the range apparel while shopping in upmarket boutiques.

A cerebral purchase designed to care for the needs of others is an activity which can be described as 'altruistic satisfaction'. The alternative cerebral option is for the individual to make a purchase entirely for their own benefit. This latter orientation is usually associated with the desire to purchase goods which the individual believes will reflect how they feel about themselves and the nature of the lifestyle which they wish to enjoy. Hence, this purchase behaviour can be described as 'self actualization satisfaction'.

**PRIMARY BENEFICIARY OF
THE PURCHASE DECISION**

	Others	*Self*
Functional	Necessity Satisfaction	Self Gratification Satisfaction
Cerebral	Altruistic Satisfaction	Self Actualization Satisfaction

PURPOSE OF PURCHASE

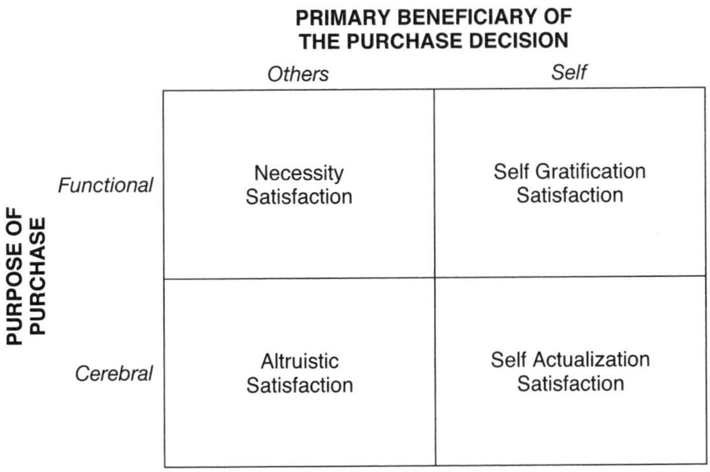

Figure 6.3 Alternative satisfaction options.

The contrast between purchase of necessity goods which is guided by logical, rational calculations and altruistic behavior is an issue which has been a matter of debate among economists for many years. This is because there is an apparent inherent contradiction between the choice by a rational individual and what represents an optimal choice for the altruist who puts the needs of others before themselves. Economic theory tends to explain the contradiction as that of the altruist in giving to others, expect something back in return from the recipient(s) at a later date (Goulias and Henson 2006). This can be contrasted with the social science view that altruistic behaviour occurs when an individual is aware of negative consequences of social conditions faced by others and takes on the responsibility for implementing a preventative or ameliorative action. In an attempt to determine the relevance of such theories in relation to an altruistic consumer purchasing scenario, Guagnano (2001) examined the willingness of consumers concerned about protecting the environment to pay a premium price for 'green' products such as recycled paper. He concluded that in this type of purchase scenario, the social science perspective is the correct explanation. His research indicated the altruistic consumer is guided not by rational self interest. Instead, the purchase decision is made on the basis of what they perceive is good for others. In the case of recycled paper, what is perceived as good for others is the growing importance of society to take greater care of the world's increasingly fragile ecosystem.

Examples of older financially attractive consumers' altruistic behaviour will be encountered in relation to actions within the home (e.g. a willingness to care for an ageing parent) and within the wider society (e.g. becoming involved in a local charity). Wolfe and Sisodia (2003) posit that altruistic behaviour among individuals is a reflection of a person who is less influenced by what is expected of them by others in society. Instead these individuals base their decision on what seems to be the most appropriate behaviour for themselves. As a result, the usual outcome is that decisions are made which are aimed at achieving greater inner personal satisfaction.

The objective of achieving inner satisfaction is also exhibited by the individual whose purchase decisions are orientated towards self-actualization satisfaction. This type of activity involves purchases and consumption that the individual perceives as a reflection of their 'real selves'. A focus on self is very different from the behaviour exhibited by younger people who are often engaged is purchases to achieve necessity satisfaction related to meeting the needs of their family. In relation to this difference, Wolfe and Sisodia have proposed that the marketer who needs to understand older financially attractive consumers, when compared with the traditional 18–49 year age group, will probably exhibit the following traits:

1   More individualistic, less materialistic and more difficult to predict.
2   Focused on being provided with truthful information from suppliers about products and services.
3   More emotionally driven, being prepared to rely more on intuition than rational logical analysis.

4 Less price sensitive when making discretionary income buying decisions, but remaining price sensitive when purchasing what they perceive as day-to-day necessities.

5 More interested in developing and sustaining a relationship with companies from whom they purchase products and services.

Maturing boomers and their cars

Case Aims: To illustrate the behavioural traits associated with self gratification satisfaction.

In order to define an appropriate consumer focused marketing strategy, suppliers need to understand the attitudes of potential customers because these are the drivers which determine the purchase decision. One of the commonest examples of self-gratification is that exhibited by maturing male boomers who purchase a luxury car upon nearing or entering retirement. Their purchase behaviour is usually very different to the selection process exhibited when they were purchasing previous vehicles. First, emotion becomes a much stronger dimension in the purchase decision because the new 'dream car' will usually cost 50–100 per cent more than they have ever spent on a car in the past (Loeffler 2002). The other important dimension in a self-gratification purchase is the consumer has very distinct perceptions of both themselves and the image they wish to communicate to others when seen using the product purchased. In the case of American maturing boomers, for example, many are adverse to the idea of buying a Cadillac or Lincoln Continental because they perceive these brands as vehicles driven by moneyed people from their parent's generation. Similarly in the UK some maturing boomers have a perception developed while still young of Britain's luxury car marque, the Jaguar, being a vehicle used by politicians, senior level staff in the police force, strike breaking company directors and well-known criminals. The behaviour traits associated with self-gratification satisfaction create certain strategic marketing implications for the luxury car maker in terms of being able to successfully market their products to the maturing boomer market. The manufacturers will need to know what key product attributes their potential customers are seeking and also the image perception which exists for their brand in a specific sector of a market. An example of a successful brand, as evidenced by their ongoing sales growth in the maturing boomer market, is the German car manufacturer, Mercedes Benz. Further understanding about the success of German brands is provided in the study of the attributes sought by American customers for luxury cars undertaken by Rosecky and King (1996). They identified some significant differing ordering of attribute priorities between consumers purchasing an American luxury car versus those opting for a European brand. In the case of the American brand, the primary consumer priorities were comfort, luxury and safety. This can be contrasted with the purchasers of European brands who gave priority to the attributes of performance, prestige, quality and romance. These respondents also admitted that they perceived their vehicles as being relatively poor in meeting the needs of a person seeking comfort. For those individuals who wanted value and reliability along with the attributes associated with European luxury cars, then their preference was likely to be for a Japanese car such as the Toyota Lexus.

Customer focused strategies

In consumer markets characterized by rapid change and an accelerating product lifecycle, it seems very possible that neither a market orientated nor a RBV-based strategy will necessarily permit a firm to achieve and sustain long-term success. As a consequence, there has been the proposal by some academics that companies need to move towards a customer focused strategy (Prahalad and Ramaswamy 2000). This alternative strategic philosophy is based upon the concept that a successful marketing strategy represents an interaction between what is desired by the customer to achieve purchase satisfaction and the ability of the firm to develop the competences required to deliver these identified consumer needs. As noted by Drucker (1973), firms adopting a consumer focused strategy must recognize that the dominant dimension which will determine business success is the consumer, not the competencies of the producer.

In developing a conceptual model of the factors which influence the successful definition of a customer focused strategy, Wang and Lo (2003) have proposed that the two drivers of delivering consumer satisfaction are superior product or service quality and superior value. The dimension of superior value should not be perceived in the traditional sense of offering a lower price. For as demonstrated by firms such as Federal Express, their customers perceive value in the much broader context of being willing to pay a relatively high price because the firm is better than competition at ensuring parcels are delivered on-time to the correct location. The other important dimension concerning achievement of consumer satisfaction is the problem that many of today's markets are continually undergoing change. Sources of change include shifts in consumer preferences, the entrance of new, more powerful competitors and the impact of a radically new technology. Hence, to sustain success the firm must have the strategic flexibility to rapidly respond to an adverse trend which emerges that indicates a revision in products or operational practices is necessary in order that the firm continues to deliver superior customer satisfaction based upon quality and value.

In relation to factors which are important in relation to being able to exhibit strategic flexibility, Grewal and Tansuhaj (2001) have proposed these include:

1   The accumulation of an excess of resources in order to be able to immediately respond to the need to change the nature of some of the firm's business activities.

2   An emphasis within the firm on exploiting the opportunities that arise from being a participant in a diverse range of market environments.

3   A priority within the firm given to rapidly moving ahead of any competitors to exploit new opportunities that will arise from being a participant in a diverse range of market environments.

4   An understanding of how to manage the risks associated with shifts in the macro-environment such as an economic downturn or worsening financial conditions.

Delivering superior quality and value

Case Aims: To illustrate how the actions upmarket service firms implement to fulfil the aim of delivering superior quality and service.

In a project aimed at gaining further understanding of how to deliver superior quality and value Bowen and Shoemaker (2003) undertook research to determine the factors influencing customer loyalty in the upmarket sector of the hotel industry. This interest in loyalty is influenced by the fact that the lifelong expenditure of a loyal customer in the luxury hotel sector is estimated to be in excess of $100,000. Furthermore, dissatisfied customers who do not return will engage in negative word-of-mouth publicity which can damage a hotel's revenue flow. A key aspect of the supplier–buyer behaviour model which the researchers constructed involves the concept that effective relationship building requires that both parties suppress opportunistic behaviour (e.g. switching accommodation because of a sudden price change by the hotel or alternatively, the hotel's competitors) and that the relationship should be based upon the creation of a mutually beneficial partnership in which both parties benefit from the actions of the other. Having validated their research model, Bowen and Shoemaker mailed a survey to American Express cardholders who were known to have stayed at least three times in one of a list of specific luxury hotels. Respondent data analysis permitted identification of the following top 10 factors influencing consumer loyalty in this market sector:

1   Hotel offers upgrades when available.
2   A guest can request a specific room.
3   The guest can check in or out at the time which best suits their needs.
4   The hotel uses information from prior visits to customize the services provided.
5   The staff communicate the attitude that solving any guest problem is an extremely important activity.
6   The staff recognize the guest upon arrival.
7   Upon a subsequent visit, prior knowledge of the guest's needs is used to expedite the check-in process.

8 The hotel has a credit card-based frequent guest programme that permits earning points towards future subsidized or free accommodation.
9 The hotel is well connected with local organizations that help the guest's stay to be more enjoyable and productive.
10 The hotel rewards guest loyalty by providing the occasional gift.

By drawing upon these data and qualitative knowledge generated from focus group studies, Bowen and Shoemaker made a number of recommendations concerning key actions by upmarket hotels that are critical in sustaining consumer loyalty. Possibly the most critical issue which they identified is to ensure that the behaviour of all employees re-enforces the trust that the guest has in the hotel. Examples include: management giving frontline employees genuine delegated authority to make financial adjustments to a guest's bill following inadequate service provision; when an employee promises an action these promises are always met (e.g. the wait time in fulfilling a room service order) and employees ensure that even the most trivial of service promises are always fulfilled.

Customizing and positioning

An important aspect of strategy development is to determine how product performance can be translated into a proposition of greatest appeal to customers. Having determined a generic strategy in relation to (a) focused versus mass marketing and (b) product performance versus price, the next step is to determine how product performance will support a specific market position in relation to whether there is greater potential in offering a standardized product or making available goods which are specifically customized to meet the needs of individual purchasers.

Data on consumers who are in a position to consider purchases based upon achieving a lifestyle satisfaction objective tend to suggest a preference for products and services which have been customized to meet their personal needs. This philosophy is described by some writers as 'mass customization' and by others as '1-to-1' marketing. One vocal advocate of the benefits of customization in consumer markets is the American business consultant Don Peppers. He has proposed that advances in information technology give enterprises the ability to develop relationships with individual customers. These advances, especially when linked to increased production flexibility in manufacturing environments, permit the supply of mass customized products and services (Peppers and Rogers 1995). Peppers feels the key benefit of customization is the success which accompanies achieving a greater long-term share of an individual customer's business. He contrasts this outcome with mass marketing where the focus is on achieving overall gains in market share which, because of the frequency and intensity of brand warfare, are often of a very transient nature.

A company faces a number of choices when considering the degree to which their products or services might be customized. Pine (1993) has suggested these choices exist on a continuum ranging from additional augmented services, adapted products, modular products through to individually tailored products. Even with the advent of new, flexible manufacturing technology and the ability of using real-time communication information via the internet to acquire customer input, mass customization will almost always involve higher operating costs. Hence, the critical issue confronting a company is the degree to which the consumer perceives that the added value which accompanies customization is justified in terms of the higher price that may need to be charged. In commenting on the issue of how consumers assess value, Roberts (1998) proposed the equation that:

$$Value = Consumer\ Alignment + Relevant\ Quality + Convenience +$$
$$Added\ Benefits + The\ Price\ for\ a\ Standard\ Product$$

Consumer alignment is the description of the degree to which the consumer identifies closely with the market image presented by the brand or supplier company. Convenience is usually assessed in terms of the time the consumer can save by being offered a faster solution or alternatively, a solution which reduces their search costs within the market. Added value relates to additional features which are provided by a customized solution. Examples of adequate added value could be apparel which is a better fit than an 'off the peg' item or a personal computer designed to undertake the data processing tasks relevant to the needs of a specific individual.

Lennart *et al.* (2002) concluded that successful customization is dependent upon customer, product, market, industry and organizational factors. In relation to the appeal of customization, this tends to be greatest where consumers have highly heterogeneous needs which are undergoing rapid change. In those cases where consumer interest in the product or service is low, or need remains reasonably constant, there is likely to be less interest in purchasing customized products. Even where consumer interest is high, purchasing will only occur if the consumer perceives the price premium for the customized product is greatly exceeded by the value of the benefits delivered. The other influencing factor is the degree to which the consumer believes a benefit exists in being seen as the owner of goods which are distinctly different from those purchased by most other members of society.

In terms of commercial and practical reality, the supplier must be able to customize the product or service. Luxury products, by their nature, tend to be of interest to consumers because they are distinctive, personalized and command a premium price. Hence, customization is much more feasible in this market than in a market supplying commodities. Another dynamic is the degree to which existing products or services might be adapted to offer greater choice to the consumer. Where existing goods are highly adaptable, this reduces the costs associated with customization. Hence, market appeal will be increased because these items can be offered at lower prices that those which require the development of an entirely new generation of products.

In relation to market factors, most consumer goods are distributed through intermediaries. These organizations may not be prepared to handle an increased variety of goods because this may increase their logistics, storage and merchandising costs. This situation is possibly most applicable to consumer products sold through national supermarket chains. These firms' operational model of profit maximization is based upon stocking only one or two top brands in each product category. Hence, to provide consumers with access to a greater variety of customized goods may require the supplier to identify another terrestrial intermediary willing to stock a wider range of goods. The other alternative is to utilize the internet to market the goods directly to the end-user.

Achieving distribution for a supplier's full range of goods is not a new problem. Manufacturers of luxury goods such as jewellery, designer apparel and upmarket furniture have always faced this problem. The usual solution is to distribute their products through specialist retail outlets. However, in order for this solution to be effective, the pricing structure must permit these specialist retailers to achieve a higher unit profit margin. This is necessary in order that the retailer is able to cover the added costs associated with offering consumers a wider product choice.

In relation to industry factors, one of the most critical factors is whether a sector is able to minimize the added costs of product line configuration that will be required to support the creation of customized output. Usually this can only be achieved by having full access to extremely accurate consumer information. For some firms, access to such information can come from the collection and analysis of data concerning the purchasing patterns of individual consumers. Hence, for example, retailers can use point-of-purchase electronic till data, credit card records and consumer membership of the firm's loyalty scheme to rapidly develop a highly accurate understanding of trends in consumer purchase behaviour. Even more useful in terms of developing a customized product line is the situation where the company has the customer data prior to the scheduling of production. This is, for example, the situation which has been achieved by Dell because the customer's placement of an online order acts as the trigger to initiate the assembly of the specific computer that has been requested.

The factor of organizational capability relates to the issue of whether the firm has the necessary internal capabilities to produce the goods at an acceptable cost, achieve the quality standards demanded by the consumer and then finally be able to make an on-time delivery. Where a company has been configured as a mass production operation, it is extremely unlikely that the manufacturing facilities would be suited to mass customization unless very significant changes are made to both the firm's production technology and logistics system. Another dilemma that can arise is where the company has previously adopted a strategy of cost minimization by relying on overseas producers or component suppliers. This type of extended supply chain is rarely capable of switching to a customized operation because of the inability or unwillingness of the overseas sources to move away from producing large quantities of standardized products and a preference of overseas producers to operate on the basis of a long lead time between order placement and delivery (Christopher *et al.* 2006). To a certain degree, the increased utilization of integrated computer systems which permits all parties within a supply chain to be immediately aware of changing consumer purchasing patterns may reduce the problems associated with firms purchasing customized products from overseas sources. Nevertheless, as demonstrated by clothing manufacturers in the USA, whose costs are much higher then their overseas competitors, these former organizations' ongoing success has been based upon the fact that, unlike their foreign rivals, they can manufacture and deliver a diverse range of products to a US retailer within less than 48 hours after receipt of an order (Doeringer and Crean 2006).

Selecting an optimal position for a firm's products or services requires an assessment of how the organization will deliver superior value to the consumer and the nature of the product configuration that will be made available. As illustrated in Figure 6.4, combining these two parameters generates four different product positioning options.

A position based upon offering a standard product is applicable in those markets where the customers are all seeking the same goods. This is typically the case with most consumer staples such as food or household products. Customization will be preferred in those situations where there are significant variations in product benefits being sought or customers are seeking a proposition specifically tailored to their own individual needs. In relation to the issue of product benefit positioning, in some markets, customers are seeking high performance (e.g. technically aware individuals purchasing a digital camera), whereas in other situations, customers

Figure 6.4 Positioning options.

may place great importance on low price (e.g. customers purchasing replacement tyres for the family car).

Deciding which of the four product position options should be selected will require the marketer to examine the inter-connected variables of demand, capability and competition. As far as customer demand is concerned, the firm should avoid making a decision based upon which positioning can generate the maximum sales volume. This is because consumers in market sectors where high sales volumes can be generated tend to be extremely price sensitive. As a result, unit margins may be small and this may drastically reduce total profitability. Hence, for most firms the marketing decision should be based upon selecting a position which can generate the highest level of long-term absolute profits. In many cases, this will be market sectors where customers are seeking customized products which offer superior performance and for which they are willing to pay a premium price. Where a high profit opportunity is identified, the next issue is to ensure the company has the internal capabilities to deliver the proposed positioning. Finally the marketer should assess the scale of competitor activity. This is because it is rarely sensible to enter an area of the market where there is a high intensity of competition. One possible exception to this suggestion, however, is where the firm is totally confident that the proposed product proposition is vastly superior to that currently being offered by other organizations.

For many consumer goods firms, entering financially attractive consumer markets will initially be considered as an incremental revenue source to compliment sales from the organization's current core market. In reaching a final positioning decision in relation to entering a financially attractive consumer market, the firm may wish to be guided by the recommendation of the business guru, Tom Peters. This individual, who wrote the book *In Search of Excellence*, concluded that firms, when considering new market or product opportunities, are more likely to succeed if they 'stick to the knitting'. Essentially this adage means that for any firm planning to expand into a new market sector, where possible the firm should select that market which permits the continued use of the mainstream marketing strategy being used in the firm's core business. This philosophy will tend to mean risk is minimized because the firm can draw upon existing trading and production experience. Nevertheless over the longer term, the firm must recognize that very major success in financially attractive consumer markets will probably require fundamental revisions in the organization's product or service portfolio in order to maximize the quality and value of the products and services to be made available to this consumer group.

In some cases, the advice of not revising the firm's marketing strategy when initially entering a new market may be inappropriate. This can occur, for example, where the firm and a number of competitors simultaneously enter a financially attractive consumer market and all continue to utilize their existing, probably not totally appropriate, core market strategies. Another scenario is where the firm is late into a new market and other firms have already attracted a loyal customer base. Under such circumstances, the firm will need to adopt a strategy based upon new product positioning that permits the organization to 'leap frog' over other companies. The most likely way this can be achieved is for the firm to identify a highly entrepreneurial proposition involving the breaking of existing market conventions through actions such as introducing a new technology, product form or operational process. If this entrepreneurial, market challenging approach is successful then a very usual outcome is that the firm will eventually become the new market leader.

The world of one (Bardaki and Whitelock 2004)

Case Aims: To review the progress which has been achieved in the implementation of the concept of mass customization.

The widespread publicity which was given to concepts such as mass customization and 1-to-1 marketing in the early 1990s persuaded a number firms to attempt to introduce the philosophy into their operations. The majority of early successes in the field were among upmarket service companies which used existing data to offer customized services to their clientele. For example the Ritz-Carlton hotel chain created a database to monitor customer preferences. This could be accessed by all of their operations around the world and permitted personalization of the guest's stay in relation to issues such as room preference, mini-bar usage and favourite amenities. Similarly, Charles Schwab, the world's first online stockbroker created a computer-based infrastructure to analyse individual investor behaviour as the basis of offering ongoing financial advice (Pine 1996). Unfortunately, problems over the lack of diversity in customer demand and the ability to move towards creating more flexible manu-facturing environments caused some of these early ventures to fail. For example in 1994, the global denim jeans company Levi Strauss announced the launch of the Personal Pair jeans. For an additional premium of $10, consumers could go into certain stores, be measured and within 2 weeks their customized jeans would be delivered to their home. Eventually, probably due to financial performance problems, the programme was withdrawn from retail outlets. General Mill's move into customized cereals was also eventually scrapped, as was the toymaker Mattell's attempt to offer customized 'friends of Barbie' dolls (Schlosser 2004). The advent of the internet did, however, permit more firms to move closer to their customers and gain real-time data on purchase behaviour patterns which have been invaluable to those firms who postponed their move into mass customization until they determined a genuine market opportunity existed by adopting this strategic philosophy. Availability of appropriate, affordable computer technology has often been the catalyst for change. For example the American leisure clothing catalogue operation, Lands' End, waited until the year 2000, until a software supplier developed a tool which can pinpoint a person's body size based upon a very small number of measurements.

Although the consumer is charged a premium of $20 for customized clothes, the company pricing strategy is merely to recover the costs of product personalization. The benefit the company receives is that re-order rates for customized clothing purchasers is 34 per cent higher than from buyers of standard products. The concept of body scanning which received widespread publicity in the mid-1990s as a revolutionary tool for supporting customized marketing of apparel suffered from the problems that the technology delivered less capability than developers had promised, at a cost much higher than originally estimated. In 2001, however, the upmarket menswear retailer, Brooks Brothers, introduced a $75,000 scanner into their New York flagship store. After the customer has been scanned and their physical details stored, they are able to order a customized suit for approximately 20 per cent more than the price of an off the peg item. Again the company's pricing strategy is only aimed at recovering added costs. The real benefit to the firm has been the ability to significantly reduce the inventory of ready to wear garments. Some apparel companies have ignored the individualized fit approach and instead offer the consumer to personalize their purchase by being offered a range of alternative styles and colours. Ralph Lauren has launched a line of 'Create Your Own' polo and Oxford shirts for which they charge a premium of between $5 and $10. Other examples of this approach are the sneaker maker Vans, the bag maker Timbuk2 and the athletic clothing manufacturer, Nike. The dominance of service firms and clothing manufacturers in the mass customization business reflects the fact that in other industrial sectors the more complex technologies or assembly processes required to support a move away from operating a traditional mass market assembly line can be too expensive or a technically impossible proposition. Nevertheless, as time passes, the success of companies such as Dell, which permits the online customer to specify their own unique machine based upon a diversity of different configurations, is now beginning to demonstrate that this philosophy is increasingly feasible in other market sectors. To-date the car companies have tended to delegate the customization market to specialist aftermarket body shops and suppliers. This situation may begin to change following BMW's creation of an online ordering system which permits consumers to purchase a Mini Cooper based upon several million specification alternatives.

References

Bardaki, A. and Whitelock, J. (2004) 'How "ready" are customers for mass customization: an exploratory investigation', *European Journal of Marketing*, Vol. 38, No. 11/12, pp. 1396–1408.

Bowen, J.T. and Shoemaker, S. (2003) 'Loyalty: a strategic commitment', *Cornell Hotel and Restaurant Administration Quarterly*, Vol. 44, No. 5/6, pp. 31–47.

Christopher, M., Peck, H. and Towill, D. (2006) 'A taxonomy for selecting global supply chain strategies', *International Journal of Logistics Management,* Vol. 17, No. 2, pp. 277–88.

Cooper, P.D. and Mialoulis, G. (1998) 'Altering corporate strategic criteria to reflect changing life', *California Management Review*, Vol. 31, No. 1, pp. 87–98.

Connolly, K. (2006) 'Who needs the new black when they sell elasticated waists?', *The Daily Telegraph*, London, 25 April, p. 15.

Doeringer, P. and Crean, S. (2006) 'Can fast fashion save the US apparel industry?', *Socio-Economic Review*, Vol. 4, No. 3, pp. 353–66.

Drucker, P. (1973) *Management Tasks, Responsibilities, Practices*, New York: Harper & Row.

Eastwood, A. (2007) 'Showing who's BOSS', *Marketing*, Toronto, 25 June, pp. 20–3.

Fraser, C.F. (1983) 'Creative strategy: a management perspective', *Journal of Advertising*, Vol. 12, No. 4, pp. 36–42.

Goulias, K.S. and Henson, K.M. (2006) 'On altruists and egoists in activity participation and travel: who are they and do they live together?', *Transportation*, Vol. 33, No. 5, pp. 447–56.

Grewal, R. and Tansuhaj, P. (2001) 'Building organizational capabilities for managing economic crisis: the role of market orientation and strategic flexibility', *Journal of Marketing*, Vol. 65, pp. 67–80.

Guagnano, G.A. (2001) 'Altruism and market-like behaviours: an analysis of willingness to pay for recycled paper products', *Population and Environment*, Vol. 22, No. 4, pp. 425–36.

Hamal, G. and Prahalad, C. (1996) *Competing for The Future*, Harvard MA: Harvard Business School Press.

Kotler, P. (1989) 'From mass marketing to mass customization', *Planning Review*, Vol. 17, No. 5, pp. 10–15.

Lennart, T., Broekhuizen, J. and Alsem, K.J. (2002) 'Success factors for mass customization: a conceptual model', *Journal of Market-Focused Management*, Vol. 5, No. 4, pp. 309–18.

Loeffler, M. (2002) 'A multinational examination of the "non-domestic product" effect', *International Marketing Review*, Vol. 19, No. 4/5, pp. 482–98.

Maslow, A.H. (1964) 'A theory of human motivation', in H.J. Levitt and L.R. Pandt (eds) *Readings in Management Psychology*, Chicago: University of Chicago Press, pp. 6–24.

Peppers, D. and Rogers, M. (1995) 'A new marketing paradigm: share of customer, not market share', *Planning Review*, Vol. 23, No. 2, pp. 14–19.

Pine, B.J. (1996) 'Service each customer efficiently and uniquely', *Business Communications Review*, January, pp. 2–5.

Pine, B.J. (1993) *Mass Customization: The New Frontier in Business Competition*, Harvard, MA: Harvard Business School Press.

Porter, M.E. (1985a) *Competitive Advantage: Creating and Sustaining Superior Performance*, New York: Free Press.

Porter, M.E. (1985b) 'Technology and competitive advantage', *Journal of Business Strategy*, Vol. 5, No. 3, pp. 60–78.

Prahalad, C.K. and Ramaswamy, V. (2000) 'Co-opting customer competences', *Harvard Business Review*, January/February, pp. 79–87.

Roberts, S. (1998) 'Harness the future', *The Canadian Manager*, Vol. 23, No. 3, pp. 11–14.

Rosecky, R.B. and King, A.B. (1996) 'Perceptual differences among owners of luxury cars: strategic marketing implications', *Mid-Atlantic Journal of Business*, Vol. 32, No. 3, pp. 221–40.

Schlosser, J. (2004) 'Cashing in on the new world of one', *Fortune, New York*, 13 December, pp. 244–9.

Strasser, S. (1989) *Satisfaction Guaranteed: The Making of the American Mass Market*, New York: Pantheon Books.

Wang, Y. and Lo, H. (2003) 'Customer-focused performance and the dynamic model for competence building and leveraging: a resource-based view', *Journal of Management Development*, Vol. 22, No. 5/6, pp. 483–527.

Wolfe and Sisodia (2003) 'Marketing to the self-actualizing customer', *Journal of Consumer Marketing*, Vol. 20, No. 6, pp. 555–69.

7 Innovation

Generic principles of marketing to financially attractive consumers (FACs)

The coverage of issues in Chapter 7 is designed to illustrate the generic principles of marketing to FACs in relation to:

1   The probability of greater success which leads to a radical change in an entire market sector is the introduction of a 'disruptive innovation'.
2   Marketers in mature, non-growth industries should avoid the mindset that no opportunities exist to exploit innovation as the basis for developing a stronger market base among FACs.
3   Significant success can also be achieved by a relatively simple innovation involving an upgrading of an existing product or service to deliver greater satisfaction to FACs to replace the existing, more generic propositions being made available to the market.
4   Innovation strategies should not be restricted to improving products or services, but instead broadened to examine opportunities to improve an organization's internal operational processes.
5   As product usage by FACs will vary over time, a useful concept for assessment of new product opportunities is to examine the Product Usage Cycle.
6   New product success is usually critically influenced by the organization maximizing the number of ideas that are generated at the beginning of an innovation programme.
7   Rigid application of the 'stage gate' new product model runs the risk that the company's new product being developed for FACs may be preempted by the launch of a new product by a competitor.
8   As the age and life experiences of the marketer is often somewhat different from that of FACs, it is critical that data are acquired from the actual target market during all stages in the new product development process.

Innovation pathways

Christensen (1997) has used the phrase 'sustained innovation' to describe how most large corporations focus their R&D efforts on introducing incremental improvements in existing products or organizational processes. The potential problem with this managerial philosophy is that the future performance of firms using this strategy is highly vulnerable to a new player entering the market offering a significantly different product or organizational process. An example of this latter proposition is Amazon's creation of a new online distribution channel into book retailing.

The conventional theory of large firm failure is of an event that occurs because an incumbent market leader fails to recognize the scale of the threat posed by a new firm entering their market or their speed of response is inadequate. More recently, however, Christensen (1997) has posited that market leaders' desire to respond to changing market circumstances is often constrained by existing customers' insistence on their key suppliers continuing to concentrate on making further improvements to existing products. As a result, many large firms tend to focus on product or process innovation which can sustain the company's current market position in terms of staying ahead of other large organizations operating within the same market sector, serving the needs of the same customer base. Thus, for example, although IBM recognized the potential of minicomputers to provide smaller organizations with access to more affordable computer technology, the firm's existing large company clients articulated a desire for IBM to continue to develop the next generation of mainframe computers capable of offering even greater, more powerful, data processing capability. This behaviour permitted an MIT-trained entrepreneur, Ken Olsen, operating from an old textile mill in Massachusetts to launch the Digital Equipment Corporation (DEC). The new firm's success was based upon the strategy of making computers affordable to smaller organizations by supplying them with the first generation of minicomputers.

The implications of Christensen's theory is, therefore, that an entrepreneurial firm seeking to achieve significant profit growth should develop a radically different product or revision to internal, organizational operational processes because this will permit delivery of benefits that are not currently satisfied by the incumbent, large firm market leader. This approach to new product or process development management is known as 'disruptive innovation'. The terminology is applicable to those situations where the new proposition is significantly different from the prevailing business conventions being followed by most of the existing firms within an industrial sector. The outcome is either the creation of a very different customer usage pattern or the provision of a radically different benefit proposition (Gilbert 2003).

The widespread acceptance of Christensen's theories has resulted in some firms assuming that disruptive innovation is the only feasible strategy through which to develop highly successful new products. This orientation ignores the fact that in many consumer market sectors, there exist extremely profitable opportunities from introducing improvements to existing products which increase their appeal to financially attractive customer segments. One consumer goods sector which has been very successful in adopting this approach is the cosmetics industry. In this sector, well known brands such as L'Oréal already have a loyal customer base. They have now enhanced brand loyalty and attracted new users by adding anti-ageing ingredients to their skin care products. Similarly in the food and drinks sector, Heinz and Minute Maid have respectively reformulated certain products to more effectively meet the nutritional and taste preferences of older, more health-orientated consumers (Janoff 2000).

New product guidelines for maturing boomer markets

Case Aims: To illustrate that by understanding certain facts about maturing boomer behaviour, a firm can increase the probability of successfully launching a new product in this sector of a market.

The greater a firm's understanding of a financially attractive consumer market, the higher the probability of success when developing new products or services (Rubel 1995). ProMatura is an American design company that specializes in advising consumer goods companies on new or improved product development opportunities suitable for maturing boomer markets. From their experience they have developed the following guidelines to increase the probability of positive new product development outcomes:

1   Understand the differences in human abilities across different age groups.
2   Understand which human abilities most affect successful use of the product or service being researched.
3   Test maturing boomer reaction to prototypes in relation to the factors of usability, usefulness and aesthetic appeal.
4   Use knowledge gained from prototyping to refine the product and to maximize the aesthetic appeal of the final design.
5   Upon launching the new or improved product, focus on marketing the design, usefulness, benefits and joy from usage.

Scope and focus

Some firms seeking to increase sales in financially attractive consumer markets will only need to make minimal changes to current marketing practices. In such cases, the most likely action will be that of redirecting promotional activity to focus on the selected customer target group. For example, many downtown restaurants in upmarket areas in large cities have usually originally been built into very successful operations by focusing on two customer targets. These are business people dining out on expense accounts and higher income, middle-aged couples. The former group tend to use these restaurants for expense account lunches on weekdays and the latter group fill the establishment over the weekend. In seeking to generate incremental revenue, many restaurant owners have recognized that an opportunity exists to fill more tables on weekday evenings. The most effective way of fulfilling this aim is to attract high income, maturing boomer couples. As this group will usually be satisfied by the existing menus, the only marketing actions required to attract new customers are those which will assist in building awareness of the restaurant among the maturing boomer market sector.

Innovation opportunities

Case Aims: To illustrate that the new lifestyle patterns of maturing boomers present opportunities for new product development in virtually every consumer market.

Up until the latter part of the twentieth century, once people entered retirement their primary demand for products and services were for those associated with a relatively immobile lifestyle, linked in many cases to the need for healthcare. The advent of maturing boomers has completely changed this scenario. This is because, to quote the phrase proposed by Ostroff (1991), individuals who constitute this market segment are 'prime life consumers'. Many are healthy, active, keen to preserve a youthful appearance and want to get as much pleasure out of life as possible. Clearly this behavioural societal shift offers firms a huge range of opportunities to develop new products and services to meet these needs of this very different group of people. In virtually every consumer market, it is apparent that the breadth of opportunity is immense. For example in relation to personal appearance, female maturing boomers want new types of cosmetics and designer clothing that make them look good by disguising their slightly less youthful appearance and shape. Having already become involved in activities to stay healthy when younger such as jogging, both sexes usually wish to sustain this aspect of their lifestyle in later life. In many cases, however, acceptance of the physical changes that occur as the body ages will mean that maturing boomers will be interested in new types of fitness regimes such as using running machines at a sports club or taking advantage of new anti-ageing treatments that may be offered by health spas. The importance that many maturing boomers place on retaining their appearance and their health will also mean that new opportunities exist for companies who focus on exploiting innovation to develop new healthier, lower calorie food and drink products. One restaurant chain in Philadelphia, for example, Thinny Delites was started by Alvin Binder. His doctor told him to reduce his cholesterol level and this was a catalyst for developing an ice cream substitute. The success of the product convinced him of the market appeal of offering fat-free desserts for maturing boomers who want to still eat out but are concerned about their waistline or their cholesterol levels.

Having determined the scale of required innovation, the firm should then make a decision in relation to the focus of the proposed innovation. There is a tendency to assume that innovation will always be based around a new product or service. This orientation ignores the fact that consideration should be given to whether opportunities exist to exploit internal process innovation as a pathway through which to optimize consumer satisfaction. Operational innovation activities that might be considered include changes to the product/service production system, promotion, distribution or logistics. The appeal of process innovation is that it frequently involves a smaller level of expenditure and is of a much lower risk than a new product development project.

Research by Ariss *et al.* (2000) has confirmed the preference of many entrepreneurs is to focus on product innovation. These researchers also concluded, however, that especially in those industrial sectors where the generic product design has been available for some years, an entrepreneurial firm seeking to achieve significant future profit growth through innovation is more likely to achieve this by concentrating upon the development of a new, more productive, operational process. In view of these findings it is recommended that upon considering the implementation of an innovation programme, the firm should undertake an assessment of the options as shown in Figure 7.1. This will permit identification of what the optimal opportunities are through which to generate revenue from a financially attractive consumer market sector.

In the context of launching a new product or service, in addition to being concerned with the benefit to be offered, a company should also be aware that customer demand will be influenced by product form. This latter product dimension relates to the product's physical appearance and attributes. These two dimensions generate the four alternative options that are summarized in Figure 7.2.

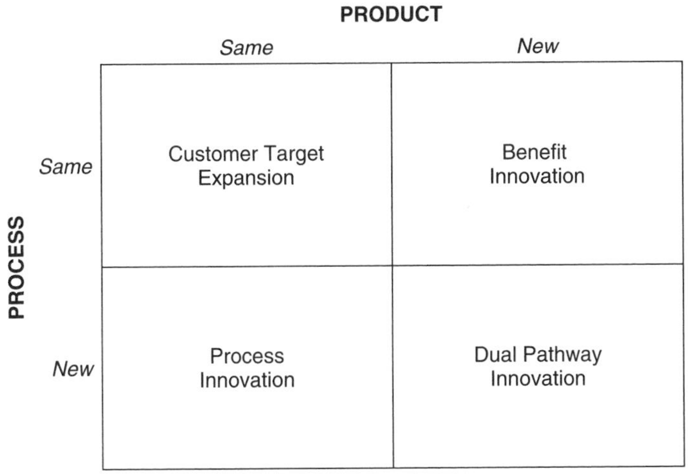

Figure 7.1 Innovation focus matrix.

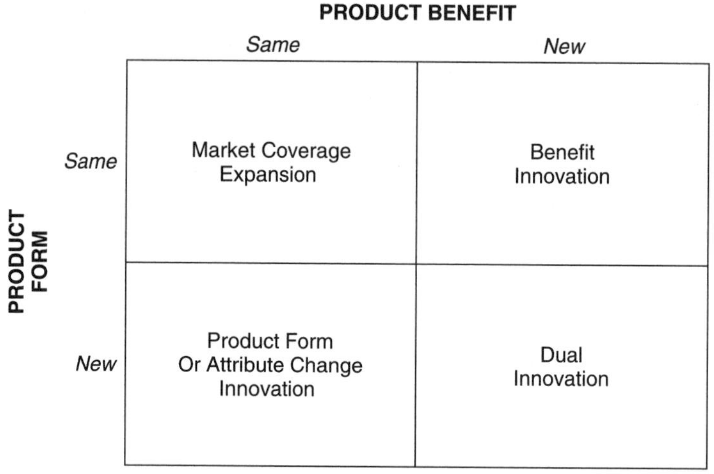

PRODUCT BENEFIT

	Same	New
Same	Market Coverage Expansion	Benefit Innovation
New	Product Form Or Attribute Change Innovation	Dual Innovation

PRODUCT FORM

Figure 7.2 Directional product matrix.

Re-focus (Keiningham *et al.* 2006)

Case Aims: To illustrate that new product development can be as simple as changing the product formulation to more effectively meet the changing needs of the maturing boomer.

For some firms, new product development can be as simple as identifying how the effects of time have impacted their existing customers and to then re-focus their innovation programme on evolving formulations that offer the benefit of helping 'turn back the clock'. One of the most obvious signs of ageing is greying hair. Hence, a number of the large major health and beauty aids (HbAs) companies, having recognized the increasing size of the maturing boomer market, have re-focused their efforts into the launch and promotion of hair colouring products targeted at older people (Rosendahl 1991). An important factor identified by Revlon's Professional Products Group in New York City is that many older people do not want to look as if they are colouring their hair. Hence, new formulations must deliver the promise of keeping the user's hair looking natural. Another important issue is that older peoples' hair is more fragile and can be more easily damaged by the application of hair dye. This has caused Revlon to develop their New Age instant hair colour which is designed to avoid damaging hair. The launch of this new product was supported with a $3.5 million promotional campaign focusing on the need for older people to give more thought about protecting their hair when selecting a colouring formulation. The other trend is that many older men are as concerned about their appearance as women. This trait has created a gold mine for Combe Inc. of White Plains, New

York. This company developed the two brands 'Just for Men' and 'Grecian Formula 16', which together have a combined brand share in excess of 60 per cent of the total male hair colouring market in the USA.

Traditionally the cosmetics industry has focused on teenagers and women in the 20–35 year age group. More recently, however, the opportunity to offer the benefit of helping maturing women boomers staying looking young has caused some of the major cosmetics brands to invest in the development of products for older age groups. One example is provided by the launch of Maybelline's Revitalizing product range which has specifically been created to help older women look younger (Stern 1993). The new range includes foundations, concealers, blushes and powders contain moisturizers, sunscreens, Vitamin A and light diffusers, all of which are aimed at counteract or hiding the signs of ageing. The product range is specifically designed to appeal to female maturing boomers by being presented in upmarket black and gold packaging. In order to achieve effective communication of the product launch among maturing boomers, Maybelline took the unusual decision of running advertisements during television programmes, such as 'Murder, She Wrote' and in magazines, such as *Ladies Home Journal.*

Usage cycle

A long established marketing theory is that the history of products can be described in terms of a Product Life Cycle (PLC). The cycle assumes products pass through the four phases of Introduction, Growth, Maturity and Decline. During each phase the nature of the marketing mix may require revision to reflect the prevailing nature of market conditions. The concept is widely accepted as an extremely useful planning tool. For example Kotler (1988) proposed 'the PLC is an attempt to recognize distinct stages in the sales history of the product. Corresponding to these stages are definite opportunities and problems with respect to marketing strategy and profit potential'.

There are, however, those who reject the PLC as a viable concept of any practical use to the marketer. One criticism articulated by this latter group is that in real life, the revenue patterns for many products have no resemblance to the classic PLC curve (Rink and Swan 1979). Another criticism is that controllable marketing variables, competitor information and other important environmental factors are ignored by the concept (Wind and Claycamp 1976). These omissions, it can be argued, may cause marketers to make inappropriate decisions. For example, a product's sales may have reached a plateau. Believing the onset of maturity has occurred, the company begins to put greater emphasis on sales promotions and price reductions, while cutting back on advertising. In fact, the sales plateau was of a temporary nature caused by an economic downturn. Had the company continued to focus more resources on further product development and sustaining advertising activity, over the longer term, further growth in market size would have occurred due to new users being attracted to the market.

In the context of the PLC, most marketers do perceive the usefulness of the concept but appreciate that blind acceptance of the validity of the model as the basis for making marketing decisions can cause errors to occur. This potential weakness of the concept in terms of reaching appropriate business decisions may point to marketers needing to consider the relationships which exist between products within a portfolio, their relative profitability and changing levels of market consumption over time (MacMillan *et al.* 1982). One approach that draws upon analysing product consumption patterns to assist the new product planning process is the Product Usage Cycle (or PUC) concept. The concept is consists of two dimensions. One dimension is that some products are only used for a specific period during a person's lifetime; whereas others which were adopted when the person was young continue to be consumed later in life. The other dimension relates to changes in lifestyle over time. The joint interaction of these two dimensions provides the basis for the PUC. Application of the tool can be illustrated in the context of the maturing boomer where the change in lifestyle dimension can be divided into an active and inactive phase. In this context, as shown in Figure 7.3(a) and (b), this generates two different PUCs.

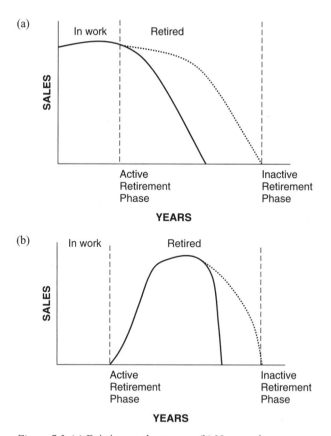

Figure 7.3 (a) Existing product usage. (b) New product usage.

In the case of existing products, the consumer is already purchasing the product and sustains usage even after moving into the active phase of their retirement. The marketer will need to determine whether the onset of retirement means that to sustain customer loyalty, there is a requirement to change either the product form or product benefit (e.g. designing a replacement for use by older, less mobile, less active people). Other products will only become of appeal upon retirement. Where the PUC indicates adoption only after retirement, to exploit this opportunity the firm will usually need to develop a radically different product than that being offered to younger people still working for a living (e.g. retirement apartments offering more security and on-site support facilities such as a social centre and 24-hour nursing care). The other issue to resolve is the question of whether product appeal will be sustained through both the active and inactive retirement phases.

Having determined which of the PUC curves is applicable and having developed a new product, the firm can also use the position of the product on the PUC to determine the optimal nature of the marketing mix. For example, with an existing customer PUC, the bias will usually be to support ongoing usage in retirement by using promotions to sustain benefit communication. There could also be a requirement to increase the level of sales promotions or to reduce the price. This situation can be contrasted with the introduction and growth phases for a new product that will only be of appeal upon entering retirement. Here, emphasis should be given to promotional activity such as advertising aimed at generating product trial and repeat usage. It is probable that sales promotion or price reductions will be of less importance within the marketing mix.

It may also be beneficial to consider the concept of a reverse PUC as a potential source of new ideas. This concept recognizes nostalgia can be an important component of older peoples' memories of happy times when they were younger. The potential opportunity that can exist in exploiting nostalgia among older people is illustrated by the average age of the audience at a Rolling Stones concert or the success currently being enjoyed by pop groups such as Pink Floyd and Queen from their revival concerts and re-issuing re-mixes of their old records as DVDs or iPod downloads. Opportunities also exist to reposition products to fulfil the urge of financially attractive consumers for products they desired or owned when young, but had to forgo when having a family placed other priorities on their spending patterns. The high level of revenue generating possibilities by exploiting this aspect of consumer behaviour is illustrated in both the USA and UK by the success car makers who are enjoying selling sports cars and convertibles to older men and women.

Identifying usage change

Case Aims: To illustrate how customer data can be utilized to understand the needs and requirements of maturing boomers at a specific key point of change on a PUC curve.

The aim of most survey-based market research projects is to assess the current attitudes of consumers to an existing product in relation to offerings from competitors. The results can be used to determine how changes in the marketing mix in the areas of promotion, price or sales could improve near-term performance. In some cases, however, surveys can provide useful early indications of shifts in product need and usage patterns. Such was the case, for example, in a survey undertaken in the late 1990s of 4,000 new-home buyers who reflect the new trend of maturing boomers purchasing properties in age restricted, gated adult communities in the USA (Schleimer 2001). Respondents were asked questions about over 100 demographic, product, feature, amenity and lifestyle issues. From the results, a number of key issues were identified about the behaviour of maturing boomers who decide to relocate just prior to, or upon, their retirement. Over 80 per cent of respondents were married, 44 per cent in the age group 55–64 and of the remainder, 41 per cent were in the age group 65–74. Annual income levels were higher than the national average, with 64 per cent indicating an income greater than $50,000 and 21 per cent with incomes in excess of $100,000. Previous property ownership was predominantly a large detached, single-family, 3–4 bedroom house sold for an average price of $270,000. This preference for a single-family dwelling was sustained in the new purchase with a wish to only marginally reduce total floor space and a preference to retain three bedrooms in the new property. Retention of this number of bedrooms reflects usage as speciality rooms for hobbies, working out and when required, being used by visitors such as children, grandchildren or friends from their old neighbourhood. There was also a preference to have a two-car garage even though many respondents only owned one vehicle. Apparently the additional space is seen as important for storage and as a place to keep the golf cart or ride-on mower. Average prices paid for the new house were in the region of $70,000 less than the money received from the sale of the previous home. Over 50 per cent of respondents then spent in the region of $30,000 of this saving in having luxury upgrades, equipment options and top of the range furnishings installed in their new home. This expenditure reflected a desire for a life of greater luxury than achievable in their previous home and the desire to own items such as kitchen appliances of the highest quality and durability. These attributes are important because they are perceived as minimizing the possibility of maintenance problems a few years later. The primary motivation of maturing boomers in moving to an adult community is to lead a more active life and to make new friends. In selecting their new home, the most important room was the kitchen.

Community facility factors of importance included having access to a clubhouse with a swimming pool and exercise rooms, the community being age-restricted and located near to medical services and shopping. The reputation of the builder, the quality of the construction, excellent customer service and a full construction warranty scheme were also important issues in selecting the community. To identify such a community, almost 40 per cent of respondents had relied on word of mouth recommendations, in many cases from relatives or friends who already lived there.

Idea generation

The potential for success in new product development projects can be heavily influenced by the quantity and quality of new ideas that are generated at the beginning of the project. As summarized in Figure 7.4, new ideas can come from a variety of different sources. Hence, it is important that the new product project leader maximizes the number of sources utilized during the idea generation phase. The advent of computer-based customer records and the internet greatly increase both the speed and breadth of data access that can be used in the identification of new ideas. It is rare that individuals will allocate equal time to mining information from every source identified in Figure 7.4. This is due to the fact that certain sources will emerge as being more fruitful than others.

Blumentritt's (2004) research on barriers to idea generation concluded that many firms in mature, non-growth industries often tend to adopt the philosophy that innovation is neither relevant nor productive in their sector of industry. He proposes that management should urgently revise their perspective on this matter. His perspective is supportive of the results from Vermeulen *et al.*'s (2005) study which identified that the following issues can act as potential obstacles to idea generation:

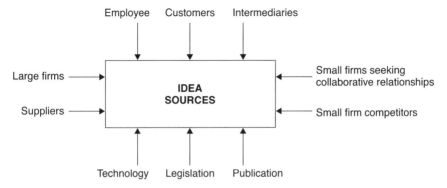

Figure 7.4 Idea sources.

1   Many organizations use 'lightweight' teams for idea generation, thereby not exploiting the best of the expertise which may exist within the company.
2   There is a tendency not to involve key customers in development activities.
3   Companies, having faced problems over incremental existing product improvements, avoid considering radically new ideas.
4   Firms suffer from a lack of resources which causes management to severely limit the scope of search permitted of employees engaged in seeking out new opportunities.
5   Those individuals assigned the idea generation have limited experience in the process.
6   Senior managers fail to provide incentives that could stimulate employees to become more involved in the generation of new product ideas.

To gain further understanding to the obstacles confronting idea generation in entrepreneurial firms and to determine how these might be overcome, Peterson (2006) surveyed 483 business leaders in the USA seeking to determine the source of their firm's most profitable ideas. Respondents indicated that the most important source were their own inspirations and spontaneous thoughts. This finding led the researcher to conclude that in some firms, the only source of new product ideas are inspirational thoughts by the company leader. These individuals apparently make no recourse to others within the firm when seeking ideas and attempt to create the more formalized, structured processes commonly encountered within the more conventionally managed companies. Peterson's conclusion was that this excessive reliance on personal judgement was the primary cause why some entrepreneurial firms failed to exploit the expertise of other sources such as employees, key customers and other external sources when seeking to maximize the number of potential ideas which could provide the basis for successful new products. The other risk associated with entrepreneurs' self reliance upon their own judgement is that ideas may not be adequately screened to assess viability. As a result, new product development may commence even though the firm's employees perceive fundamental flaws exist that will cause the idea to fail upon market launch.

It is important not just to focus on positive information. This is because negative data, such as customer complaints or an e-mail from an angry supplier, can sometimes lead to the identification of a new idea. For example, the Coleman Corporation, a US pioneer of camping equipment such as lanterns and stoves, launched a smoke detector with a big 'broom button' alarm tester. The idea came from newspaper articles about some older people, frustrated with the kitchen fumes repeatedly triggering their alarms, were removing the batteries from their existing alarms as a way to achieve peace and serenity.

This added feature is specifically aimed at older people who cannot climb onto a stool or ladder to turn off an alarm that has been accidentally triggered by burning the toast. The added benefit from this innovation is that it saves lives.

The reason some idea sources are relied upon more heavily than others is the empathy which may exist between the employee and the information source. Computer techies, for example, prefer talking to other computer techies. Hence this type of individual is likely to concentrate on dialoguing with suppliers they know in the computer industry. An individual motivated by finding ways of delivering customer satisfaction may exhibit the inclination of relying heavily on discussions with customers to identify new opportunities. Hence, in the case where the firm is adopting a team-based approach to researching a variety of idea sources, it is useful to decide which individuals should concentrate on what sources of information.

When exploiting any idea source, it is important to recognize that the information provided may be biased. This can occur when a source lacking in commercial integrity has a vested interest in gaining acceptance for their suggestions. For example, a supplier wishing to sustain future sales may propose a design idea to ensure their own company's components will remain an integral part of any new product. Intermediaries such as large retailers will typically favour a new product idea capable of maximizing their profit per unit of retail space. They will have little concern about whether the innovation will significantly improve their supplier's financial performance.

Mature mart

Case Aims: To illustrate how observations of potential customers and their needs can provide the basis for new product ideas.

For those individuals willing to undertake some form of market assessment to identify a business start-up idea, there are undoubtedly a whole range of opportunities out there just waiting to be harvested. Support for this view is provided by the case of Alexis Abramson who founded Mature Mart in Atlanta, Georgia (Mimms 1996). With a Masters in Gerontology, Alexis was appointed as Director for the 60+ programme at the Atlanta Jewish Community Centre. Every day she observed examples of older peoples' physical state causing them problems. For example, older people with limited vision being unable to read the numbers on a standard telephone dial. Having spent time seeking out solutions, she realized that an opportunity existed to launch a business supplying older people with products that permit them to overcome their physical limitations. Alexis borrowed $50,000 from her father to launch Mature Mart in 1995. Initially the business was just a website offering a one-stop shopping outlet. She knew older people in those days were not computer literate. Hence, promotional activities were directed at building awareness among younger people who were providing care to their parents or older relatives. To expand market coverage, the company introduced a catalogue featuring over 20,000 products and a free phone number. Like many successful entrepreneurs, Alexis prefers to avoid spending money on advertising or buying mailing lists. Instead, she wrote articles for small-town newspapers and subsequently gained national coverage through appearances on programmes such as the NBC Today show. Never satisfied with the company's performance Alexis has continually sought ways of expanding the business. She moved in wholesaling by persuading retail outlets such as pharmacies and grocery stores to stock her products. This was followed by becoming a supplier of retiree products for the United States Franchise Systems Inc. (USFS) which owns the franchising rights for Microtel Inns. Subsequently, Mature Mart has expanded into older person consultancy providing assessments of buildings being senior friendly, advising firms how to become senior-orientated and delivering care provision training.

New product management

The linear (or 'stage gate') new product management model is to be found in virtually every marketing text ever published. As illustrated in Figure 7.5 it is a straight line, sequential process typically constituted of the seven components of: idea generation, idea screening, concept development, business planning, prototype development, test marketing and launch (Cooper *et al.* 1997). Originally evolved to assist large firms minimize the risk of new product failure, the model is an excellent example of the 'moving from one box to the next' managerial philosophy often communicated as the 'holy grail of best management practice' to MBA students at Business Schools around the globe. Supporters of the model strongly adhere to the view that firms should execute every component within the model prior to market launch. Furthermore, the user is urged to adhere to the rule of totally completing all the activities associated with the tasks specified within each box before progressing to the next stage in the model (Lester 1998).

In recent years, in seeking to understand why many Western companies have been unsuccessful in the development and launch of new products, there have been some questions raised about the universal validity of the stage gate model. One of the concerns is that the process involves a significant period of time between idea generation and the eventual launch of the new product. As demonstrated by the Japanese car and electronic consumer goods industries, a firm can gain a massive market advantage by implementing certain components of the model on a concurrent basis because this will dramatically reduce 'time to market' for their new venture (Vesey 1991). However, it is worth noting that Wansink and Gilmore

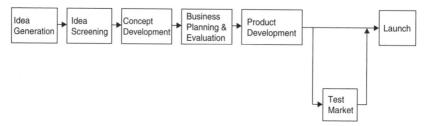

Figure 7.5 A traditional linear new product process management model.

(1999) identified in some cases firms suffering from the delusion that a very rapid new product development process is always justified because it will lead to much faster generation of a positive cash flow. A risk with this viewpoint is the outcome of potential product failure because of insufficient attention being given to market research to ensure there is convergence of opinion between the firm and potential customers.

Millier and Palmer (2001) note the utilization of the stage gate model also involves making other certain critical assumptions. These are that the product can be characterized as having features or benefits which potential customers can understand and that the market for such a product is readily identifiable. In those cases where these assumptions are invalid, they posit an alternative new product process system will be required. As summarized in Figure 7.6, there are three scenarios where due to lack of understanding by either customers or producer, it would be inadvisable to use the conventional linear new product process model in isolation of the market while progressing through the stages of concept definition, prototype development and subsequent market launch.

In all of the scenarios where at least one party has a low understanding of the proposition under consideration, successful new product development will require collaboration between the company and key customers. This is because collaboration is necessary in order for the producer to acquire sufficient understanding of how to maximize the market appeal for the new product under development. Even where the producer has an understanding of the proposition, customers need to be involved at some stage in the development process in order that, upon the subsequent market launch, they comprehend how they can benefit from purchasing the new product.

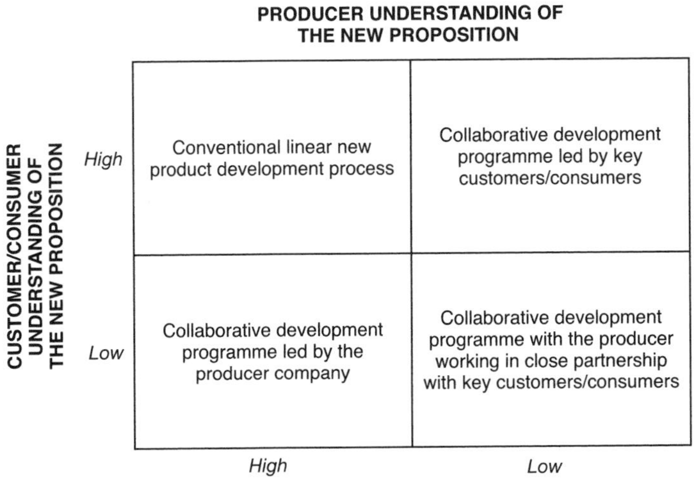

PRODUCER UNDERSTANDING OF
THE NEW PROPOSITION

CUSTOMER/CONSUMER UNDERSTANDING OF THE NEW PROPOSITION		High	Low
	High	Conventional linear new product development process	Collaborative development programme led by key customers/consumers
	Low	Collaborative development programme led by the producer company	Collaborative development programme with the producer working in close partnership with key customers/consumers

Source: Modified from Millier and Palmer (2001)

Figure 7.6 Consumer/supplier interaction matrix.

Some common problems

Case Aims: To illustrate that compared with the 18–49 year age group, marketing new products to maturing boomers is usually a more difficult task. The success of the new product is often reduced because of a failure of a company to recognize that their marketing campaign can have generated an adverse reaction among older consumers.

Lunsford and Burnett (1992) posit that new product marketing is the most difficult and challenging of all of the marketing tasks because the innovation must be capable of encouraging consumers to alter their purchase or product usage behaviour. Furthermore, they believe that the successful introduction of a new product into the maturing boomer market is made more difficult because the barriers that need to be overcome are greater than those encountered when marketing new products to the 18–49 year age group. As a consequence, success rates in the maturing boomer market are often lower because there is a tendency of firms to make mistakes while introducing a new product into this market sector. One issue is the compatibility of the new product with older peoples' reduced vision capacity, touch sensitivity and muscular strength. Hence, new products must be designed for ease of use in order to accommodate the influence of these factors on the consumers' willingness to adopt the product. Maturing boomers, when compared with young people, are also more objective when determining whether the promised benefits of a new product are of a sufficient scale to prompt a change in purchase behaviour sufficient to want to switch to the new product. In those cases where the only product claim being made for the product is that of 'newness', maturing boomers' reaction will often be that their current product has not reached the stage where a replacement is needed. Another potential problem is to ensure that the new product is portrayed in a way which is perceived as compatible with the maturing boomer's own self image. Most maturing boomers perceive themselves as feeling and looking younger than their actual age. Failure to recognize this attitude can result, for example, in a firm running a television commercial featuring the actors who the maturing boomer viewers conclude are much older than they currently perceive themselves to be. An even greater error is to portray the older person as a hard-of-hearing busybody whose only pleasures in life are being miserable and criticising the behaviour of others. Maturing boomers are usually less impulsive than younger people when making a purchase decision. They are also strongly in favour of being able to easily gain access to additional information about a new product. Hence, those firms which focus on distributing the new product via a self service environment and make no attempt to provide access to additional information by creating a website or toll-free telephone enquiry service will find these decisions can significantly lower the number of individuals who are willing to purchase the product.

Various researchers have used survey data or case studies to assess whether the linear model is in wide-scale use among entrepreneurial firms. Typically they discover it is not (De Toni and Nassimbeni 2003; Vinson *et al.* 1975). The conclusion that some academics have reached when encountering this finding is new product failure rates would be greatly reduced if only entrepreneurs could learn from their counterparts in more conventional companies and adopt a structured, stage gate management model. Such views have caused some Government-funded business support programmes concerned with stimulating greater innovations to promote utilization of a stage gate model on the basis that this will improve new product success rates. The usual reaction of entrepreneurs attending training programmes is this recommendation about the stage gate model merely confirms their existing opinion that most Government-funded support schemes are of minimal benefit to their business operations.

In the real world, entrepreneurs have a tendency to ignore strict adherence to the stage gate process model. Nevertheless, they often perceive there are clear advantages in using one or more of the components contained within the model. As is shown in Figure 7.7, actual utilization, however, tends to be less formalized, with the entrepreneurial firm exhibiting a menu-based orientation in the selection of those components which are deemed to have a useful function in assisting the new product development process. As a result, use of the process usually involves varying the order of action sequencing and in many cases, totally ignoring certain component activities within the model.

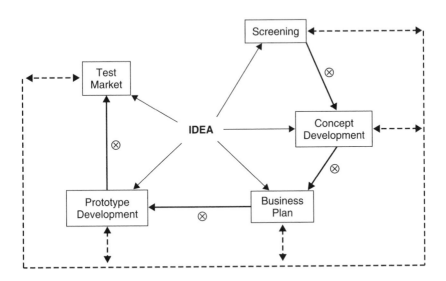

Key: ⊗ = Conventional sequential linear model

◀---▶ = Menu-based approach to innovation management

Figure 7.7 Alternative innovation process management model.

There are a number of reasons to explain this difference in the use of the process model by conventional vs. entrepreneurial firms. In some cases it is a reflection of managerial culture. For example some entrepreneurs, such as enthusiastic engineers, enjoy jumping immediately from idea generation to prototyping because they want to prove the technical practicality of their latest idea. Another common scenario, especially in the small firms sector, is that a poor cash flow situation may mandate there can be no delay in bringing the new product to market. There are also some company leaders who based on previous success, hold the view that their proven entrepreneurial skills totally justify their decision to move from idea identification to market launch without any attempt to validate project viability. Whichever is the reason influencing how the process model is utilized, the critical issue is that these firms understand the purpose of every component in the model. This understanding can then lead to acceptance of the advisability of implementing one or more additional stages of the model as a path by which product success rates may be increased and product failures reduced.

Whether the entrepreneurial firm accepts the validity of using the stage gate model for managing new product development, research by individuals such as Owens (2007) and Pons (2008) has revealed that project success can be undermined due to certain other failures in the project management process. Included in such findings are the following factors, which respondent firms indicated that in their organizations led either to project failure or the project breaching agreed time schedules or financial budgets:

1   Lack of overall strategic thinking and purpose to guide the development process.
2   Failure of senior management to exhibit strong commitment to new product development because of a tendency to be more involved in resolving crises that arise in day-to-day business operations.
3   A failure to ensure that adequate financial and staff resources are assigned to the project.
4   Lack of scientific, technical or engineering skills to overcome unexpected technological problems.
5   Inadequate skills within the manufacturing operation to convert a prototype into a viable product suitable for manufacturing in large quantities or an inability to produce the new product that meets specified cost or quality specifications.
6   Poor communications between different departments causing delays or miscommunications that lead to incorrect decisions being reached.
7   Poor decision-making due to a tendency to use a hierarchical structure accompanied by limited interaction between the different departments involved in the project.
8   A failure to involve potential customers in the development process at a sufficiently early enough stage that lessons learned from their feedback can be incorporated into the final product specification.

Another key factor that can strongly influence the successful implementation of a new product development project is for the company to be able to acquire appropriate information from potential customers that can assist in the launch of a proposition which has strong market appeal. The conventional view that entrepreneurial firms do not engage in formal market research has led to the assumption that many new product failures can be attributed to inadequate data acquisition and analysis during the new product development process. Sultan and Barzack (1999) have challenged this view on the grounds that (a) the evidence of entrepreneurial firms not valuing market research tends to be of a limited, anecdotal nature and (b) where formal academic research studies have been undertaken, the results typically indicate that most entrepreneurial firms do draw upon market sources to assist their product development activities.

In their study, Sultan and Barzack did find that the nature of the market interaction process rarely involved the classic, positivist approach of undertaking large scale, quantitative consumer surveys. Instead, they found entrepreneurial firms tended to rely on a more informal, qualitative approach where data about markets and views of customers are generated through 1-to-1 meetings between a key customer and the company. Additionally, the firms also often arranged focus groups constituted of intermediaries or potential end-users.

People power

Case Aims: To illustrate the importance of ensuring that in developing a new or improved service, managers need to ensure that employees have the necessary skills to deliver the revised service proposition.

A factor well understood by successful firms, especially those operating in the service sector, is the importance of employees being able to deliver the new benefit proposition that is to be offered. Hence, as part of the innovation planning process, managers will need to assess, prior to any market launch, whether the staff do have the capability to deliver the new or revised product proposition (Carrigan 1999). In those cases where an area of employee vulnerability has been identified, the wisest course of action is to delay new product market introduction until the identified weaknesses have been remedied. An example of the importance of internal people power is provided by the case of the Moor Hall Health and Leisure Club located in Sutton Coldfield, UK. An area traditionally associated with traditional industries such as steel and coal, the economic decline of the smoke stack industries has meant that the local population is increasingly constituted of older people with ample leisure time. This caused the Moor Hall manage-ment to decide that expanding the business would require focusing on developing new and revised health and fitness services aimed directly at the needs of the local people. A lifestyle analysis of local people in the Sutton Coldfield area identified that older users of fitness centres are predominantly individuals seeking to retain their health while concurrently being involved in social interaction with other people. Analysis of staff roles in delivering new or revised services to retirees, permitted the Moor Hall owners to identify the following three different, but equally important, roles within their organization, and the associated conclusion that some staff would need further training in order to deliver customer satisfaction:

- *Interfacers* who have most contact with customers, delivering or supervising sports and exercise training. These individuals should not just have qualifications in sports management, but also have to be trained in the understanding of relevant physiological conditions such as osteoporosis. They also need to understand older people and be able to relate to them when providing guidance on exercise regimes.
- *Interadjacents* such as receptionists and cafeteria operatives, are critically important in building customer loyalty. These individuals would have to further develop their skills of being warm, flexible and understanding of the social needs of retirees.
- *Interplayers* are support staff including people such as maintenance workers and cleaners. They have infrequent contact with customers and may be unaware that failing to maintain high standards in their work could create an adverse image among Moor Hall members. Hence, further training would be necessary to develop a pride in achievement, sufficient to positively impact customer perceptions over, e.g. equipment cleanliness and appearance of changing and bathroom facilities.

The benefits associated with ensuring Moor Hall staff had the ability to deliver the new strategy of creating a health, fitness and social products portfolio of appeal to older people is demonstrated by over 80 per cent of members now being maturing boomers with high levels of disposable income. The club's 76 per cent member annual retention rate is much higher than the industry average. Furthermore, the club's long waiting list of people seeking membership is totally generated by word-of-mouth promotion by existing members.

References

Ariss, S.S., Raghunathan, T.S and Kunnathar, A. (2000) 'Factors affecting the adoption of advanced manufacturing technology in small firms', *S.A.M. Advanced Management,* Vol. 65, No. 2, pp. 14–23.

Blumentritt, T. (2004) 'Does small and mature have to mean dull? Defying the ho-hum at SMEs', *Journal of Business Strategy*, Vol. 25, No. 1, pp. 27–34.

Carrigan, M. (1999) 'Old spice–developing successful relationships with the grey market', *Long Range Planning*, Vol. 32, No. 2, pp. 253–62.

Christensen, C.M. (1997) *The Innovator's Dilemma,* Boston, MA: Harvard Business School Press.

Cooper, R.G., Edgett, S. and Kleinschmidt, E.J. (1997) 'Portfolio management in new product development: lessons from the leaders', *Research Technology Management,* Vol. 40, No. 6, pp. 43–53.

De Toni, A. and Nassimbeni, G. (2003) 'Small and medium district enterprises and the new product development challenge: Evidence from Italian eyewear district', *International Journal of Operations & Production,* Vol. 23, No. 5/6, pp. 678–98.

Gilbert, C. (2003) 'The disruption opportunity', *Sloan Management Review,* Vol. 44, No. 4, pp. 27–36.

Janoff, B. (2000) 'The aging of Aquarius', *The Progressive Grocer,* New York, Vol. 79, No. 8, pp. 79–83.

Keiningham, T.L., Vavra, T.G and Aksoy, L. (2006) 'Managing through rose-colored glasses', *Sloan Management Review,* Vol. 48, No. 1, pp. 15–22.

Kotler, P. (1988) *Marketing Management: Analysis, Planning, Implementation and Control,* 8th edn., Englewood Cliffs, NJ: Prentice Hall.

Lester, D.H. (1998) 'Critical success factors for new product development', *Research Technology Management,* Vol. 41, No. 1, pp. 36–44.

Lunsford, D.A. and Burnett, M.S. (1992) 'Marketing product innovations to the elderly: an understanding of process', *Journal of Consumer Marketing,* Vol. 9, No. 4, pp. 53–64.

MacMillan, I.C., Hambrick, D.C. and Day, D.L. (1982) 'The product portfolio and profitability – a PIMS-based analysis of industrial product businesses', *Academy of Management Journal,* Vol. 25, No. 4, pp. 733–56.

Millier, P. and Palmer, R. (2001) 'Turning innovation into profit', *Strategic Change,* Vol. 10, No. 2, pp. 87–98.

Mimms, C. (1996) 'Mature Mart's marketing plan', *Atlanta Business Chronicle,* Atlanta, 12 July, p. 4.

Ostroff, J. (1991) 'Targeting the prime-life consumer', *American Demographics,* Vol. 13, No. 1, pp. 30–5.

Owens, J.D. (2007) 'Why do some UK SMEs still find the implementation of a new product development process problematical?; An exploratory investigation', *Management Decision,* Vol. 45, No. 2, pp. 235–47.

Peterson, R.T. (2006) 'Development of useful ideas in the new product development process of small manufacturing firms', *Journal of Applied Management and Entrepreneurship,* Vol. 11, No. 3, pp. 23–40.

Pons, D. (2008) 'Project management for new product development', *Project Management Journal,* Vol. 39, No. 2, pp. 82–98.

Rink, D.R. and Swan, J.E. (1979) 'Product life cycle research: a literature review', *Journal of Business Research,* Vol. 78, pp. 219–42.

Rosendahl, I. (1991) 'Aging consumers brighten hair color sales', *Drug Topics,* Oradell, 17 June, pp. 65–7.

Rubel, C. (1995) 'Mature market often misunderstood', *Marketing News,* Chicago, Vol. 29, No. 19, pp. 28–30.

Schleimer, J. (2001) 'Active adults uncovered', *Builder,* Vol. 24, No. 2, pp. 336–40.

Stern, G. (1993) 'Aging boomers are new target for Maybelline', *Wall Street Journal,* New York, 13 April, p. B1.

Sultan, F. and Barzack, G (1999) 'Turning marketing research high-tech', *Marketing Management,* Vol. 8, No. 4, pp. 24–31.

Vermeulen, D., Patrick A.M., Jeroen P.J., De Jong, P. and O'Shaughnessy, K.C. (2005) 'Identifying key determinants for new product introductions and firm performance in small service firms', *Service Industries Journal* 25, No. 5, pp. 625–40.

Vesey, J.T. (1991) 'The new competitors think in terms of speed-to-market', *SAM Advanced Management Journal*, Vol. 56, No. 4, pp. 26–34.

Vinson, D.E., Jackson, J.H. and Ray, G.D. (1975) 'A pragmatic approach to new product planning', *Journal of Small Business Management*, Vol. 13, No. 2, pp. 37–48.

Wansink, B. and Gilmore, J.N. (1999) 'New uses that revitalize brands', *Journal of Advertising Research*, Vol. 39, No. 2, pp. 90–103.

Wind, Y. and Claycamp, H. (1976) 'Planning product line strategy: a matrix approach', *Journal of Marketing*, Vol. 40, pp. 2–9.

8 Promotion

Generic principles of marketing to financially attractive consumers (FACs)

The coverage of issues in Chapter 8 is designed to illustrate the generic principles of marketing to FACs in relation to:

1 The role of promotion is communication, the effectiveness of which in the case of FACs will be enhanced by the advertiser having knowledge of the self image, role assumption and purchase behaviour of this target audience.

2 Target audience definition for FACs is complicated by the heterogeneous needs of this customer group.

3 The nature of the promotional message will be influenced by both the involvement and information needs of the FACs to whom the communication is being directed.

4 Where a cost-effective proposition, personal selling is the preferred promotional channel for reaching FACs. This is because this group places great importance on developing a close relationship with suppliers.

5 Although social networks and the internet have caused media channel fragmentation, FACs remain major users of the conventional terrestrial advertising media channels.

6 Electronic marketing such as tele-sales tends to be less acceptable to FACs as an effective method of communicating information.

7 Where possible, the benefit message directed at FACs should seek to communicate the claim that product usage can deliver benefit in relation to the enhancement of mental states such as happiness, love or caring for others.

8 In the case of older FACs, the promotion should usually feature individuals who are younger than the target audience and to present

these featured individuals in the context of enjoying life and being involved in social activities.

9 In the case of older FACs the promotion should usually avoid communicating a message which evokes negative connotations in the minds of the target audience.

10 For products and services purchased by most age groups, the promotional message should be split and delivered via those channels most widely utilized by each consumer target audience.

Process

The fundamental aim of any form of promotion is to build awareness among potential and/or existing customers through the provision of appropriate information. Optimizing the cost/benefit outcomes for a promotional campaign requires a detailed understanding of buyer behaviour. Large companies can draw upon the skills of their advertising agencies to assist in the acquisition and exploitation of these market data. An obstacle often facing smaller firms is their inability to afford the fees charged by agencies for the provision of such services. Barriers such as these can cause smaller firms to conclude that promotion is an expense they cannot afford. This attitude will mean some small firms miss out on the additional sales that can accrue from allocating an appropriate level of funds to supporting promotional activity.

Achieving success in building market awareness will involve a promotional process management model of the type illustrated in Figure 8.1. The effectiveness of the planning process will be strongly influenced by the degree to which the company has knowledge of the self image, role assumption and buying behaviour of the financially attractive consumers to whom the promotional information is to be communicated. There is a minor difference between the process model shown in Figure 8.1 and the models presented in most standard marketing texts. This is because the latter sources tend to recommend determination of the promotional budget prior to the development of the promotional message or the selection of a promotional channel. In contrast, observations of firms in the real world tend to support the view that determining the promotional budget usually involves a reiterative approach based upon the knowledge generated about market conditions and consumer behaviour which emerge during the message development and channel selection process.

Prior to defining a promotional objective, the firm should identify the target audience to whom the promotion will be directed. Usually this target will be that group who are the highest potential users of the product or service. Target definition in the world of conventional mass marketing is relatively simple because the definitions tend to be quite generalized. For example, the promotional plan for many dishwashing liquids will involve a target audience definition of women in

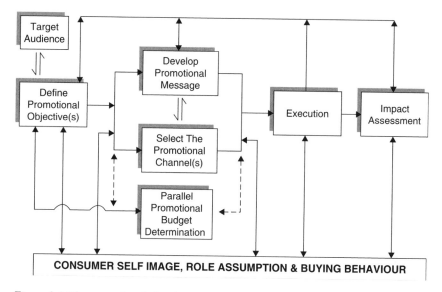

Figure 8.1 The promotional planning process.

the age group 18–49 years old who have children. This can be contrasted with the case for many financially attractive customer markets where target market definition can be quite difficult (Stephens 1991). This is because the heterogeneous nature of these latter consumer groups will usually require greater target audience accuracy and specificity in terms of variables such as sociodemographics or lifestyle.

The target definition process for certain groups of financially attractive consumers can be further complicated because buyer behaviour within the specific consumer group may change over time. For example in the case of maturing boomers, buyer behaviour may change over time due to the influence of factors such as ageing, loss of mobility, death of a partner or declining health. The maturing boomer target market definition may be further complicated when illness begins to severely restrict the independence and decision-making ability of the older person. In these scenarios, other people such as their own children may begin to exert increasing influence over the purchase decision (Gilbert *et al.* 1994). Should this trend be identified as occurring in the market of interest to a firm, then promotional activity may have to re-directed towards whoever has taken responsibility for the ongoing welfare of the financially attractive consumer. Data from studies in both the USA and the UK, for example indicate the selection of a residential care home often becomes the responsibility of the maturing boomer's children.

The promotional objective is a specification of the communication task to be undertaken (Jones 1994). In those cases where the aim is building new demand, the primary target audience will be new customers and the promotional task is to be informative. Where the aim is to communicate to existing customers that the product is superior to competition, the task becomes one of persuasion. Once customers have become regular purchasers, the aim may switch to sustaining loyalty and the task of promotion is to act as a reminder of benefit. As illustrated in Figure 8.2, in the period prior to the first purchase decision being made, informative advertising is likely to be the dominant promotional task. Once customers are nearer to making a purchase decision, the promotional task will shift towards being persuasive. In the case of a product only ever purchased once, or a product which will not be replaced for some years, such as a household appliance, no further promotion will probably need to be directed at the purchaser. Where the product is purchased frequently, the promotional task may remain that of persuasion. However, in the case of those products for which the consumer exhibits high brand loyalty, then the task may switch to reminder communication concerning the product or service's primary benefit claim of superiority.

Communication

No matter which promotional channel is selected, as shown in Figure 8.3, in all cases there are certain standard, common components influencing the communication process. The volume of information that can be delivered may be constrained by delivery time (e.g. the 30-second television commercial), available space (e.g. the size of a print advertisement) and the time the consumer is prepared to allocate to receiving the information. This requires that the key information upon which the firm's promotional story is based will have to be distilled down into a much brief communications message (Graeff 1995). In most cases, the outcome is the promotional message which will focus on communicating the product's primary benefit claim and the attributes of the product which provide justification for this claim.

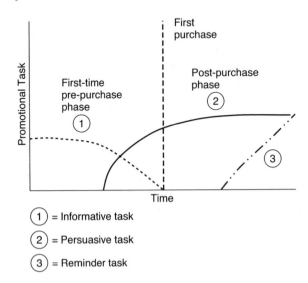

Figure 8.2 Promotional task phases.

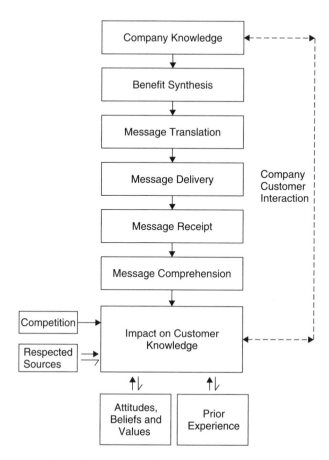

Figure 8.3 The communication process.

As companies and customers rarely share a common language, the product benefit claim will have to be translated into a form understood by the target audience. Once the promotional message has been received, the customer will process the information to comprehend what has been communicated. This new information will add to the customer's existing level of knowledge about the product which is being promoted. The impact of the promotional message will be influenced by a number of factors. Factor importance will vary between product categories. Persons with a satisfactory prior experience with a product will have a more positive reaction to a benefit claim being presented in a promotion.

Customer response to a promotion will also be influenced by their existing attitudes, beliefs and values (Bailey 2004). Above average income Germans, for example, tend to be more receptive to promotional messages communicated by domestic producers of both cars and home appliances. This is because they consider these firms are more strongly committed to engineering excellence than any foreign supplier of the same goods. For certain product categories and companies, people may have an innate suspicion of the benefit claim being communicated. In those cases, consumers will rely very heavily upon the opinions expressed by respected sources. In the case of many financially attractive consumers in the UK, for example, when selecting high unit price durable household goods and consumer electronic products, their purchase decision will be heavily influenced by recommendations made by the advocacy magazine, *Which.* Firms also need to be aware that potential customers' degree of receptivity to a promotional message may be influenced by the information being communicated by competition.

An important factor influencing the development of an effective promotional message is the degree to which the financially attractive consumers are interested (or 'involved') in the product (Park and Moon 2003). Interaction between involvement and level of promotional information required by the customer will result in four different outcomes (Figure 8.4). To demonstrate the interaction between information needs and consumer involvement, examples of how different product or service promotional propositions might be handled are presented in Figure 8.4a.

Where the financially attractive consumer has a high level of involvement in the product and needs a high volume of information to acquire an adequate understanding of the offered benefit, promotional budgetary constraints may require that the message be targeted at a relatively narrow target audience. Message effectiveness can sometimes be amplified where the benefit proposition is endorsed by a respected source such as a popular figure from the world of sport or entertainment. In those cases where the financially attractive consumer is highly involved in the product but only needs a minimal volume of additional information, the promotional message should be directed at closing the sale. Low information needs occur when the financially attractive consumer feels sufficient knowledge has already been acquired through prior product usage experience or input from respected sources. The attraction of this type of high involvement product is that even firms with very limited promotional budgets can expect to enjoy promotional success.

Low involvement products will normally require a high level of promotional expenditure to achieve high customer awareness. Products exhibiting this requirement are less appealing to many firms because a large promotional budget will be necessary to achieve an adequate level of customer awareness (Grunert 1996). The scenario of low consumer involvement and high information need implies the product does offer enjoyment or pleasure, but has become perceived as a necessary purchase. Consumers will require information to increase their knowledge of the product category and to understand the product benefit being communicated. This scenario can involve the phasing of the promotional message, moving the consumer through the stages of the purchase process from initial limited interest to finally making a purchase decision.

Given those situations where the consumer has very high information requirement and the time or space constraints which exist in most advertising channels, until recently the perceived most effective promotional solution was to

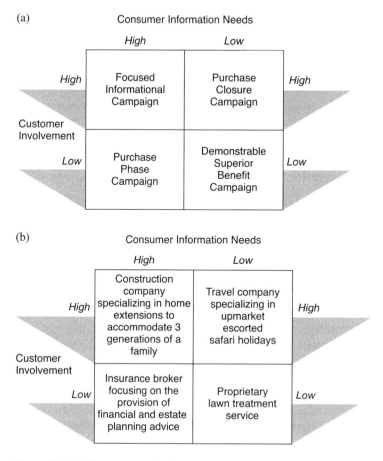

Figure 8.4 (a) The customer involvement matrix. (b) Application examples of the involvement matrix.

deliver the information via a supplier or intermediary sales person. The arrival of the internet has altered this situation because by establishing a company website or being featured on a third party website, the organization can provide an almost infinite amount of information at virtually zero cost. Firms in the healthcare sector such as clinics, private hospitals, pharmaceutical firms and providers of alternative therapies have significantly benefited from the advent of the internet as a medium through which low cost promotional information can be delivered to the older, financially attractive consumer. This outcome has occurred because within this consumer group, there are individuals concerned about remaining healthy, others seeking further understanding of a healthcare problem facing a friend or relative and those who need guidance for themselves having been diagnosed as suffering from an illness (Jones and Mullan 2006).

The standard scenario facing mass market, branded goods is of a low involvement product for which there is a low information need, but numerous companies are all seeking to influence the consumer's purchase decision. It is the most expensive situation confronting a firm because high levels of promotional expenditure are demanded in order to negate the influence of competitors' promotional campaigns. Only those firms with extensive financial resources would be advised to operate in this area of a consumer market because a successful campaign will require a very large promotional budget.

Personal selling

Firms selecting an appropriate promotional channel are able to choose from the following options:

- *Personal selling,* which permits representatives of an organization to enter into a dialogue with potential customers.
- *Advertising,* which involves paying a fee for time or space to a third party such as a radio station or a local newspaper.
- *Direct marketing,* which are activities concerned with personalized communication to individual customers using techniques such direct mail or the telephone.
- *Public relations,* which, to a large degree, is concerned with generating awareness of a firm's activities through information appearing in the media.
- *Collateral,* which is an umbrella phrase covering a diversity of activities including brochures, letterhead, the visual impact of physical facilities, employee appearance and employee behaviour.

Personal selling is the most effective form of promotional communication because the process permits face-to-face dialogue between customer and supplier. Given access to an unlimited promotional budget, a firm should usually opt to rely on personal selling as the primary channel through which to deliver customer information. The drawback is that personal selling is the most expensive medium through which to communicate to a large number of customers. Hence, in a world where cost/benefit outcomes determine promotional channel decisions, the use of sales people will tend be restricted to those situations where there are few customers; interactive dialogue will be required to assist the customer reach a decision and each customer makes a purchase which represents a significant proportion of the supplier's total sales.

This situation means that personal selling is more commonly utilized in industrial markets and is rarely encountered in most consumer markets. One consumer market where the criteria concerning customer type is supportive of personal selling is the promotion of pension and investment products to high net worth, financially attractive consumers. Even in this sector, however, firms will seek to reduce promotional costs by utilizing a multi-channel medium through which to communicate with their clients. For example Charles Schwarb, the

California-based stockbroker who pioneered the introduction of the electronic share trading systems for US consumers, still retains a chain of terrestrial offices where clients can meet with a Schwarb advisor. This communications channel is complimented by a tele-sales/advisory operation, downloadable electronic stock analysis tools and a real-time website offering rapid up-dates about emerging trends in the world's financial markets.

Available research on promotional channel preferences among older financially attractive consumers is somewhat contradictory. In seeking to explain this variance between research studies, Tongren (1988) undertook an extensive review of published studies (1988). He concluded that part of the problem is caused by poor research methodology. This includes actions such as not specifying exactly which age group has been studied or not attempting to obtain data from younger consumers which would permit a comparison of different age groups in relation to purchase behaviour. Despite this problem, a common conclusion across a number of studies is that financially attractive consumers do prefer a promotional channel which supports interaction with a sales person because this is beneficial in terms of acquiring an adequate level of information about a product or service. It would also appear that older consumers prefer to interact with sales people who are of a similar age. Additionally this consumer group is less trusting of promotional information communicated by very young sales people.

This preference for being provided with promotional information via an older sales person becomes increasingly important to financially attractive consumers who are seeking to make a purchase decision concerning a complex issue, such as pension or stock market investment. In their review of what enhances the capability of a financial advisor when interfacing with financially attractive consumers, Resnick and Lillis (2001) have proposed the key top skills requires of the sales person are education, commitment and credibility. Knowledge of product features is necessary, but is not the most critical requirement. It is also important for the financial advisor to be fully informed about the client in terms of lifestyle changes, financial planning and personal insurance history. Furthermore, the advisor must fully comprehend a country's healthcare system, medical delivery options, patient–provider reimbursement, and health insurance coverage options.

Financially attractive consumers want their financial advisors to exhibit genuine commitment and integrity. This means the individual is expected to only recommend financial services companies that have existed for many years, have a reputation for being conservative and are reliable in terms of being organizations with whom one can safely invest money. This consumer group also prefers to work with advisors who they perceive as partners in any purchase decisions. A related issue is the need for the advisor and the companies they recommend to be perceived as credible. Many financially attractive consumers have acquired extensive experience of purchasing complex service propositions at work or in the context of being the head of a family. These experiences have caused these individuals to develop a strong preference for the sales person's promotional communication based on facts, clear illustrations and practical explanations.

Questionable personal selling

Case Aims: To illustrate how personal selling techniques in the financial services industry may be focused more on the success of the sales person and less on the provision of advice about what is best for the client.

In the last few years, the media and the financial regulatory authorization have highlighted the dubious quality of some of the financial advice given to consumers. Many of the recipients of such advice have been maturing boomers because their above average net worth has made them a prime target of the consumer financial services industry (Avery 2004). A very common example of dubious practice in recent years in the UK has been older people having stated their requirement for a steady income flow, capital preservation and minimal risk, being persuaded by their financial advisor to invest in 'with profits' or mixed share/corporate bond funds, where over time, both the income flow and the value of their investment has subsequently gone down. Another common example of questionable advice has been consumers persuaded to shift their money from a savings account into a commercial money fund which only performs marginally better in terms of interest paid, but the consumer is charged a front end arrangement fee in the region of 20 per cent of the value of their investment to switch into the fund. The occurrence of these questionable activities in the USA is assisted by the training offered by individuals such as Mr Tyrone Clark, the president of Brokers' Choice of America Inc. The company based in Glendale, Colorado runs a programme called Annuity University, which trains financial advisors in the selling of financial products such as annuities. In their article about Mr Clark's activities, Schultz and Opdyke (2002) reported that this individual advises participants when working with older consumers to 'treat them like they're blind 12-year-olds. They thrive on fear, anger and greed. Show them their finances are all screwed up so that they think, Oh, no, I've done it all wrong'. He also proposes that the first step to wooing older people is to get them to attend introductory seminars, and the best way to attract them is a free meal. The Annuity University training manual notes that 'they like freebies and like to eat one major meal a day'. Another Annuity University lecturer, Mel Brandon of Memphis, Tennessee is described as telling course participants that educational seminars offer a good way to find out which seniors are well off and worth concentrating the sales pitch on. When people arrive at his seminars he has 'spotters' in the parking lot 'checking out what kind of car each person drives. That way we'll know who has the money'. Class members are taught that whatever the consumer's particular financial concern, taxes, investments or asset protection, the recommended solution for the client is almost always the same, an annuity. These products are insurance contracts in which the earnings are tax-deferred. Fixed annuities have returns that are guaranteed for a short period such as 12 months, while variable annuities are essentially a collection of tax-sheltered mutual funds. Annuity University participants are advised that providing detailed information about annuities can complicate the selling process. Mr Clark suggests that in relation to annuities 'There's the technical answer' and 'there's the senior answer. Tell them it's like a CD – it's safe, it's guaranteed'. Mr Clark maintains that his teachings at Annuity University are not designed to belittle consumers or to help sales agents persuade older customers to make incorrect investment decisions. Mr Clark insists that his training events focus on communicating the idea that 'agents can come across as too technical and people don't understand them'. Mr Clark says he makes agents sign a code of ethics pledging that they will not misrepresent information when selling to older people. He also admits, however, that 'the problem is agents take the classes and abuse the information everyday. And I have no control over that. These [agents] are independent and want to pitch high-commission products, and we can't stop them'. Maturing boomers are increasingly the most likely consumer group to receive sales presentations about annuities because they have a high net worth. A salesman who persuades a US maturing boomer to move $50,000 from bank certificates of deposit or an individual retirement account into an annuity will generate a commission of $3,000–$4,000. In reality, annuities are complex products and have downside risks of which consumers should be made aware. The higher fees of most annuities can often negate any tax advantages, most annuities lock in the investor for a number of years and annuities can result in a person's heirs facing a significant tax bill. For these reasons, many investment experts say annuities are usually not suitable for many older investors. With annuity sales generating high commissions for the sales person, regulators in America such the National Association of Securities Dealers have expressed concern that many of the sales are transacted merely to generate income for the sales person.

Other promotional channels

Western nation maturing boomers were the first generation in the world to be exposed to television advertising from the day they were born. The arrival of commercial television channels created a new medium, which was hugely attractive to the major consumer goods companies. This is because television can deliver large audiences and the promotional communication is enhanced by the combination of sound and vision. In recent years, however, the television broadcasting industry has suffered from audience sizes being reduced by a fragmentation (Gersham 1988). This has occurred due to the influence of technological advances such as cable TV or satellite television, Governments approving the establishment of numerous new television channels, conversion from analogue to digital transmissions and consumers accessing information via the internet. Further reduction in total audience size has occurred because young people prefer other entertainment media such watching DVDs or engaging in online social networking, via sites such as Facebook (Kaye and Johnson 2003).

The price to the advertiser of any medium is determined by both the absolute size of the consumer audience and the prevailing demand for advertising space. For smaller firms, the absolute cost of certain media and a constrained geographic customer footprint may prohibit the use of many advertising vehicles used by the national consumer goods companies. In those cases where the communication is aimed at financially attractive consumers located within a small geographic area, advertising choice is often restricted to the use of local newspapers. An advantage in promoting to commercially attractive consumers is that they usually exhibit a high level of newspaper readership and tend to have an above average interest in local affairs. This means local newspapers can often be a very effective promotional channel for this consumer group. This rule only remains valid, however, where this group constitute a significant proportion of total readership. Where financially attractive consumers are a relatively small proportion of total readership, one solution to avoiding expending funds communicating to individuals outside this target audience group is buy time on local commercial radio stations. The medium offers limited geographic coverage and air-time can be purchased for programmes where the dominant listening audience are the financially attractive consumers who constitute the advertisers primary target audience.

The nineteenth century invention of the telephone offered the potential to make interactive personal selling more cost-effective. Commercial feasibility for utilization of the technology in most consumer markets did not occur until the late 1950s. This was when market penetration for home ownership of the telephone started to rise, accompanied by declining call costs. By the 1980s, tele-marketing had become an extremely popular channel through which to deliver promotional information. Unfortunately, the uncontrolled behaviour of some companies such as making cold calls, calling at inconvenient times and contact generation through random dialling, has alienated many consumers, especially among the older age groups.

The subsequent move by large service sector firms such as banks to seek to reduce operational costs by closing retail outlets and concurrently persuading consumers to seek information via the telephone was followed by these organizations outsourcing their operations to countries such as India and Pakistan. This latter move has compounded tele-marketing's poor image. Studies undertaken with maturing boomers confirm that in relation to complex products, especially where users are concerned about confidentiality when seeking information, individuals feel more comfortable with personal face-to-face contact with the financial institutions (Grougiou and Wilson 2003). As shown in Figure 8.5, there are a number of variables which can contribute towards higher satisfaction from for face-to-face interaction rather than using a call centre.

Public relations can be an effective low cost promotional vehicle whereby the firm is the source of a newsworthy story of interest to the broadcast and print media. Sometimes smaller firms may be able to self manage regular contact with

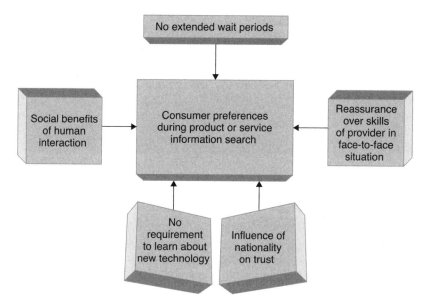

Figure 8.5 Factors of influence in information search.

their local media. Additionally, there is always the chance that a story run in the local media may subsequently become an item of national interest. In most cases, however, where the firm is depending upon public relations to ensure regular appearances in the national media, this will usually require the services of a public relations agency. Furthermore, a public relations agency can become a mandatory expenditure in those cases where the business needs to deflect the potentially damaging influence caused by media interest in an organizational problem (e.g. an upmarket hotel being forced to temporarily close due to an outbreak of Legionnaires disease).

Direct marketing involves a diversity of techniques. They share the common characteristic of being directed at a specific person with the potential to personalize the promotional message. This medium has gained in popularity due to the influence of advances in IT across areas such as word processing, automated letter customization, electronic data storage and automated data retrieval. By the 1990s, in many Western nations, these advances resulted in expenditure on direct marketing; expenditure exceeding that of television advertising. Further acceleration in the usage of direct marketing targeted at consumers has been caused by people using electronic media for financial transactions and the ability of commercial websites to support real-time capture of vast amounts of customer information (Polyak 2000). Originally pioneered by large firms, once database management platforms moved from requiring a mainframe computer to becoming suitable for installation on PCs, this permitted direct marketing to become a highly popular medium for promotional campaigns by even the smallest of companies.

The development of the e-mail has been another major accelerator in the use of direct marketing (Haste 2005). Firms are able to construct, at relatively minimal cost, a consumer database drawing upon their own records, secondary data sources and data swaps with other firms. At the touch of a button, thousands of promotional messages can be instantly distributed. Regretfully, 'spammers' have damaged the appeal of the medium. In some countries, legislation has banned unsolicited e-mails being sent to consumers unless the addressee has given prior permission to be contacted. Message delivery has also been further reduced by consumers, or their internet provider, installing anti-spam software to reject messages based either on content or having originated from a non-approved address source. Despite these drawbacks, recent research indicates that although 79 per cent of older UK consumers delete between 50 and 100 per cent of the e-mails they receive, these same consumers consider e-mail as their preferred option for receiving promotional messages (CACI and the Customer Partnership 2005).

As the firm progresses through the process of developing a promotional plan, it may be decided there is a need to use more than one channel to deliver all components of the information that should be made available to the consumer (Berman and Thelen 2004). For example, a clothing company selling fashion goods to financially attractive consumers may use their own website to feature their top selling products, but have found that many of their customers also want a printed catalogue containing the entire product line before they are willing to make the final purchase decision. Where a multi-channel approach is used, the communications' objective for the promotional message should be consistent across all channels (Anon 2007). Actual structure and content of the communication, however, will usually need to be modified to achieve compatibility with the medium being utilized. For example, a local newspaper advertisement for a health resort specializing in treatments for ageing skin will contain significantly less informational content than the company's own brochure distributed via mail shots.

Direct marketing and the mature consumer

Case Aims: To examine the behaviour of maturing boomers in relation to purchasing goods from direct marketing sources vs. the alternative of shopping in retail outlets.

Utilizing data from the Market Facts Consumer Mail Panel in the USA, Chonko and Caballero (1989) were able to identify specific behavioural issues in relation to maturing boomers' response to direct marketing campaigns. On average, this group are less frequent users of this mode of purchase when compared with the 18–49 year age group. Furthermore, maturing boomers are often one-time shoppers from a specific source such as a speciality mail order company or a department store catalogue. Maturing boomers appear to dislike buying from salespeople at home, whether these individuals are door-to-door sales people or the organizer of a party plan selling event. Although maturing boomers acknowledge the convenience of in-home catalogue shopping, they sometimes feel there is greater risk in making a purchase in this way when compared with purchasing the same item from a retail outlet. The level of risk is perceived to increase in direct relation to the increasing price of an item. Those maturing boomers who use catalogues on a regular basis feel that the product offerings are as good as, or better, than local retailers in relation to product claims, price and quality. They do not hold a similarly favourable view of suppliers who use tele-sales, door-to-door sales staff or advertising on a television shopping channel. Another reason that mature boomers favour purchasing from retail outlets is that shopping is perceived as an enjoyable recreational or social occasion. Additionally, those who favour terrestrial shopping exhibit a high sense of loyalty to their local retailers. This reduces their inclination to purchase products via a direct marketing channel. In relation to direct marketing companies wishing to increase their market share among maturing boomers, Chonko and Caballero make a number of recommendations. One is that the companies should try to reduce the complexity of the purchase process by providing easy-to-read catalogues and very simple order forms. Another suggestion is that, as maturing boomers tend to favour paying a premium price to obtain higher quality over the alternative option of purchasing average quality goods at lower prices, the recommended focus of direct marketing efforts should be on upmarket, high quality items produced by well-known prestigious brand names or companies.

Budgeting

Determining the appropriate size of the promotional budget remains one of the greyer areas of marketing decision-making. Some branded goods companies have evolved very sophisticated computer models to assist their decision-making (Lancaster and Stern 1983). They can also afford the fees associated with employing the services of a major international advertising agency offering extensive experience about developing promotional campaigns and calculating promotional budgets. Smaller firms who often have limited internal marketing expertise may face the problem that their local advertising agencies tend to be good at creativity but have limited skills in the area of promotional planning and budget optimization (Mitchell 1993).

There are a number of options available to firms when seeking to determine an appropriate promotional budget, all of which have both strengths and weaknesses. The simplest, and possibly most commonly used approach in the small firms sector, is to set the budget based upon what management feel can be afforded. This is a reasonably safe approach where the firm has a successful track record using an intuitive decision-making approach to budgeting. The major drawback is that the method ignores the relationship which exists between economic trends, competitor promotional activity and sector sales rates. Another commonly utilized approach is based upon the concept of setting the budget in relation to expenditure patterns across a market sector. In the event data are available on average spending by other firms, this figure can be used as a benchmark. This benchmark allows the firm to assess whether the level of forecasted sales justifies spending more, the same or less than the competition. A similar approach may be used where the firm knows a sector's average level of promotional spending expressed as a percentage of sales.

Where possible, however, the preferred approach to promotional budgeting is to adopt an objective-task method (Barnes *et al.*1982). This involves determining a quantitative specification of what is required from a promotional programme. Some situations do exist where a direct relationship between a promotional activity and resultant sales can be established. One example is the average sales generated by a sales person and the size of the salesforce required to achieve the company's total sales forecast. Another example is the number people redeeming a 'money off' voucher distributed via a newspaper advertisement. In many cases, however, being able to specify an accurate quantitative relationship between promotional activity and sales is virtually impossible. Thus, firms may be forced to adopt an objective-task approach in which the level of promotional spending will be based upon a non-financial objective such achieved overall customer awareness.

Management texts recommend that firms should assess the effectiveness of all promotional campaigns. This is because such actions permit determination of whether revisions are required to improve future promotional cost-effectiveness. Even in some large branded goods companies, however, marketers have a tendency to ignore such advice (Wilhelmsson 1992). Nevertheless, both anecdotal evidence and research studies indicate that where promotional campaigns are monitored and evaluated, this can greatly assist the firm to achieving the aim of optimizing the cost-effective provision of information to their customers.

In cases of the promotional budget being determined using affordability, percentage of sales or spending relative to competitors approach, it is usually only feasible to operate a somewhat generalized promotional assessment monitoring system. Such systems might involve observing indications of changes in overall total customer contact or a qualitative assessment of the total number of customers who are active purchasers. Assessment accuracy will only improve when the firm has adopted an objective-task approach to promotional budgeting.

Self image

There are a plethora of articles about what terminology should be avoided when referring to older financially attractive consumers in promotional campaigns. This is an important issue because past research studies have shown that in the USA, for example, over 70 per cent of maturing boomers are dissatisfied with the way companies market products to them (Speer 1993). Frequently, mention is made concerning which names may have a negative connotation with this customer group. Labels such as greys, silvers or golden age people have, quite rightfully, been heavily criticized. In the USA, the recommendation proposed by AARP is to refer to older people as 'mature'.

In reaching a decision about appropriate nomenclature for use in a promotional message aimed at older financially attractive consumers it seems wisest to follow the long established rules which apply to campaigns directed at any target audience. Possibly the most important of these is wherever possible, avoid communicating a negative message. Instead, campaign development should focus on positive communication because this is much more likely to re-enforce purchase intent. Achieving this communication objective does require ensuring that variables are incorporated into the promotional execution which can have a positive influence on the understanding, attitudes and values within the customer audience (Schewe 1990). As illustrated in Figure 8.6, there are a number of variables that can contribute towards enhancing consumer purchase intentions.

There are limited research data available which permit a very accurate prioritization of the relative importance of the variables shown in Figure 8.6. Nevertheless, it seems reasonable to assume the communication of a benefit specifically relevant to the needs of the target audience is a fundamental requirement for any promotional message. Market research studies confirm that many older financially attractive consumers are concerned about the impact of ageing on themselves and also about how their physical appearance will influence how they are perceived by others. Most people over the age of 35 have a self image of being younger than their actual biological age. In the case of older consumers, this self image effect usually creates a belief that their appearance and behaviour causes their age, as perceived by others, to be reduced by about 15 years (Carrigan and Szmigin 1999).

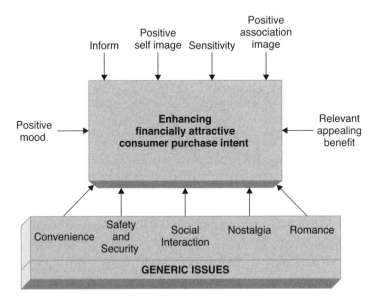

Figure 8.6 Factors influencing promotional effectiveness.

The related dimension concerning self image and effective communication which needs to be understood in the development of an effective promotional campaign is that as people grow older, there is a change in the way they are influenced by message content (Williams and Drolet 2005). One dimension of change is that as people grow older they tend to move away from an objective, factual approach to information processing and instead adopt a more subjective, evaluative, emotional mode of thinking. This change is associated with ageing, not retirement. Hence, promotional messages aimed at any 50+ individual, whether they are in work or retired, are more likely to generate higher awareness when the product benefit claim focuses on mental states such as happiness, love and caring for others (Tenser 2006).

Another area of mindset change which is found among older financially attractive consumers is whether they perceive themselves as beginning to approach the end of their lifespan (Divine and Lepisto 2005). Younger individuals tend to perceive their lifespan as sufficient that they need not yet to be concerned about dying. This group of individuals will respond to the emotional content of a promotional message framed in either a positive or negative way. In contrast, older people who perceive their remaining lifespan as very short tend to react adversely to any promotional message which is framed in an emotionally negative context. Hence, a younger individual would perceive an advertisement about how funeral insurance can absolve the burden of funding their future death as an informative, practical message. In contrast, older people are likely to exhibit a less positive reaction to an advertisement about funeral insurance.

The ongoing debate in many academic articles is how to portray older financially attractive consumers so that the target audience react positively to a promotional campaign. It is generally recommended that with the exception of certain role models such as Jane Fonda or Clint Eastwood, people featured in an advertisement aimed at older consumers should be younger than the target audience. What seems just as obvious, but not widely accepted by some within the advertising industry, is to use images which do not include humans. Whichever approach is selected, the critical aim is for the promotional communication to re-enforce older consumers' own self image of appearing younger than their biological age (Polyak 2000).

Older consumers are usually concerned with sustaining self respect and minimizing their reliance on others. Any promotional message needs to be sensitive to these concerns. Sensitivity is also critical when handling issues of a personal nature which confront older people, such as everyday hygiene or potentially embarrassing medical conditions such as incontinence. A promotional approach which has been validated in relation to medical conditions is to portray a person enjoying life as a result of the advertised product providing a complete solution to the socially sensitive problem. Further positive impact will be achieved by presenting the product as being used by a younger person. This approach implies the condition is more widespread across the population; thereby dampening an individual's personal resentment that ageing is the cause of their medical condition (Minkus-McKenna *et al.* 2006).

A possible exception to the use of much younger actors and models in promotions aimed at older consumers may apply in the context of products or services which offer relief for certain types of illness. In relation to scenarios such as a television commercial for a product offering pain relief from a condition such as arthritis, the use a relatively old person in the advertisement may be perceived by sufferers as acceptable because they personally identify with the life problem being presented. Older financially attractive consumers are both aware and worried that ageing will be accompanied by events such as aches and pains, lower energy levels or financial problems. These events are recognized as having the potential to exert a negative influence over the way people feel about both themselves and life in general. Hence, to counter this effect, where possible any promotional message directed at this target audience should seek to stimulate a positive mood by positioning product consumption as a mechanism which can contribute to greater overall happiness and where relevant, closer warmer relationships with partners and friends (Cooper and Miaoultis 1988).

Further gains in striving to enhance purchase intent can come from the promotion re-enforcing the consumers' self image by portraying the product user as a person whose image is appealing to the potential customer. For example, in a promotion for a drink brand targeted at older female consumers, added positive enhancement would occur by presenting the product user in an advertisement as a well dressed lady standing on the deck of a cruise liner alongside a male partner. Older consumers also have aspirations of being involved in associating with other people who are enjoying life. Thus, the drinks brand may wish to run a parallel campaign of showing a male enjoying a game of golf with friends in an upmarket golf resort. In fact, the importance that older financially attractive consumers place on achieving life satisfaction can often mean that some of the most successful promotions are those which focus on individuals enjoying a social experience while only giving secondary attention in the advertising to the actual attributes of the product.

There are a number of product categories such as de-caffeinated instant coffee, shampoo, suntan products and laxatives where both young and old people and are purchasers. In the case of the product categories mentioned, older people are above average consumers of these items. The issue confronting the advertiser is whether the same advertising message and execution can be directed at both market segments or is there a requirement for some form of promotional segregation (Greco 1989). As shown in Figure 8.7, using the dimensions of breadth of product usage and the ability to achieve promotional segregation generates four different scenarios.

In those cases where promotional segregation is achievable and the product has broad appeal, then the advisable strategy is to implement two separate independent campaigns aimed at the older financially attractive and younger consumer market segments. Where market appeal is broad and segregation is not feasible for reasons such as cost or promotional channel availability, then the usual solution is to direct the advertising towards the younger consumer. By presenting a youthful image, the proposition will not alienate the younger consumer. Concurrently, the user

AUDIENCE SEGREGATION

		Feasible	Impractical
BREADTH OF PRODUCT OR SERVICE APPEAL	*Broad market appeal across generations*	Separate promotional campaigns targeted at financially attractive consumers and younger consumers	Single promotional campaign directed at all consumers, but execution content biased towards presenting a youthful image for the benefit proposition
	Restricted to financially attractive consumers	Promotional campaign directed specifically at financially attractive consumers	Promotional campaign directed at financially attractive consumers but featuring characters whose visual image will not alienate other consumers

Figure 8.7 Promotional campaign options.

image portrayed in the advertisement will also appeal to the older customer. In those cases where market appeal is narrow and the primary customer target is financially attractive consumers, then these individuals should be the primary focus of the promotional campaign. Where it is not feasible to segregate the promotional message, then again a youthful image should be presented in order not to alienate any potential customers among older consumers.

There are also some generic concerns to be remembered when determining whether promotional message is supportive of issues that are important to older consumers (Tongren 1988). These include offering convenience, safety, personal security, contributing to reducing isolation, re-kindling nostalgic memories and romance. There is also a requirement to recognize certain practical issues in the execution of a promotion. Effective communication directed at older consumers does require the understanding that ageing leads to deterioration in the senses such as sight and hearing. Print size may need to larger and dialogue pitched at a somewhat louder level. Speed of comprehension may be lower, which in turn requires a slower pace in the promotional presentation. The impact of the promotional message will also be reduced by using language or visual images popular with very young people because in many cases, the older consumer may have limited understanding of these images or words.

References

Anon (2007) 'Promotions and incentives: make it a season to remember', *Marketing Week*, London, 18 October, p. 35.
Avery, H. (2004) 'America's wealthy get picky about advice', *Euromoney*, London, October, pp. 1–3.

Bailey, A.A. (2004) 'The interplay of social influence and nature of fulfilment: effects of consumer attitudes', *Psychology & Marketing*, Vol. 12, No. 4, pp. 263–76.

Barnes, J.D., Moscove, B.J. and Javad, B. (1982) 'An objective and task media decision model and advertising cost formula to determine international advertising budgets', *Journal of Advertising*, Vol. 11, No. 4, pp. 68–76.

Berman, B. and Thelen, S. (2004) 'A guide to developing and managing a well-integrated multi-channel retail strategy', *International Journal of Retail & Distribution Management*, Vol. 32, No. 1/2, pp. 147–56.

CACI and the Customer Partnership (2005) 'Understanding ambiguous relationships between UK consumers and the direct marketing channel', *CACI*, London, www.caci.co.uk

Carrigan, M. and Szmigin, I. (1999) 'The portrayal of older characters in magazine advertising', *Journal of Marketing Practice*, Vol. 5, No. 6/7/8, pp. 248–56.

Chonko, L.B. and Caballero, M.J. (1989) 'The mature consumer: how successful are direct marketing and direct selling in this segment of the population', *Baylor Business Review*, Vol. 7, No. 1, pp. 9–14.

Cooper, P.D. and Miaoultis, G. (1988) 'Altering corporate strategy criteria to reflect changing markets', *California Management Review*, Vol. 31, No. 1, pp. 87–97.

Divine, R.L. and Lepisto, L. (2005) 'Analysis of the healthy lifestyle consumer', *Journal of Consumer Marketing*, Vol. 22, No. 4/5, pp. 275–84.

Gersham, M. (1988) 'The twilight of advertising', *Management Review*, Vol. 77, No. 6, pp. 22–33.

Gilbert, F.W., Tudir, K.R. and Paolillo, J. (1994) 'The decision making unit in the choice of a long term health care facility', *Journal of Applied Business Research*, Vol. 10, No. 2, pp. 63–74.

Graeff, T.R. (1995) 'Product comprehension and promotional strategies', *Journal of Consumer Marketing*, Vol. 12, No. 2, pp. 28–40.

Greco, A.J. (1989) 'Representation of the elderly in advertising', *Journal of Consumer Marketing*, Vol. 6, No. 1, pp. 37–44.

Grougiou, V. and Wilson, (2003) 'Financial service call centres: problems encountered by the grey market', *Journal of Financial Services Marketing*, Vol. 7, No. 4, pp. 360–71.

Grunert, K.G. (1996) 'Automatic and strategic processes in advertising effects', *Journal of Marketing*, Vol. 60, No. 4, pp. 88–102.

Haste, H. (2005) 'Joined-up texting: mobile phones and young people', *Young Consumers*, Vol. 6, No. 3, pp. 56–62.

Jones, D.B. (1994) 'Setting promotional goals: a communications' relationship model', *Journal of Consumer Marketing*, Vol. 11, No. 1, pp. 38–50.

Jones, S.C. and Mullan, J. (2006) 'Older adult's perceptions and understanding of direct-to-consumer advertising', *Journal of Consumer Marketing*, Vol. 23, No. 1, pp. 6–15.

Kaye, B.K. and Johnson, T.J. (2003) 'From here to obscurity: media substitution theory and traditional media in an on-line world', *Journal of the American Society for Information Science and Technology*, Vol. 52, No. 3, pp. 260–71.

Lancaster, K.M. and Stern, J.A. (1983) 'Computer-based advertising budgeting practices of leading US consumer advertisers', *Journal of Advertising*, Vol. 12, No. 4, pp. 4–10.

Minkus-McKenna, D., Beckley, J. and Moskowitz, H.R. (2006) 'Evaluation of in-market communications of selected OTC products targeted to older consumers', *Journal of Medical Marketing*, Vol. 6, No. 3, pp. 222–31.

Mitchell, L.A. (1993) 'An examination of methods of setting advertising budgets: practice and the literature', *European Journal of Marketing*, Vol. 27, No. 5, pp. 5–22.

Park, C. and Moon, B. (2003) 'The relationship between product involvement and product knowledge: moderating roles of product types and product knowledge', *Psychology & Marketing*, Vol. 20, No 11, pp. 977–89.

Polyak, L. (2000) 'The center of attention', *American Demographics,* Vol. 22, No. 11, pp. 30–3.

Resnick, L. and Lillis, M. (2001) 'Selling in senior market requires education, commitment, credibility', *National Underwriter*, Erlanger, 28 May, pp. 7–9.

Schewe, C.D. (1990) 'Get in position for the older market', *American Demographics*, Vol. 12, No. 6, pp. 38–42.

Schultz, E.E. and Opdyke, J.D. (2002) 'Annuities 101: how to sell to senior citizens', *Wall Street Journal*, New York, 2 July, p. C1.

Speer, T.L. (1993) 'Older consumers follow different rules', *American Demographics*, Vol. 15, No. 2, pp. 21–4.

Stephens, N. (1991) 'Cognitive age: a useful concept for advertising', *Journal of Advertising*, Vol. 20, No. 4, pp. 37–48.

Tenser, J. (2006) 'New old won't go quietly', *Advertising Age*, Chicago, 2 January, pp. 20–2.

Tongren, H.N. (1988) 'Determinant behaviour characteristics of older consumers', *Journal of Consumer Affairs*, Vol. 11, No. 1, pp. 136–56.

Wilhelmsson, T. (1992) 'Administrative procedures for the control of marketing practices–theoretical rationale and perspectives', *Journal of Consumer Policy,* Vol. 15, No. 2, pp. 159–78.

Williams, P and Drolet, A. (2005) 'Age-related differences in response to emotional advertisements', *Journal of Consumer Research*, Vol. 32, No. 3, pp. 343–55.

9 Pricing and distribution

Generic principles of marketing to financially attractive consumers (FACs)

The coverage of issues in Chapter 9 is designed to illustrate the generic principles of marketing to FACs in relation to:

1   The higher income enjoyed by FACs means their purchase preferences tend to be biased towards higher quality goods for which they are willing to pay a premium price.
2   Bias towards buying premium priced goods among FACs is influenced by their desire to own products which support self actualization or communicate their higher income status to friends and relatives.
3   FACs are less price sensitive than consumers living on an average or below average income.
4   FACs' financial situation means this group are less likely to radically alter their purchase patterns during an economic downturn.
5   FACs are less likely to become highly price sensitive during an economic downturn.
6   Older FACs' purchase decisions are rarely motivated by an age-related discount. Hence, offering blanket market age-related discounts can often have no influence on sales revenue but may significantly reduce net profit.
7   FACs' purchase decisions are less influenced by the availability of sales promotions than those of younger consumers or those living on a below average income.
8   FACs' preference for high quality goods, a broad range of product choice and personalized service means than the distribution of durable goods should usually be directed through retail channels such as department stores and speciality retail outlets.
9   Over recent years providing access to goods via the internet has become an effective alternative distribution channel for reaching FACs. This is because their level of usage of online sites is now very similar to that of younger people.

Demand based pricing

A preference of managers, especially those in the small firm sector, is to use what appears to be the logical and most easily applied concept in reaching a decision. Unfortunately, on occasion this perspective can sometimes cause the firm to make a significant error. One such example is provided by the concept of *cost plus pricing*. This is based upon the formula that *price = cost/unit + desired/profit*. Although the formula is intuitively appealing, it will be purely fortuitous for the resultant price to be acceptable to the firm's customers. This is because customers, not firms, determine price. In the case of cost plus pricing the supplier is attempting to mandate the price to the market. As a consequence there is a reasonable probability that the calculated price will be perceived by customers as being either too high or too low (Shapiro 1973).

Once a firm understands the risks associated with cost plus pricing, hopefully the organization will perceive the benefits of adopting a demand-orientated pricing philosophy. This approach is based on the premise that customer expectations are the source of decision and behaviours that provide the basis upon which the firm should set prices. Obtaining an understanding of customer price expectations can be achieved by seeking the views of potential customers or by observing prevailing prices of successful competitors. Once the prevailing price has been determined, then the firm by re-stating the cost plus formula in the form of *profit = prevailing average market price – company costs*, can calculate whether an acceptable level of profit per unit can be achieved. Should the resultant profit figure be unacceptable, the options available to the business are to examine whether opportunities exist to either increase price or reduce operating costs. If neither action is feasible, it is probably advisable to avoid operating in this sector of the market.

The implications of altering price or operating costs are summarized in the conceptualized diagram, Figure 9.1. This diagram indicates that as a firm moves from a low to a high standard of product performance specification, costs will rise.

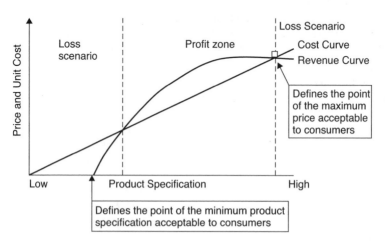

Figure 9.1 Price and cost relationships.

Customers are normally willing to pay a higher price for products delivering superior performance. With most products or services, however, there is a minimum and maximum specification below and above which customers will not purchase. This means there is only a restricted product specification range within which costs and customer expectations will permit the generation of an adequate level of profit.

In terms of determining an appropriate price, the firm can explore consumer expectations through the medium of focus groups. For example a group of financially attractive consumers can be provided with a product description for an average product and asked to identify their price expectation for the item. By repeating this process for the alternatives of a higher and lower product specification, data can be generated that permit an evaluation of the price expectations of customers in relation to variations in quality or performance. This knowledge provides the basis for constructing a graphical price assessment of the type shown in Figure 9.2.

Variations in consumer response can be described by adding a scatter plot of individual responses. This distribution of response permits identification of the acceptable price zone within which the majority of responses fall. By plotting data on prices for both the firm and competition, this graphical tool can also be useful in determining whether customer expectations are capable of being fulfilled. In Figure 9.2, price point A would be perceived as unbelievable by the majority of potential customers and total sales would be lowered. This is because customers would consider the price is too low in relation to the product's performance claim. At price point B, sales will be optimal because the product is fulfilling consumers' price/value expectations. Price point C would usually mean product sales will be lower because the item is perceived as making an unbelievable performance claim relative to the quoted price.

Premium pricing

In view of the preference many financially attractive consumers exhibit for purchasing higher quality goods, then entrepreneurs seeking to achieve success

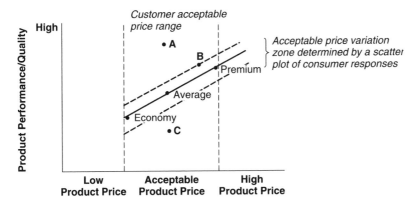

Figure 9.2 Value price relationships.

in this market sector should probably focus on the development of products or service propositions which greatly exceed the performance standards of goods offered by existing companies (Flanagan 1994). The reward for their endeavours will be an ability to command a higher (or 'premium') price. There may exist, however, consumers for whom the premium price offering is not perceived as an appropriate proposition because their expectations are that of desiring to purchase lower priced goods. To respond to this situation the firm, as summarized in Figure 9.3, can assess what other options might exist. These alternative options are dependent upon whether de-engineering to reduce costs is a feasible action. Under most circumstances, the most effective path to support market expansion outside a premium price sector is to implement a strategy of offering a higher value proposition. This involves entering that sector of the market sector containing consumers with lower price and product performance expectations. Where cost savings cannot be achieved because product or service de-engineering is not a viable concept, then the only option for expanding market coverage without having lowered the price, is a consumer education campaign. The aim of this campaign would be to generate greater consumer understanding that the nature of the product or service can only be made available at a premium price. The other, somewhat rarer option, is where de-engineering would support a reduction in price, but consumer price expectations remain relatively high. Under these circumstances, the solution is to charge a price higher than is justified by the cost saving achieved through de-engineering. Known as 'price skimming', the strategy only remains viable while consumers are willing to pay a price higher than is justified by the level of performance for the product being offered.

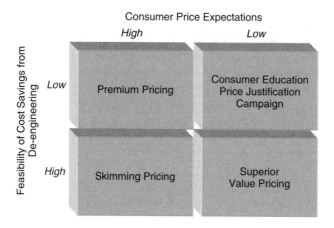

Figure 9.3 Product performance/pricing options.

Inconvenience pricing

Case Aims: To illustrate that consumers are willing to face a degree of inconvenience in return for paying a lower price for a product or service.

Firms need to understand how price expectation in their specific market sector will be influenced by the degree of inconvenience or purchase dissatisfaction the consumer is willing to accept. The degree of inconvenience is influenced by consumers' income and the scale of the financial savings that are available. An illustration of maturing boomers expecting lower prices in return for greater inconvenience is provided by their purchasing behaviour for prescription medicines in the USA (Brink 2003). The total annual drugs bill in the USA is $160 billion and retired people have five times as many prescriptions filled as individuals still in work. In Europe, the welfare system permits prescription drugs to be made available for free or at a subsidized price. This is in contrast with the situation in the USA, where retirees in receipt of Medicaid or covered by a private health insurance scheme, still have to find a significant proportion of drug costs themselves. To this burden has to be added the fact that US consumers pay the world's highest prices for prescription drugs. The solution, which has been adopted by a significant number of maturing boomers, is to travel across the country's borders to either Canada or Mexico where drug prices are significantly lower. In theory, it is illegal for private citizens to import prescription drugs into the USA. As long as people cross the border with prescriptions and return with not more than a 3-month supply of medicines for personal use, the customs and other federal officials leave them alone. The State of Maine is bounded on the north by Canada, where on average, the drug prices are 60 per cent lower. Not surprisingly, a large number of Maine's elderly population is willing to suffer the inconvenience of participating in organized bus trips across the border to gain access to these lower prices. Similar behaviour is to be found in the USA's Southern States, such as Nevada and Texas. In this instance, people head south to cities such as Tijuana in Mexico where savings of up to 70 per cent are available on prescription drugs. In some parts of middle America, where certain illnesses cause drug costs to be especially high, some people are saving money on their medications by flying across to Europe to make their purchases. Not surprisingly, the American Food and Drug Administration has stated that it cannot guarantee the safety of imported drugs. Consumers making overseas trips have no concerns about product quality. This is because they are purchasing the same drugs from the same pharmaceutical firms which supply the market in the USA. For individuals who are unable to travel to another country, there are now a number of alternative ways of purchasing drugs from outside of America. In Minneapolis, the Minnesota Senior Federation helps people get the forms and information they need to purchase their prescriptions by mail order from Canada. More recently, individuals have increasingly turned to the internet where there are a growing number of Canadian pharmacies willing to supply the American market. In a partial attempt to reduce the level of cross-border purchasing, the pharmaceutical industry, private companies and not-for-profit organizations have started to sponsor prescription drug discount cards which are administered by pharmacy benefit managers. Although there is some variation in the savings offered by such cards, on average consumers can at best expect to receive a price reduction of not more than 20 per cent when taking advantage of this system.

Behaviour shifts

Few marketers would rely on an economics text to guide their pricing decisions. This is fortunate because many of these texts tend to suggest that firms should determine price only after all other decisions such as product specification, promotion and distribution have been decided. Additionally, economic theories usually ignore that selecting an appropriate price involves examining the interactions of various other influencing variables. The importance of understanding these variables is especially relevant in the case of older financially attractive consumers because some marketers appear to assume that all older people live on low incomes. Hence, their tendency is to conclude that all consumers in this sector of the market base their purchase decision on always opting for lowest priced goods (Leech 1988).

The price a consumer is willing to pay is strongly influenced by the individual's net income. However, if the marketer can be persuaded to ignore the stereotyped image of all older people are living on low incomes, then it becomes possible to recognize that the high net worth of the average older financially attractive consumer will mean their purchase preference will be biased towards premium priced goods in many market sectors (Schufeldt *et al.* 1988). The reason for this price preference is that financially attractive consumers use higher prices as an indication of higher quality. Also being able to pay a higher price is a self-authentication of success or alternatively offers an individual the opportunity to communicate a higher social status to friends, relatives or the world in general.

Allsop (2005) has posited that in today's world, some traditional price/value perceptions are being complicated by a variety of factors. One factor is brands which were previously perceived as luxury goods being de-engineered by the supplier such that saleability can be expanded to include consumers who previously could not afford the product. An example of this approach is provided by the car manufacturer Mercedes Benz in launching their A-Class people carrier. The risk for companies implementing this strategy is that as product usage is extended across more of the market, existing customers may perceive the brand as less exclusive and switch to an alternative, high status competitor.

When setting and reviewing prices, firms have to be aware there a number of variables that can cause price expectations of financially attractive consumers to change over time. Some of these factors are summarized in Figure 9.4. As described in this diagram, one factor is the level of personal income. Older financially attractive consumers, for example, who feel financially secure will tend to purchase higher quality goods than they would have done in the past when their children were still at home. This trait explains why many individuals during the early years of their retirement make purchases such as upmarket furnishing or take a world cruise (Wei *et al.* 1999). The existence of such variables shown in Figure 9.4 means that firms serving this market sector must remain extremely alert to any evidence that behaviour shifts are occurring among their target audience.

In the case of high technology goods such as DVD players or televisions, consumers who have been purchasing goods over a number of years are influenced by their prior purchase experience. Where prices within a category have tended to decline over time due to ongoing technological advances, this trend causes consumers to expect lower average prices in the future. The consumers' assumption that further price declines will occur in the future for a specific product category can have significant profit margin erosion implications for suppliers. This trend is illustrated in the UK where consumers have become increasingly price sensitive in relation to audio-visual electronic goods. The outcome is that when a new technology first appears in the market and unit prices are high (e.g. plasma screen televisions), most of the early purchasers will tend be young people. This is because older financially attractive consumers will postpone their purchase based upon their prior experience that prices can be expected to fall significantly in the relatively near future (Guy *et al.* 1994).

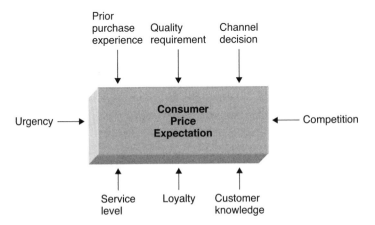

Figure 9.4 Category level price influencers.

Eating out

Case Aims: To illustrate that among maturing boomers, factors other than low price are often perceived as more important when reaching a purchase decision.

The highly heterogeneous nature of the maturing boomer market is reflected by the fact that significant variation in relation to the importance of price can be demonstrated in market sectors where there is a wide range of choice in terms of the prices charged for products or services (Moschis *et al.* 2003). To gain further understanding of the importance of price in reaching a purchase decision, these researchers undertook a study of the factors influencing purchase decisions by maturing boomers in the US restaurant market. At a macro-level, the data revealed that on average, maturing boomers were more influenced by price than younger consumers. Further data analysis involving segmentation of the maturing boomer respondents, however, revealed significant variation in factors affecting the restaurant selection decision. Using a consumer segmentation system previously validated by Professor Mouchis, respondents were classified into four gerontographic groups: *Healthy Indulgers, Healthy Hermits, Ailing Outgoers* and *Frail Reclusives*. The two healthy segments still perceive their lives as enjoyable, but unlike healthy hermits, the indulgers strongly prefer a busy social life, most of which is enjoyed outside of their home. Ailing Outgoers and Frail Reclusives both have to cope with factors such as illness and reduced mobility impacting their lives. The main difference is the outgoers do not perceive their impairments as totally stopping them enjoying social activities outside the home. The research study identified the following top six factors influencing the choice of restaurants among the four groups:

Factor*	Healthy indulgers	Healthy hermits	Ailing outgoers	Frail reclusives
Comfortable place to socialize	1	1	2	2
Location near to home or work	3	2	3	1
Special pricing for older patrons	2	3	1	3
Recommended by other people	4	4	4	4
Location near to other places patronized	5	6	5	5
Have personnel orientated to your needs	6	5	6	6

*Source: Moschis *et al.* 2003.

The way price influences customer loyalty is not always easy to predict. Loyal customers for branded goods are usually willing to pay a higher price when purchasing their favourite brand in most product categories. In other cases, however, consumers expect their loyalty to be rewarded through being offered repeat purchase discounts or receiving higher service priority when making a subsequent purchase. The degree to which loyalty is influenced by price appears to vary with age (Mogelonsky 1995). Research on American consumers undertaken by the *Better Homes and Gardens* magazine revealed that although lower prices were the dominant factor in causing people to switch supermarkets, this variable has declining influence as people grow older. Financially attractive consumers are much more loyal to their primary retail outlet and are less likely to be influenced by lower prices available elsewhere in their immediate neighbourhood. Instead, other variables such as attentive employees, rapid response to requests for assistance, positive reaction to complaints and store cleanliness are all factors which are usually much more important in determining loyalty to a specific retail store (Patterson 2007).

Most consumers, no matter their age, expect to save money when they switch to a lower cost supply channel. Thus, for instance, many people expect to pay a lower price when switching from a terrestrial to an online source when purchasing upmarket branded domestic appliances. Lack of variation between age groups is also present when consumers expect a firm to match price reductions announced by competitors. Should the firm fail to respond, many customers can be expected to switch to the lower cost supplier. This has been the case in the European travel industry, for example, where major international airlines have lost a significant proportion of their customers of all ages to the budget airlines.

Macro-influencers

Macro-level factors can influence customer price sensitivity across most market sectors. Unlike category level factors where the firm is often able to forecast the impact of impending change, assessing the potential impact of macro-level factors on consumer behaviour is more difficult. Examples of some of these factors are summarized in Figure 9.5.

Most macro-level influencers can cause entire groups of consumers to change their attitude about their wealth and financial security. People feeling less secure or less wealthy will become more price sensitive. A Government increase in income tax rates, for example, will cause consumers to become concerned about their disposable income. The outcome will be to cut back on personal expenditure and to actively seek out lower priced goods.

The reverse scenario is also applicable when consumers believe they have increased spending power; namely the feeling of greater personal wealth fuels a higher level of consumption accompanied by a decline in price sensitivity. The scenario of consumption pattern variation has been demonstrated in recent years, when financial institutions exploited a period of low interest rates to relax their lending rules (Mollenkamp and Whitehouse 2008). The banks expanded their

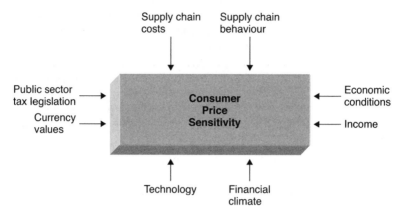

Figure 9.5 Macro price sensitivity influencers.

mortgage business by offering increasingly tempting lending terms. House buying activity increased which in turn drove up house prices. Higher property values caused consumers to feel wealthier, motivating them to purchase more goods funded via the medium of their credit cards or loans. In 2007, the meltdown in US sub-prime mortgage was the initial spark which burst this lending bubble. Then in 2008, as the world began to comprehend the other dubious practices by financial institutions, this led to a massive liquidity problem followed by a severe tightening in consumer lending. Falling house prices and credit restriction have caused consumer spending to decline dramatically. Consumer price sensitivity has risen which means most suppliers seeking to sustain sales, especially of non-necessity goods, have been forced to severely reduce prices.

Macro-influencers of price sensitivity may not have the same effect across an entire group with a nation's population. For example financially attractive consumers who thought their savings had been lost during the 2007 collapse of the UK bank Northern Rock and those whose funds became inaccessible following the 2008 collapse of the Icelandic banks were both forced to immediately adjust their spending plans and have become more price sensitive. Furthermore, it is also probable that these traumatic experiences will continue to dampen their purchasing propensity for the foreseeable future (Anon 2008). Similarly the 2008 banking crisis severely impacted those UK financially attractive consumers who decided that the road to a secure future was to build up a portfolio of buy-to-let properties (Macwhirter and Wake 2008). These individuals, having heard how others were making their fortunes in buying houses and apartments, found certain banks very willing to lend money to support the purchase of investment properties. Unfortunately, when the UK housing market collapsed, the banks' response to the liquidity crisis was to tighten lending terms and raise interest rates. The outcome is many of these new breed of landlords have lost virtually everything and again these individuals will be forced to radically alter their spending plans in retirement.

These two groups, however, only represent of small proportion of the UK's total number of financially attractive consumers. The majority of this group have not been adversely impacted by the turmoil these events have caused in the financial markets. This is because they avoided placing their savings with an insecure bank or investing in the buy-to-let property market. Consequently, these latter individuals can be expected to retain a more positive orientation in relation to their future spending plans and will probably also retain a reasonably high level of price insensitivity.

Clearly it is impossible to accurately predict the long-term impact of the 2007/2008 financial crisis on the future spending patterns of financially attractive consumers. Nevertheless, some understanding can be gained from consumer reaction to earlier severe stock market downturns in the second half of the twentieth century (Sternlieb and Hughes 1987). For example, analysis of the late 1990s dotcom stock market crash would suggest that changes in the expenditure patterns of financially attractive consumers following the 2007/2008 financial crisis will depend on a number of factors (Punch 2004). Included in these factors are issues such as the perceived security of their pensions, the degree to which those in work are hoping the sale of the family home will fund their retirement and the proportion of retirement portfolios individuals are holding in company shares which have massively declined in value during the mid-2008 market crash.

Variation in response to recent macroeconomic events will also occur across different socioeconomic groups. Higher social class maturing financially attractive consumers in receipt of an adequate pension, for example, will be less concerned about the low interest rates on savings accounts than people reliant upon their savings to fund their retirement. Based upon prior spending patterns during the last severe economic downturn in the early 1990s, higher social class maturing boomers are unlikely to significantly reduce personal spending levels or switch to suppliers purely on the basis of being offered a lower price (Schieber 2004). In the past, gender has not been considered to exert a strong influence over purchase behaviour. Many of the studies that provide the basis for this conclusion have usually made no attempt to assess the interaction between age and gender of respondents. When Sherman *et al.* (2001) compared what they described as the 'new age elderly' with 'traditional elderly', however, they concluded that gender has little influence in the case of the traditional elderly group. This is not found to be the case, however, with the new age elderly. The group perceives themselves as financially secure and equate wealth as determining happiness or success. Within the new age group, gender is found to influence spending patterns. Women tend to be more price conscious than men. However, women perceive themselves more adventurous than men, being involved in meeting new people, seeking out sources of new ideas, having greater market knowledge in relation to stores offering greater value and are more likely to be influenced by discounts or retailer sales.

Dining incentives

Case Aims: To illustrate how service providers can use price incentives to attract retired boomers at times of the day when employed people will not be a significant element of an organization's customer base.

Service providers are aware that as their products are perishable, a failure to sell capacity is revenue that is lost forever. Examples of this scenario include the empty airline seat or the vacant hotel bedroom. To minimize the impact of perishability, firms use a variety of price-based incentives. Retirees are often the target of such incentives because their more flexible lifestyle permits them to purchase services at times of the day, week or month when younger, employed people are not able to participate in the market. In the USA, some of the most active users of incentives are small service firms located in areas such as Arizona and Florida where retired boomers constitute a significant proportion of the total population (Carlin1994). Data on the social activities of this group indicate that over 55 per cent eat out at least once a month and that over 50 per cent of their restaurant visits are to mid to upscale establishments. The attraction of this customer group to restauranteurs is their ability to be able to dine earlier than people in work. To exploit this behaviour pattern as a way of filling capacity at times when otherwise the outlet would be relatively empty, most restaurant owners offer some form of price discount or sales promotion to retirees willing to dine between late afternoon and early evening. In Florida, most restaurants have found that all inclusive meals for a fixed price are perceived as highly attractive by retired boomers. Examples of outlets using this approach are Shells in Tampa, Laverocks Seafood House in St Petersburg and The Crab House in Hollywood. All three of these operations offer a complete dining package priced at approximately 50 per cent of the price paid by their evening patrons.

Price-based incentives

As prices fall, demand for most products will rise. This means firms can use temporary variations in price as a short-term sales incentive. These incentives can be classified into three types: discounts, sales promotions and sale pricing. As far as price discounts, one of the commonest practices in consumer markets is to offer all pensioners a reduced price. This discount philosophy has existed for many years and in most markets it is a tradition that is rarely questioned. For example, arts cinemas in the UK follow the national mass market cinema industry practice of offering pensioner discounts. Given, however, that the older patrons of arts cinemas are essentially all from the AB social group, removal of the pensioner discount would have zero impact on audience size. Hence, the only outcome from this unquestioning provision of a pensioner discount is to lower the profit margin on sales.

Some sectors of US industry, where older financially attractive consumers are now a major component of total sales, have begun to recognize that their blanket approach to offering senior citizen discounts is a massive source of profit erosion (Knutson *et al.* 2006). This realization has been followed by firms either reducing or abolishing this type of consumer incentive. In the airline industry, for example, American, Continental, Delta, Northwest, United and US Airways have drastically reduced the breadth of their senior citizen airfare discount schemes. In Colorado, large ski resorts have abolished their decades-old programme of free lift tickets for skiers aged 70+ . General Cinema Theatres have been forced to withdraw from the Florida market because of the operating losses generated by a huge proportion of their audiences who were people aged 65+ and who qualified for the company's national discount scheme for retirees.

For those individuals surviving on just a state pension, discounted prices can provide the difference which makes the purchase affordable. In the case of individuals receiving an adequate retirement income even though these individuals expect to be offered a price discount when booking an upmarket hotel or restaurant, the existence of the discount has little or no influence over their purchase decision. This attitude was confirmed in research undertaken by Knutson *et al.* (2006) concerning the factors influencing restaurant choice in the USA. These researchers concluded the relative importance of discounts as a factor of influence in relation to a purchase decision declined in direct proportion to the increasing size of the financially attractive consumer's net income.

In some cases, firms may also encounter the problem that age-related discounts may generate a negative reaction from older financially attractive consumers (Tepper 1994). Society's emphasis on retaining a youthful appearance means that image conscious financially attractive consumers are unwilling to accept their visual appearance will decline with age. These individuals also have a stereotyped image of pensioners being very old, shrunken, inactive people. This causes some older financially attractive consumers to wish to avoid others realizing they are now pensioners. The outcome is these individuals will decline a pensioner discount because they feel it stigmatizes them in front of other people. Only after these individuals have become comfortable with their own self image, will discounts become acceptable and thereby have a positive influence on purchase intent.

Sales promotion is a term given to a range of offers all of which share the common characteristic of providing a temporary increase in the value of goods. Examples include free product, price pack, coupons, premiums (e.g. a free towel with every purchase), competitions and sweepstakes. This type of promotion is a dominant feature of branded goods marketing. Although precise data on large firm sales promotion expenditure is unavailable, for most brands it is very probable that over 70 per cent of their marketing budget is allocated to supporting sales promotions. There is a diverse range of reasons to explain this scale of expenditure. Probably the most important reason is supermarkets recognizing the appeal of in-store specials, and demanding that leading brands fund these events. Another

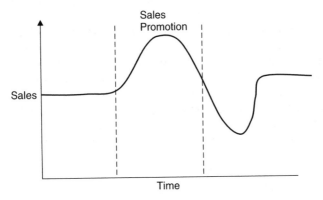

Figure 9.6 Sales promotion revenue curve.

important influence is that brand managers know sales promotion have an immediate impact on sales and hence, can be used to delay a downturn in sales. What seems to be ignored by most manufacturers and major retailers is that, as shown in Figure 9.6, sales promotions merely bring forward future sales. Unfortunately, the higher sales during the promotional period are generated at a reduced price. Hence, the outcome over the medium term is, therefore, that total overall net profit will be reduced (Kimball 1989).

Most retailers, especially in areas where there is a high proportion of retirees, appear to perceive that sales promotions are an effective tool through which to increase sales among this consumer group. Similar to the evidence on pensioner price discounts, there is little evidence to suggest that sales promotions are a key purchase decision influencer among older financially attractive consumers. A study by Krinshna *et al.* (1991) concluded that the families, especially those with a large number of children, are the most responsive consumer group in relation to their purchase behaviour being influenced by in-store promotions. A key reason for this situation is that sales promotions permit them to save significant monies by purchasing a larger than usual quantity of goods when the item is on deal. The family then ceases further purchases until their on-hand stock at home of the purchased item has declined. The study also revealed that older financially attractive consumers are much less likely to be motivated by in-store offers. Although this group recognize sales promotions can offer savings on their grocery bill, they perceive their much smaller consumption of most items does not justify buying larger quantities of items during a sales promotion. Their view is that sales promotions are not designed to attract their custom because most sales promotions are directed at increasing sales volumes among families with children.

Distribution

The era of low-cost hydrocarbon fuels which the world enjoyed in the twentieth century has gone forever. This has a number of implications, not least of which is the issue of seeking to utilize the most economical approach for product distribution to minimize transportation costs (Balakrishnan *et al.* 2004). The solution for most large firms is to exploit the economies of scale that can be achieved through the utilization of an intermediary to link the company with the end-user. Supermarkets, for example, achieve economies of scale by purchasing truck load quantities of goods and then using a centralized warehouse storage system through which to re-distribute a variety of products out to their stores. By bringing together a variety of goods, the intermediary also provides additional added value by featuring goods from different suppliers; thereby providing consumers with the opportunity to view a broad range of goods at a single location.

There are a number of factors that will influence what is the optimal distribution system through which a producer should make contact with the consumer (Rangan *et al.* 1986). These are summarized in Figure 9.7. One of the factors influencing any distribution strategy is the degree of price sensitivity among consumers. In those cases where price sensitivity is high, then distribution channels will be selected on the basis of the lowest possible operating costs, because these can be passed on to consumers in the form of more competitive prices. In those cases where the lowest possible price is not an issue, channels can be selected in terms of being the most effective approach for responding to consumer preferences. For example Johnson-Hillary *et al.*'s (1997) research on consumer shopping patterns in America confirmed earlier studies that many financially attractive consumers place greater importance on factors such as high levels of product choice, an enjoyable shopping experience, store personnel on-hand to provide information, product selection assistance from staff and high service quality. As a consequence, this group of consumers prefer to shop in department stores and speciality outlets such as boutiques and thus, producers who restrict distribution of their goods to mass merchandise outlets or discount stores are unlikely to achieve a high market share among the financially attractive consumer sector of a market.

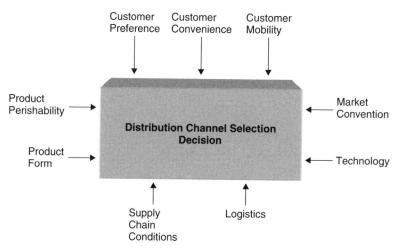

Figure 9.7 Distribution decision influencers.

Cutting distribution costs

Case Aims: To illustrate how revised operational processes and computer technology can be utilized to reduce distribution costs.

The focus of many intermediaries in the past has been to seek a unique selling proposition based upon variables such as store layout, range of merchandise carried and in-store service quality. More recently, however, there is growing acceptance that emphasis on improved logistics as a route through which to save costs that can be passed along to consumers in the form or lower prices may be more important (Koselka 1992). The individual who first demonstrated the advantages of this concept in the supermarket industry was Sam Walton, the founder of Wal-Mart. This retailer was among the first to invest heavily in computerized scanning equipment for cash registers. With real-time information about what customers wanted, Wal-Mart could tell manufacturers what to produce and where and when to deliver. To reduce delivery times, Wal-Mart also started to require manufacturers to ship goods already tagged and hung, ready for the sales floor. This eliminated some of the need for warehouse space and reduced shipment processing costs. Wal-Mart stores have only about 10 per cent of their square footage allocated to product storage compared with other supermarkets who need about 25 per cent of their physical facilities to this same task. Manufacturers have not been slow to learn from Wal-Mart's success. For example the US consumer goods company Helene Curtis has built a vast new distribution centre in Chicago. The $32 million facility has no paper order tickets or shipping tags. Computer-controlled forklifts place packages on conveyors that laser-read the barcodes and send the packages to their destinations. This single facility employing 225 people can handle more than twice as many goods as the six older company warehouses which it replaced and has reduced distribution costs by over 40 per cent.

Another dimension influencing the selection of an optimal distribution channel is that the shopping patterns of older financially attractive consumers may be influenced by illness or limited mobility. In these cases, a key preference will be a desire among consumers for convenience in terms of minimizing travel or some cases, never having to leave home. Under such circumstances an intermediary such as a small local shop may be an optimal distribution channel solution. Alternatively, the producer may need to create a system where the goods can be delivered direct to their consumer's home.

For some products, over the years consumers may have developed a preference for using one specific delivery channel. Their purchase behaviour will be based upon a well established convention (e.g. home purchase of cosmetics from an Avon representative). Conventions can be broken, however, where technological change offers a more attractive distribution proposition (e.g. saving money by switching from a local travel agent to an airline website). In some cases, a firm which breaks a distribution convention can ultimately become a leading national or international brand. For example some years ago, the UK company Direct Line came into existence because the entrepreneurial founder recognized that major insurers and their broker affiliates were operating from an expensive network of terrestrial offices. His solution was to launch a centralized, tele-sales and tele-services operation which permitted a dramatic reduction in car insurance premiums. The company rapidly moved to market leader and by expanding into other areas of consumer insurance, has retained a dominant market position in the UK consumer insurance industry.

Another factor that influences the distribution decision is that delivery of certain goods involves the provision of a service process at or in the consumer's home (e.g. garden maintenance, house repairs). This situation has created numerous opportunities for a diversity of small businesses to become engaged in the direct supply of services to consumers. Financially attractive consumers exhibit a higher than average *per capita* consumption of domestic services. One reason for this situation is financially attractive consumers' net incomes allow them to afford to employ others to undertake domestic tasks. Another reason for the high utilization levels of home delivered services is that immobility or illness among older financially attractive consumers means that fulfilling their needs can only be achieved by an in-home delivery of the service proposition.

Exclusivity

Case Aims: To illustrate the importance of using distribution and product mix to sustain the exclusivity image of a successful upmarket brand.

Major retailers' primary market tends to be the 18–49 year age group and the items they stock are reflective of the purchasing behaviour and *per capita* spending levels of this consumer group. This means that higher priced, more upmarket goods aimed at financially attractive consumers are not perceived by most mass market retailers as generating an adequate profit per square foot. On the other side of the equation, status orientated people such as financially attractive consumers who feel able to purchase more expensive items, prefer to shop in outlets which they perceive as unafford- able to the majority of the population (Rock 1989). This fact is fully understood by the major upmarket brands. Hence, their distribution strategies are orientated towards achieving market exclusivity either by operating their own outlets or only being stocked in upmarket speciality retailers and department stores. An example of a company which has successfully utilized distribution as a key element in their desired image to be perceived as an exclusive, upmarket brand is the French jewellery and luxury goods group, Cartier. The company's top markets are the USA, France, Italy, Hong Kong, Germany, the UK and Switzerland. Across the company's global operation, there are 10 flagship, luxury Cartier outlets that only sell jewellery. The remaining 120 outlets stock jewellery but just as critical to the revenue generated by these other stores, are sales of watches and other Cartier branded goods such as leather goods and perfume. With watches becoming an increasingly important component of the firm's overall product mix, in 1988 the company purchased two luxury Swiss watch companies, Piaget and Baume et Mercier as part of a strategy to challenge the market dominance of the world's leading luxury brand, Rolex. Cartier has also entered into a number of licensing agreements, such as that signed with Yves St Laurent, to permit the brand to expand into the fashion accessories market. Management are very aware, however, that excessive and uncontrolled market expansion could damage the Cartier name among the core customers who might come to perceive the brand as no longer sufficiently exclusive. Hence, any action, even where significant incremental sales are available, is strongly resisted by management if they consider the new idea would move the company downmarket or erode the Cartier image for exclusivity.

Online distribution

Many of the technologists involved in the creation of the internet wanted this to be a completely democratic medium, free from the influences of large private or public sector organizations. They were successful in relation to certain issues such the use of open source programming languages and the insightful decision to establish a global not-for-profit organization to manage domain name allocation. This democratic philosophy caused some individuals to predict that the internet would 'level the playing field' because firms of any size would be free to start selling and distributing goods on a global scale. Events in the early-1990s appeared to support this perspective of a brave new world. The internet was dominated by the launch of totally new, online small enterprises. Tragically, however, the hopes of business democratization were soon defeated by commercial reality. Once the viability of the technology was proven, large firms took actions to dominate this new distribution channel. By spending large sums of money, large firms were able to obtain a prime page position with the online search engines. Additionally, consumers have a preference to purchase online goods from firms with whom they are already very familiar. Consequently, existing large 'bricks and mortar' firms enjoy higher website visits than most purely cyber world firms. This outcome validates the age old business adage that when a new distribution channel emerges that is attractive to existing large companies, these organizations are usually able to ensure no new entrants are likely to pose a threat to their existence (Chaston 2000).

Early studies on internet usage indicated that younger people were more likely to make online purchases than older individuals. There were some researchers in the mid-1990s who predicted that online buying would never be of appeal to older financially attractive consumers. Such forecasts have since proved to be incorrect because, over time the relationship between age and internet usage has all but disappeared. For example by 1999 consumers aged 55+ in the USA accounted for 9 per cent of all online sales. The stockbroker Charles Schwarb estimated that older financially attractive consumers represented almost 20 per cent of their total online client group (Oberndorf 1999). An exception to this generalization does currently remain valid among consumers aged 65+ where usage continues to decline with age. This probably reflects among this group either a lack of IT skills or alternatively, no access to a home computer.

One study which sought to apply existing terrestrial retail buyer behaviour theory to online purchasing was that undertaken by Wolfinbarger and Gilly (2001). By the use of a qualitative methodology to generate data, these researchers concluded there are two types on online shoppers; namely experiential and goal-orientated individuals. The experiential shopper uses the internet to expand their knowledge and involve more classes of product. This type of consumer, who is in the minority, spends significant periods of time browsing the internet, visiting auction and hobby-related sites. In contrast, goal-orientated consumers perceive the medium as an alternative distribution channel which offers the appeal of convenience, informativeness, wider selection and the ability to control the timing of the shopping experience.

Scorce *et al.*'s (2005) study attempted to quantitatively determine whether a relationship exists between the age of the consumer and whether they are experiential or goal orientated internet users. The researchers concluded that their selected methodology was unable to draw any solid conclusions about the influence of age on experiential user behaviour. In the context of goal-orientated behaviour, however, they determined that younger people were more likely to search online for a broader range of products than older financially attractive consumers. However, once the older consumer had located the goods online, they were then more likely to make a purchase than a younger person. There was no statistically significant difference between the scale of online purchasing across different age groups. Where buying difference did exist, these reflected age-related interests (e.g. young people bought music whereas older consumers bought garden tools). Individuals of all ages who perceive the internet as offering significant information and convenience benefits, are more likely to use the medium to locate and then purchase goods online.

Another study which sought to determine the factors influencing internet usage among older consumers was undertaken by Trocchia and Janda (2000). This study identified that in the case of individuals age 50+, key influencing variables included reference group affiliation, nature of social relations, response to technology, resistance to change, perceptions of reality and dexterity. In relation to reference group affiliation the study found that individuals are influenced by the behaviour and knowledge of others within their social group. As a consequence, those individuals who were members of a social group where others were already using the internet were more likely to become interested in the medium. A related factor in the context of social group participation is where individuals are interested in strengthening or expanding their social relationships. In these cases, internet usage is higher because the technology is perceived in assisting social interaction through activities, such as visiting chat rooms or e-mailing friends and relatives.

Those individuals who have an aversion to new technology such as DVD recorders or mobile telephones are less likely to consider using the internet. This attitude is compounded if the same individual is a traditionalist who is resistant to making changes in their lifestyle or shopping habits. In terms of perceptions of reality some individuals only feel comfortable when purchasing goods after being able to touch the product or interact on a terrestrial basis with a service provider employee. Such individuals tend to feel uncomfortable replacing these terrestrial reassurances by moving to what they perceive as the machine world of online purchasing. The final factor influencing internet usage is the somewhat obvious variable of dexterity. Those people who suffer from problems such as arthritis or have poor eye sight face real problems using a computer. Hence, these individuals find online shopping an activity in which they feel reluctant to participate.

Missing the opportunity

Case Aims: To illustrate how the increasingly important online maturing boomer audience has yet to be effectively exploited in the promotional strategies of major brands.

Many branded goods companies have yet to recognize the importance of older financially attractive consumers and remain focused on using terrestrial advertising and distribution channels that favour the sale of goods to the 18–49 age group. This same trend appears to also exist in relation to marketers' exploitation of the opportunities available through the Internet (Anon 2006a). In the UK, for example, 86 per cent of maturing boomers own a computer with an internet connection. Almost 60 per cent shop online, 47 per cent bank online and 26 per cent use the internet to research products which they then purchase from a terrestrial outlet. Despite this fact, the majority of online brand advertising which appears on commercial websites is directed at either teenagers or the 18–49 year age group. As noted by the market research firm Starcom, older financially attractive consumers now represent approximately 80 per cent of the UK's personal wealth, yet in relation to many of online advertising strategies used by the major branded goods companies, virtually none appear to target their communications at this vital consumer group (Anon 2006b). This latter study suggested that older financially attractive consumers tend to exhibit a lower level of trust in online advertising than younger people. Furthermore, the primary reason older financially attractive consumers log onto the internet is to obtain information, manage their hobby, obtain up-dates on current affairs or to communicate with friends and relatives. This means online shopping is a less important activity. This situation probably explains why the majority of older financially attractive consumers ignore banners and pop-up advertisements. The other key influencer is the majority of older financially attractive consumers believe online advertisements are aimed not at them, but at younger people. Given this attitude, then possibly a more effective advertising campaign aimed at older financially attractive consumers might be to use a mix of media channels to communicate the brand message. For example a brand might use traditional print advertising such as magazines to communicate the primary benefit message and to purchase online advertising space as a mechanism through which to enhance awareness of financially attractive consumers when they are engaged in making an online purchase.

References

Allsop, J. (2005) 'Premium pricing: understanding the value of premium', *Journal of Revenue and Pricing Management*, Vol. 4, No. 2, pp. 185–94.

Anon (2008) 'Frozen in Iceland; UK investors need certainty on bank deposit protection', *Financial Times*, 10 October, p. 8.

Anon (2006a) 'Silver surfers: golden opportunities for brands?', *Brand Strategy*, London, 18 December, pp. 44–6.

Anon (2006b) 'Interactive: targeting the silver surfers' pot of gold', *Marketing Week*, London, 28 June, p. 34.

Balakrishnan, A., Geunes, J. and Pangburn, M.S. (2004) 'Coordinating supply chains by controlling upstream variability propagation', *Manufacturing & Service Operations Management*, Vol. 6, No. 2, pp. 163–84.

Brink, S. (2003) 'Health on the border', *US News & World Report*, 9 June, p. 3.

Carlin, B. (1994) 'Operators strike gold with service', *Nation's Restaurant News*, 3 October, pp. 53–5.

Chaston, I. (2000) *E-Commerce Marketing Management*, London: McGraw-Hill.

Flanagan, P. (1994) 'Don't call 'em old, call 'em customers', *Management Review*, Vol. 83, No. 10, pp. 17–22.

Guy, B.S., Rittenberg, Y.L. and Hawes, D.K. (1994) 'Dimensions and characteristics of time perceptions and perspectives among older consumers', *Psychology & Marketing*, Vol. 11, No. 1, pp. 35–48.

Johnson-Hillary, J., Kang, J. and Tuan, W. (1997) 'The differences between elderly consumers' satisfaction and retail sales personnel's perceptions', *International Journal of Retail & Distribution Management*, Vol. 26, No. 1, pp. 126–37.

Kimball, R. (1989) 'An exploratory report on sales promotion management', *Journal of Consumer Marketing*, Vol. 6, No. 3, pp. 65–75.

Knutson, B., Elsworth, J. and Beck, J. (2006) 'Restaurant discounts for seniors: perceptions of the mature market', *Cornell Hospitality and Restaurant Administration Quarterly*, Vol. 47, No. 1, pp. 61–76.

Krinshna, A., Currim, I.S. and Shoemaker, R.W. (1991) 'Consumer perceptions of promotional activity', *Journal of Marketing*, Vol. 55, No. 2, pp. 4–17.

Koselka, R. (1992) 'Distribution revolution', *Forbes*, 25 May, pp. 54–6.

Leech, R.E. (1988) 'On the verge of a golden age', *Trusts & Estates*, Vol. 127, No. 1, pp. 29–38.

Macwhirter, I. and Wake, K. (2008) 'Crash: the housing crisis is just beginning', *New Statesman*, London, 9 June, pp. 28–31.

Mollenkamp, C. and Whitehouse, M. (2008) 'Lehman's demise triggered cash crunch around globe: decision to let firm fail marked a turning point in the crisis', *Wall Street Journal*, New York, 29 September, p. A1.

Mogelonsky, M. (1995) 'Satisfying senior shoppers', *Marketing Tools*, Vol. 2, No. 2, pp 4–5.

Moschis, G., Curasi, C.F. and Bellenger, D. (2003) 'Restaurant-selection preferences of older consumers', *Cornell Hotel and Restaurant Administration Quarterly*, Vol. 44, No. 4, pp. 51–62.

Oberndorf, S. (1999) 'Targeting the senior surfers', *Catalog Age*, Vol. 16, No. 1, p. 53

Patterson, P.G. (2007) 'Demographic correlates of loyalty in a service context', *Journal of Services Marketing*, Vol. 21, No. 2, pp. 112–24.

Punch, P. (2004) 'Older debtors, new problems', *Credit Card Management*, Vol. 17, No. 5, pp. 26–30.

Rangan, V.K., Zoltners, A.A. and Becker, R.J. (1986) 'The channel intermediary selection decision: a model and application', *Management Science*, Vol. 32, No. 9, pp. 1114–23.

Rock, S. (1989) 'The luxury of being Cartier', *Director*, London, May, pp. 82–5.

Shapiro, B.P. (1973) 'Price reliance–existence and sources', *Journal of Marketing Research*, Vol. 10, No. 3, pp. 286–97.

Schieber, S.J. (2004) 'Pensions in crisis', *Pensions: An International Journal*, Vol. 9, No. 3, pp. 212–27.

Schufeldt, L., Oates, B. and Vaught, B. (1988) 'Is lifestyle an important factor in the purchase of OTC drugs by the elderly?', *Journal of Consumer Marketing*, Vol. 15, No. 2, pp. 111–20.

Scorce, P., Perotti, V. and Widrick, P. (2005) 'Attitude and age difference in online buying', *International Journal of Retail & Distribution Management*, Vol. 33, No. 2/3, pp. 122–32.

Sherman, E., Schiffman, L.G. and Mahour, A. (2001) 'The influence of gender on the new-age elderly's consumption pattern', *Psychology & Marketing*, Vol. 18, No. 10, pp. 1073–82.

Sternlieb, G. and Hughes, J.W. (1987) 'The mortgage market', *American Demographics*, Vol. 27, No. 2, pp. 26–31.

Tepper, K. (1994) 'The role of labelling in elderly consumers' response to age cues', *Journal of Consumer Research*, Vol. 20, No. 4, pp. 503–20.

Trocchia, P.J. and Janda, S. (2000) 'A phenomenological investigation of Internet usage among older individuals', *Journal of Consumer Marketing*, Vol. 17, No. 7, pp. 605–14.

Wei, S., Ruys, H. and Muller, T.R. (1999) 'A gap analysis of perceptions of hotel attributes by marketing managers and older people in Australia', *Journal of Marketing Practice*, Vol. 5, No. 6/7/8, pp. 200–11.

Wolfinbarger, M. and Gilly, M. (2001) 'Shopping for freedom, control and fun', *California Management Review*, Vol. 43, No. 2, pp. 34–55.

10 Health and beauty

Generic principles of marketing to financially attractive consumers (FACs)

The coverage of issues in Chapter 10 is designed to illustrate the generic principles of marketing to FACs in relation to:

1 Companies considering entry into the provision of private sector residential care for older FACs should recognize this is already an overcrowded and not very profitable market.
2 Profitable opportunities possibly exist in the 'assisted living facilities' market where residential complexes offer the provision of services to FACs ranging from minimal support through to 24/7 nursing care.
3 The most profitable areas associated with the provision of services to older FACs are those which fulfil these consumers' lifestyle aspirations.
4 Significant marketing opportunities exist for companies which can assist FACs' desire to remain healthy well into later life.
5 Older FACs are very interested in services which increase their involvement in physical or mental activities. This because these activities are seen as offering the potential to postpone or avoid the onset of mental illnesses such as Alzheimer's or dementia.
6 FACs' strong interest in remaining young looking makes this consumer group a prime target for non-medical solutions such as eating specific foods which producers can claim contain anti-ageing properties.
7 Female FACs' strong commitment to their personal appearance means this group are the prime target for both medical and non-medical solutions associated with postponing the visual impact of ageing.
8 Female FACs are the largest group of clients within the market for anti-ageing medical treatments such as cosmetic surgery.
9 Cosmetics offering superior skin care and anti-ageing benefits can usually command a premium price, thereby causing these products to be extremely profitable.

10   Companies interested in generating profits from involvement in the anti-ageing segment of the cosmetics industry should recognize competition in this market has become more intense following the entry of major branded goods companies such as Proctor & Gamble.

A crowded market

Some 50 years ago the opportunities to build successful new enterprises through the provision of products and services to older people in the healthcare sector were excellent. Forward thinking companies exploited the impact of rising incomes, higher living standards, increased welfare state funding and advances in medical technology which together led to a rapid expansion in market demand for this sector of the healthcare market.

Entrepreneurs either launching a new business idea or seeking to expand an existing operation would be wise to avoid markets containing numerous other firms all competing for the same customers. This is especially important in market sectors where there are few opportunities to compete other than on the basis of price. Additional warning signs that sustaining an adequate profit margin could become increasingly difficult are provided by indicators such as the rising cost of fixed assets, a decline in the scale of public sector subsidies, the impact of new legislation on operating costs and wage rates rising faster than revenue. The variables have all been present in the residential care market in many Western nations for some time, with the consequence that in most countries, sector profitability has declined.

In the UK for more than three decades the residential care sector attracted numerous small firm owner/managers because of the ease of market entry and the demand for care services trending upwards as improvements in healthcare resulted in more people living longer but unable to cope living alone. As a consequence, an increasing number of people started new small residential care enterprises or purchased existing residential businesses. Market entry was made even more attractive because business revenues were partially guaranteed under a scheme whereby by the UK Government funded a significant proportion of the residents' fees. Since the late 1980s, however, there has been some degree of flattening in the number of small firms participating in the UK residential care market. This is due to a number of factors (Calhoun 2006). First, as property prices have continued to rise, it has become more difficult to enter the industry via the traditional route of purchasing a large house and converting this into a new residential home. Second, with national and state Governments struggling to fund their ever-increasing welfare budgets, these public sector bodies have been forced to freeze or even reduce their spending on paying the fees for people who have been taken into care. Third, operating costs have been forced upwards by numerous legislative changes impacting residential care homes such as health and safety regulations necessitating expenditure on facility upgrading, lowering of the minimum ratio of residents to carers and requirements in relation to the number of professionally qualified staff that must be on-site. This issue of workforce costs was further complicated by the advent of minimum wage legislation in the 1990s which led to a dramatic increase in the sector's wage bills (McCune 1995).

By the beginning of the twenty-first century, price competition at the lower end of the residential care market, high wage costs, reduced Government funding and new legislation together resulted in a severe reduction in care home profit margins. In the UK, the impact of these external variables has been to drive enterprises into bankruptcy. Today, in many Western nations, most small, single unit care homes struggle to make an adequate level of profit unless they acquired their premises many years ago when property prices were significantly lower. Larger multiple unit operations, usually owned by national companies, are able to survive because they use a strategy of operating high bed number facilities while concurrently exploiting economies of scale in areas such as procurement of medicines, disposable materials and food. In the light of these trends it is probably inadvisable for entrepreneurs to now consider entry into the residential care home market.

Future opportunities for firms in the most Western countries providing care for the elderly may follow the US trend of older people now opting for what are known as 'assisted living facilities'(Castle 2005). These are operations which are designed as a bridge between traditional nursing homes, which offer round-the-clock, skilled medical care in an institutional setting, and independent retirement housing, in which residents receive no outside help. In assisted living, the elderly live as independently as possible, usually in apartments or cottages, but also have access to central meal and laundry facilities. If needed, residents can get assistance with daily chores such as bathing or dressing. Many of these operations are now beginning to offer on-site medical support to treat illnesses that do not require hospitalization. Creating these new entities requires a significant upfront investment to acquire sufficient land and to then construct the multi-unit accommodation. Such levels of expenditure are well beyond the capabilities of the average small firm. Hence, the most likely creators of such operations are large companies from either the home construction industry or from a relevant service sector such as corporations operating large hotel chains.

The other opportunity which many smaller firms recognized years ago is that old people who remain living in their own homes may need assistance over issues concerning mobility and many are also concerned about their personal safety. The scale of opportunity in these market sectors is reflected in the number of advertisements in magazine and newspaper advertisements aimed at older readers seeking to generate awareness for products designed to assist those facing mobility problems or to improve in-home safety. The insertions are predominantly from small firms offering extremely similar products in categories such as stairlifts, showers with safety features, easy entry baths, burglar alarms and personal monitoring systems. These organizations appear to rely on price-based competition because very few use concepts such as superior design or advances in technology as a route to differentiate themselves from others in the market.

Another important source of self-employment opportunities is the provision of at home support services to financially attractive consumers. This group, for either personal preference or for health reasons, are major purchasers of services such as decorating, minor house repairs and garden maintenance (Miller and Kim 1999). The ongoing existence of many small independent food retailers is also often critically influenced by their ability to provide a local purchase source for less mobile financially attractive consumers who are unable to travel a longer distance to shop in a large retail chain outlet. The success of many of these independent retailers is assisted by the fact that some older consumers do not like the shopping environment offered by large retail multi-chain companies. Instead, the consumer group prefers to purchase goods from an outlet where they receive a personalized service and preferably, one where they can establish a close relationship with the owner and the shop's sales assistants (Yu *et al.* 1996).

Early bird success

Case Aims: To illustrate that early entry into a market followed by sustained investment in innovation can permit an entrepreneurial firm to continue to operate a profitable business.

Despite the crowded nature of the healthcare market for the elderly, innovative firms who identified and exploited new opportunities in the 1970s and 1980s can even today, continue to enjoy growth in sales and profitability. One such firm is the UK company, Mangar International. The company is planning to double sales to £10 million by the year 2010. Achievement of this target will be through higher penetration of their domestic market and by overseas market expansion (Smith 2006). The business was founded 25 years ago by an accountant, David Garman. He was concerned about problems his elderly parents were facing using the bath, so he designed and manufactured a pneumatic lifting device. The business is still family owned with Mr Garman, now 84, occupying the role of chairman. Since successful market entry for Mr Garman's first product, the company has continued to focus upon developing new specialist equipment to move, handle and position elderly or disabled people. Although David Garman's aim has always been to make life more bearable for individuals with limited mobility, with the unit price for some products in excess of £500, the company has found that selling products to UK consumers for in-home use is a restricted market opportunity. The majority of sales now come from customers in the healthcare sector such as hospitals, care homes and occupational therapists. The company is seeking to grow sales in the USA, but is very aware of the highly competitive nature of the healthcare market in that country. To ensure success in this and other overseas markets, the current focus is on two activities. First is the aim of reducing product costs through actions such as investing in technology to improve efficiency in their Glamorgan factory and by outsourcing the manufacturing of some products to China. The second aim is to avoid price competition. This has been achieved by the company acquiring other, entrepreneurial smaller firms operating in the healthcare market and by investing in R&D to develop new, innovative products that can be protected from price by the existence of patents. The current expenditure on patents is in the region of £60,000 per year.

Another example of success achieved through being an early entrant into the maturing boomer sector based upon the provision of supplementary support for less mobile maturing boomers is provided by Arlene Harris. Ms Harris is the founder of the American Jitterbug mobile technology company (www.gojitterbug.com). Recognizing that older people need to stay in touch but have problems learning how to operate complex electronic devices, she exploited Samsung's innovative approach to create a mobile phone with a restricted number of usage features. This reduction in the number of features lowers the likelihood of the user becoming confused by having to use the highly complex keyboard and screen options found on the standard mobile phone. The jitterbug telephone has help features such as oversized buttons for emergency speed dial or frequently called numbers. Phone users, typically retirees or their children, have the option of making direct calls or using a live operator. This latter individual can help connect a call, retrieve messages and monitor whether a phone battery is remaining adequately charged.

Diversity of need

Over the last 50 years, rising living standards, social housing, subsidized healthcare, advances in medical technology and increased *per capita* incomes have all combined to dramatically alter the nature of the lives of older people. Although there will always remain a significant proportion of less active, older people in need of medical services and residential care, the number of active, financially secure individuals is, however, increasing dramatically. Furthermore, this latter group is forecast to grow in size for at least another 30 years in most developed nations.

Market success for any business is usually dependent upon understanding and fulfilling the needs of customers. Some the best commercial opportunities are those generated by the provision of goods and services which ensure individuals can totally fulfil their aspirations for an enjoyable lifestyle. To achieve this aim, however, the marketer must be aware that the older consumer market is segmented by factors such as health, mobility and level of desire for increased sociability (Guy *et al.* 1994). This means that financially attractive consumers, as summarized in Figure 10.1, exhibit a very diverse range of needs in terms of seeking to achieve lifestyle satisfaction. The probability of delivering this satisfaction, and

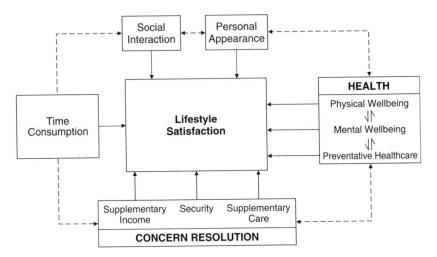

Figure 10.1 Lifestyle influencers.

consequently building customer loyalty, is increased by a firm's product or service proposition that has the potential of fulfilling two or more benefits.

In determining market opportunity, a priority for many older consumers is to resolve concerns they may have about access to supplementary care, feeling secure in their own home and supplementing their income. Some individuals will face the devastating physical and mental pressures of coping with one of the partner's health deteriorating over time. Examples of how declining health will affect older people include reduced mobility, a prolonged illness, a lengthy period of recovery from major surgery or chemotherapy or in the worst case scenario, the illness being diagnosed as terminal. Another increasingly major problem facing some older consumers is the need to provide 24/7 support for a partner whose mental faculties are deteriorating due to Alzheimer's disease or dementia (Dilworth and Kingsbury 2005).

Most people develop a very strong sense of loyalty to their partner when this person's physical or mental condition begins to deteriorate. They will endeavour to do as much as possible to create a caring, supportive environment (Merlis 2000). There is a growing trend of wishing to avoid the infirmed partner being taken to a residential home. This means the more active partner will have to commit themselves to the role of being the primary carer for what can be many years. This is a stressful and a physically draining role. In theory, public sector agencies are supposed to provide respite and ancillary services to private citizens who have accepted the responsibility for being the primary carer. In reality, however, the low social services budgets in many countries means that carers are forced to purchase support services from the private sector (Donelan *et al.* 2000). The higher than average *per capita* income of older financially attractive consumers will be a primary source of demand for services to supplement and support their role as primary carer. Examples of service provision demand include being a companion, shopping, transportation, housework, house maintenance and nursing support. One US national company which is already exploiting this market sector is Home Helpers which provides a one-stop-shop for people seeking third party assistance (www.homehelpers.cc).

As people retire, they develop very understandable concerns about their financial, personal and physical security. In relation to financial security, opportunities exist for financial services firms to provide guidance, support and a portfolio of different products to assist maturing boomers manage their wealth. Concerns over personal security are exacerbated by the media's deep and abiding interest in featuring old people who have been victims of crime. As a consequence, many older people have been sensitized to the issue of remaining secure, especially at night, in their own homes. These concerns provide a diverse range of opportunities for companies in sectors such as home construction, building maintenance, security services, remote alarm products and personal safety monitoring services (Powell and Wahidin 2008).

With state pensions in most nations not increasing at a rate anywhere near the rate of inflation, this means older consumers do need access to other sources of income. Their additional income need can range from being able to fund even just a minimum standard of living through to fulfilling an aspiration to be able to afford some luxuries in life. Sources of additional income may be generated by releasing funds through house downsizing, finding a new job or starting a small business. Based on recent trends in America, there are indications that in the future, an increasing number of older people will re-enter the workforce or start a new business (DeVaney and Haejeoing 2003). These older consumers can be a new opportunity for organizations who are (a) having difficulty recruiting younger employees and (b) seeking to improve workforce productivity by hiring older personnel who often are more highly motivated than their younger counterparts.

The traditional management perspective is that younger people are preferred over older people because the latter are paid a higher than average salary, are slower at doing their jobs and are frequently off sick (Minda 2004). As demonstrated by retailers such as Home Depot in America and Tesco in the UK, today's actual reality is very different. Older people will accept relatively low paid jobs, are grateful to be offered employment and to prove their ongoing value work harder than many younger employees. Furthermore, older people can draw upon their industrial and life experiences to provide levels of customer service greatly exceeding those delivered by their younger colleagues.

Older consumers expect to have lots of free time. Some individuals such as those on low incomes, living in poor accommodation, in poor health or with limited social skills, can encounter difficulties when attempting to find ways of occupying their time. It will probably be difficult to generate awareness and interest in new activities among this group within society. Consequently, these individuals do not represent a significant revenue source for many commercial businesses. Individuals with adequate incomes and interested in being outgoing, social individuals, however, are of interest because these individuals represent market opportunities for firms offering to support them in finding ways of successfully occupying their spare time in retirement (Calver *et al.* 1993). Many of this latter group tend to engage in the same activities as those enjoyed before retirement (e.g. gardening, golf, etc.). Some, however, may decide to experiment with completely new life experiences. In relation to these different approaches to occupying time, firms wishing to determine potential revenue from this group of financially attractive consumers will need to research the number of new customers entering their market sector, the amount of time potential customers wish to allocate to specific activities and the probable level of *per capita* expenditure.

High on the agenda of many older financially attractive consumers is to sustain or even expand their level of social interactions with others. Reasons underlying this aim are somewhat varied. Some individuals may have moved to a new location where initially, they do not know anyone. Others remain in their old neighbourhood, but had previously been too busy as working people or parents to find the time to build a large circle of friends. There are also those people who are divorced or their partner have died. A proportion of these individuals want to find someone with whom a new relationship can be established. All of these different reasons for a desire to build new social networks are exploitable by firms operating in sectors such as tourism, sports, home building and hospitality (Mathur and Moschis 1999). Customer appeal will be heightened by a firm offering a proposition that provides satisfaction across two or more influencing variables. One dual benefit is to offer financially attractive consumers the opportunity to fill their free time while concurrently being involved in social interactions. This type of dual benefit is exemplified by rural golf clubs with on-site accommodation generating incremental revenue by offering retirees out-of-season, holiday golfing packages.

Health

The advent of scientific thought was a new guiding social philosophy in Europe which in the eighteenth century led to the emergence of professionally-trained and educated doctors. These new professionals eventually eroded demand for incumbent healthcare suppliers such as apothecaries and butchers or blacksmiths acting as part-time surgeons. A lack of effective drugs and a limited understanding of human physiology meant that many of the early treatments developed by these new doctors were based upon invasive surgery. Although subsequent advances in medical science, diagnostic equipment, drugs and vaccines have supported the emergence of other treatment regimes, surgeons and their professional bodies still have a major influence over the funding and delivery of healthcare (Guadilliere and Lowy 1998).

During the twentieth century, the discovery of new drugs to treat medical conditions such as heart problems, mental illness and serious infections permitted the pharmaceutical industry to compete with surgeons in exerting influence over healthcare provision. In recent years, however, the continuing upward spiral in the costs of drugs and surgical treatments has accelerated acceptance of preventative medicine as an alternative, more cost-effective form of healthcare provision. One area of growth in preventative healthcare is the use of screening programmes to provide early warning of developing conditions. Early diagnosis may permit the use of non-invasive treatments to either cure or delay the onset of a major illness. Older people are the primary market source for many of these screening programmes because this group in society are often more likely to be affected by major illnesses that demand the most expensive forms of medical treatment (Daemmrich 2004).

For many years, industrialized countries have subsidized the costs of the drugs needed by retirees. It is only more recently, however, that Governments have recognized the cost/benefit advantages of funding screening programmes for older people. In the USA it was not until 2005 that the Government decided to create fund free and subsidized preventative healthcare services for retirees (Center for Medicare Services 2004). Upon retirement, all Americans are now offered a subsidized medical examination by a doctor under the 'Welcome to Medicare' scheme. This programme also includes ongoing regular screening for illnesses such as cardiovascular disease, breast cancer, cervical cancer, colorectal cancer, prostrate cancer and osteoporosis. Medicare, similar to many other countries' welfare provision, also offers retirees free vaccines for influenza and pneumonia. As many doctors are self-employed, the growth in diagnostic medical examinations, issuance of prescriptions and screening services mean this sector of the healthcare industry will continue to enjoy increasing revenue from older consumers, especially those in retirement who enjoy average or above average incomes.

Legislation has been in place for many years that requires medical providers to be qualified and licensed. This means the market opportunities to offer professional medical services to financially attractive consumers' medical market are closed to the vast majority of small firms. Nevertheless, the general public is exhibiting growing concerns with the cost of medical services, and the well publicized cases of the identification of dangerous side-effects requiring a drug to be withdrawn from the market has led to increased interest in alternative treatments (Harmon and Ward 2007). These alternatives include provision of manipulative approaches such as those offered by chiropractors, oriental treatments such as acupuncture, health foods and homeopathic medicines. Professional bodies representing some of these alternative treatments specify training and licensing for their membership. This ensures the delivery of appropriate standards of treatment. In these sectors, entry by new providers is restricted by the requirement to undertake training before being able to practice. There are other sectors, however, such as health foods where there is no competency requirement of individuals offering advice to consumers. This situation may change in the future because some Governments are considering new legislation in the health foods sector that may severely limit sector participation by unqualified individuals.

The probability of developing many mental illnesses increases with age. The two commonest age-related mental illnesses are Alzheimer's and dementia. In recent years the discovery of new drugs is permitting psychiatrists to deliver more effective treatments for mental illness. In the case of age-related conditions, however, the currently available treatments rarely offer a cure, but merely delay the onset of the final stages of the illness (McDermott *et al.* 2005). As drug-based treatments can only be prescribed by qualified professionals, opportunities for individuals or small firms who lack such qualifications are limited to the provision of at-home or residential care home services or involvement in the supply of alternative herbal remedies. As the medical profession has gained understanding of the impact of ageing on mental competencies, it is apparent, however, that a lifestyle in retirement which stimulates intellectual and physical activities can play an important role in postponing a decline in people's mental faculties. This means there are opportunities for smaller firms to provide services that deliver mental stimulation or exercise programmes to older financially attractive consumers.

High death rates and widespread disease among people living in the urban environments during the Industrial Revolution demonstrated health is strongly influenced by adverse environmental conditions such as inadequate sewage treatment systems. Public health bodies in Victorian times led to the creation of healthier towns and cities in developed nation economies. The advent of the welfare state after the Second World War further contributed to improving general living standards and the creation of healthier environments. More recently, public health bodies are beginning to emphasize the importance of exercise and nutrition as a fundamental element in remaining healthy in retirement (Anon 2006a). Exercise can contribute to overall wellbeing and lead to improvements in medical conditions such as poor blood circulation, high blood pressure and asthma. More recently, some evidence has emerged that a healthy lifestyle may be beneficial in delaying the onset of dementia and Alzheimer's.

A major problem associated with ageing is declining mobility. People who exercise regularly are less likely to encounter mobility problems in their declining years. Influenced by the trend of younger people in the 1980s starting to jog and power walk, an increasing number of retired financially attractive consumers now consider exercise as an important component of their lifestyle. In the UK, research suggests that more older women than men believe exercise is important. For example in a Key Note Survey (2003), 80 per cent of female maturing boomers agreed with the statement 'I make a point of taking some exercise at least once a week'. This compares to agreement by only 57 per cent of respondents in a similar in survey in 2000. Traditionally a positive attitude towards exercise tends to be prevalent among higher social classes. Awareness of the benefits of exercise is now beginning to emerge among older people in the lower social classes. This is because public sector healthcare providers such as doctors and health visitors are now placing greater emphasis on promoting the importance of exercise as an important ingredient for remaining healthy in old age (Brownson *et al.* 2001).

The increasing interest in remaining active during retirement presents major opportunities for firms in sectors such as fitness, sports, leisure and tourism. Some companies have already implemented strategies to exploit these opportunities. In the USA, for example, Fit After Fifty Corporation offers people the chance to purchase a franchise based around a fitness studio specifically targeted at providing moderately paced exercise programmes for old people (www.fitafterfifty.com). Many golf and tennis clubs now have special programmes, customized facilities and targeted events aimed at attracting more maturing boomers to become members. Within the travel industry, tour operators and hotels are offering a wide range of services aimed at older financially attractive consumers who want to activity-based vacations.

Alternative choices

Before the existence of the pharmaceutical industry, many of mankind's medical and nutritional treatments were based upon products made from a diverse range of different plants. In the last 50 years, consumer demand for health food products mainly from natural, chemical free ingredients has created new opportunities for entrepreneurs in both manufacturing and retailing. At the beginning of the 1990s there were indications that the health food market in some Western nations might be in decline. By the end of the decade, however, this trend had been reversed. A major catalyst for a return to sales growth was consumers' increasing concerns about animal husbandry practices and agricultural chemicals. These factors caused more people to become interested in the nutritional and healthcare benefits of eating natural or organically produced foods. Further stimulus to growth in the health food market occurred with creation of healthcare edu-informational internet sites. People, especially financially attractive consumers, are using search engines to gain a greater understanding of health and nutritional issues. Some of these sites also offer information about herbal products as alternative treatments for medical conditions.

The internet has permitted rapid access to the online purchasing of a wide range of different food products. Nutrition is now considered as possibly the most critical dimension of preventative healthcare. The medical profession is expressing increasing concerns about obesity damaging the quality of life for older people (Herne 1995). This is because obesity reduces mobility and raises the probability that retirees will develop chronic conditions such as cardiac problems and diabetes. Public sector organizations such as the FDA in the USA are investing in promotional and educational campaigns aimed at persuading maturing boomers to take more interest in their diet. Much of the nutritional advice being communicated is about food's calorific and nutritional content. The older population are being urged to 'go back to basics' by eating more fresh meat, eggs, dairy produce, fruits and vegetables.

The interest among financially attractive consumers in eating healthy food is a major source of new opportunity for entrepreneurial firms. Consumers seeking nutritional solutions for staying looking younger are an increasingly important source of sales revenue. Many of the new products coming onto the market are specifically targeted at the provision of products promising to fight the ageing process. Until recently, the large multinationals appeared to be uninterested in products designed to deliver nutritional benefit to older consumers. These organizations whose primary customer target remained the 18–49 age group are, however, beginning to revise the focus of their marketing efforts. National brands such as Kellogg's high fibre breakfast foods or Weight Watcher low calorie frozen meals have moved towards promoting an age-neutral positioning when communicating their products' nutritional benefits. This situation means that smaller entrepreneurial firms, which until recently have been relatively unopposed in sectors such as specialist retailing and the provision of weight control counselling services, now face competition from national brands with huge financial resources capable of supporting massive promotional campaigns.

With financially attractive consumers realizing that nutrition is an important component of a healthy lifestyle, multinational companies are directing R&D activities towards products of appeal to older people. For example an increasing number of older consumers are becoming more interested in low calorie, low fat products. The response of major manufacturers has been to seek ways of supporting maturing lifestyle aspirations by offering products that can assist in reducing the risk of certain medical conditions (e.g. low fat, low sugar content and low cholesterol products) (Business Insights 2001).

One of the fastest areas of growth for products claiming nutritional benefits has been yoghurts. Yoplait's products, for example, contain probiotic bacteria which are claimed to contribute towards supporting healthiness (Business Insights 2004). Another example is provided by Raisio, a Finnish firm, who discovered that stanol esters can reduce cholesterol levels. This led to the launch of their Benecol product range of margarines and cheeses. These firms have been followed into the market by firms such as Unilever marketing their cholesterol reducing margarine brand, Pro-Activ. The success of brands marketed on a health platform has caused other companies to offer products which contain ingredients believed to exhibit anti-ageing properties. Some of the new products being introduced are being referred to as 'nutraceuticals' because they are functional foods which blur the traditional dividing lines between foods and medicine. Antioxidants are one example of chemicals which are attracting interest in both the healthcare and the food industry. These compounds are believed to combat premature ageing by protecting the nervous system and the brain from damage leading to memory loss. There is also evidence indicating antioxidants can protect diabetics from kidney damage.

Small firm success

Case Aims: To demonstrate how American food companies are currently able to make claims for their products about their contribution towards healthier living without being required to meet FDA guidelines that apply to other healthcare products and services.

In the USA, the health food industry seeks to avoid introducing new products which could fall foul of the Federal Drug Administration. A recent example of where the developers were able to avoid the FDA demanding clinical trials prior to market launch is the product Juvenon™

(www.juvenon.com). The product is a cellular health supplement based upon a patented combination of natural micronutrients. The producer company, which is based in California, has a mission to develop and market products that help maintain vigour and functionality as we age. The product's proprietary technology was originally developed at the University of California, Berkeley where researchers discovered a nutritional supplement that enabled elderly laboratory animals to function at levels characteristic of much younger animals. The researchers found that by combining a natural, energy-boosting component (acetyl L-carnitine) with a powerful antioxidant (alpha lipoic acid) they could slow the ageing process of cells. In humans, the Juvenon™ Cellular Health Supplement has an overall effect of promoting a healthier, more energetic body. It is particularly effective in protecting tissue from toxic oxidants, which increase with normal daily stress-producing activities and exercise, as well as delaying the ageing process. The Juvenon health supplement acts on the mitochondria, the organelles within the cell where energy is produced. As we age, oxidants cause cellular damage, which accumulates over time. Oxidants affect mitochondria by causing damage to DNA, lipids and protein. The Juvenon product facilitates the entry of fuel (starches and fatty acids) into the mitochondria and stimulates production of natural antioxidants that protect the cell from age-associated increases in tissue-damaging oxidants. By marketing the product as a dietary supplement, the company has avoided FDA approval and has not been subjected to the pre-market clearance requirements that apply to the drugs industry. Another success story provided by a smaller company exploiting antioxidants to support anti-ageing claims is PomWonderful, a Californian pomegranate grower (www.pomwonderful.com). This firm has planted many acres of the Wonderful variety of pomegranate in the sunny San Joaquin Valley in Central California. The fruit which they grow has been used as basis their rapidly growing internationally distributed, Pom drink brand. The other increasingly popular anti-ageing agent is omega-3. Research appears to suggest the product keeps saturated fats moving in the bloodstream and assists kidney function. These are properties of great interest to retirees. Consequently, the CAFL Corporation in the USA has launched a range of yoghurt which produces containing omega-3.

Personal appearance

The human race has always been deeply interested in finding ways of postponing physical deterioration caused by ageing. One example from history is provided by the portraits and writings about Britain's Queen Elizabeth 1st. During the later years of her reign, she relied heavily on wigs, face paint and supportive clothing in an attempt to sustain the impossible myth of still appearing youthful. Today, with older financially attractive consumers enjoying a high level of disposable income, these individuals can be expected to purchase more products that offer the benefits of improving appearance or delaying the onset of ageing (Schindler and Holbrook 1993).

The steady rise in *per capita* income in Western nations during the last half of the twentieth century has already led to the creation of a large, global cosmetics market. This is in part reflective of society's desire to stay younger looking. Hence, firms offering products perceived as improving self image can expect to enjoy further sales growth in the future. The ability of some of today's products that claim to postpone the impact of ageing can range from the minimal (e.g. soap products containing moisturizing creams) through to rendering a complete physical transformation. However, to actually achieve this latter outcome may involve significant invasive plastic (or 'cosmetic') surgery (Gardener 2002).

The pioneering work by surgeons during the two World Wars to treat the horrendous injuries inflicted by twentieth century warfare provided the basis for the development of plastic surgery. In America during the 1930s, the leading practitioners of what was then known as 'restorative surgery', were Drs Aufricht and Maliniac. During the Second World War, another individual who extended the boundaries of rebuilding horrific facial injuries was the British surgeon, Sir Archibald McIndoe. The Hollywood studios have always sought to prolong the popularity of their top movie stars and organizations such as MGM were the first members of the entertainment industry who used plastic surgery to sustain the youthful appearance of their leading actors and actresses. Concern over the potential negative impact on cinema audiences of discovering how their favourite stars were retaining their looks meant that until the 1960s, few of the general public were aware plastic surgery had moved from a medical to a cosmetic treatment.

The first important catalyst which catapulted plastic surgery into being accepted by the general public was the introduction of silicon as a breast implant device. Despite the subsequent safety scares about breast implants during the 1990s, the whole area of cosmetic surgery has continued to prosper. In the 1970s and 1980s, some of the richest individuals in the world were surgeons based in the City of Dreams, Los Angeles. Their financial success has stimulated a rapid increase in the number of doctors wishing to become certified as plastic surgeons. This increase in the supply of qualified doctors, the development of less invasive techniques such as liposuction, and nations such as Poland offering low price surgery, have together permitted a growing number of consumers being able to afford plastic surgery to deny the impact of ageing on their physical appearance. By 2005 the global annual revenue for the cosmetic surgery industry was estimated to exceed $20 billion (Hanson 2008).

Beauty and other services

Case Aims: To illustrate how the growing demand for enhancing physical appearance has led to the emergence of new businesses involved in the health tourism industry.

Independent hospitals and clinics in nations which have lower than average health costs have moved to exploit the growing demand for plastic surgery by making their services available to consumers living in the Western world (Anon 2006b). Mills & Mills Medical Group, a cosmetic surgery and aesthetic medicine company are based in Marbella, Spain. Founded by David and Debra Mills, the company benefit proposition is their 'Circle of Care' healthcare. This involves cosmetic surgery in a modern, upmarket clinic, financial loans, travel to Spain and accommodation. The firm's emphasis is on surgery accompanied by more enjoyable recuperation and aftercare (www.millsmedical.com). Another example is provided by the Australian company Gorgeous Getaways, which offers a complete cosmetic surgery package in a private hospital in Malaysia. The firm specializes in offering what they call an holistic experience. Their focus is upon refreshing and restoring the body and spirit with personal beauty packages, including cosmetic surgery procedures, and complementary services such as dentistry, optical, diet, exercise and pampering packages. They promise the retirees that they will return home with an inner sparkle and renewed energy for life (www.gorgeousgetaways.com) In the UK, the use of overseas providers is not just restricted to plastic surgery. Older people, frustrated by long wait times in the National Health Service and the high prices quoted by British private sector providers, are becoming 'healthcare tourists'. Their horizons are not limited to traditional holiday destinations such as France or Spain but include Eastern Europe and the Far East. Eastern Europe is enjoying a huge increase in people arriving for medical treatment, particularly Poland, Hungary and the Czech Republic. India is also targeting the UK as a prime market for health tourism. The Indian government has introduced a special visa for people going to the country for healthcare. The Medical Tourist Company was set up in 2005 and through hospitals in Delhi, Chennai and Bangalore, offers hip and knee replacement, cosmetic surgery, dental treatments, weight-reduction programmes, corrective eye surgery and heart procedures (www.medicaltourist.co.uk). For a knee replacement, the company charges £5,000, which includes the cost of transport and accommodation. This compares with the £10,000 quoted for just the operation alone in the UK.

(Source: Horowitz and Rosensweig 2007)

Traditional solution

Plastic surgery is still a very young product when contrasted with the health and beauty industry, which has been offering skin care treatments since almost the beginning of time. The Romans, for example, were strong believers in the ability of mineral waters and salt water to treat a range of ailments, many of which were associated with ageing. Long after Rome became an empire, Europeans continued to believe in the benefits of mineral springs. Down through the centuries, spa towns remained the chosen destination of the wealthy. 'Taking the waters' began to decline in popularity between the two World Wars, in part because the availability of cosmetics marketed by major firms had become a more widely, socially acceptable alternative for sustaining a youthful appearance. Recently, there has been recognition that the resort spa concept is in need of rejuvenation, but that any rescue attempt would have to go beyond just offering mineral water or salt water treatments. This has led to beauty spas being opened, which offer a much broader range of skin care treatments to residential and non-residential clients. Treatments include services such as massage, health diets, saunas and skin toning therapies using their proprietary brands of creams and lotions (McNeill and Ragins 2005).

A Swedish miracle?

Case Aims: To illustrate how science and an entrepreneurial orientation can permit a new small player to enter the ageing skincare market.

Lifes2good is an Irish-based company who distribute a range of health, beauty and lifestyle products. In 2006, the company launched an anti-ageing product range, Nourella Delay, which had been developed by Professor J. Wandstein. He is a Swedish dermatologist whose research led to the identification of the anti-ageing product formulation (Anon 2006c). This scientist spent 10 years researching why Eskimos have hair and skin which is much healthier than other European races. He concluded Eskimos' diet being rich in marine protein, was probably a key factor. This led him to develop a food supplement using marine protein and organic silica. His skin cream product also contains these ingredients and is fortified with vitamin C plus a soluble form of vitamin A. The food supplement is claimed to rejuvenate the skin's inner structure by improving thickness and elasticity. By penetrating down to the skin's dermis, the cream can repair visible damage and reduce signs of ageing. Clinical trials by the University of Helsinki revealed that the supplement can improve the skin's ability to retain moisture by 300 per cent, increase thickness by 200 per cent and improve elasticity by 68 per cent.

Until the twentieth century, the cosmetics industry tended to be dominated by pharmacists and herbalists formulating products for sale to their local customers (Rose 2002). Many of today's multinational beauty companies started life as small business run by an innovative entrepreneur. In 1909, Eugene Schueller founded the French Harmless Colouring Company, which evolved into L'Oréal. Two years later, Paul Biersdorf, a German chemist, developed the first cream to bind together oil and water. This innovation led to the creation of the Nivea Company. Meanwhile in the USA, two twentieth century industry giants were still running small beauty shops: namely Elizabeth Arden and Helena Rubinstein. As these various businesses grew in size, they began to use mass marketing techniques to communicate the importance of remaining youthful and beautiful. The promotional focus of these companies has primarily been the 18–49 year age group. This focus on the 18–49 age group by large companies has left smaller firms free to supply products and services targeted at older women seeking ways of postponing or hiding the impact of ageing. The vast majority of these small firms operate with single outlets such as hairdressers and beauty salons. Some entrepreneurial companies have developed proprietary formulations of tonics, creams or lotions which they distribute through pharmacies and independent grocery stores.

With their origins rooted in soap manufacturing, the multinational giants such as Unilever and Proctor & Gamble have been in the skin care business for well over a 100 years. Brands such as Dove Soap with added moisturizer were among the first to exploit a mass marketing approach to persuade women of the benefits of including health and beauty aids (HbAs) as part of their weekly shop. By dominating the supermarket shelves, these companies now command a lion's share of categories such as soaps, shampoos, toothpastes and deodorants. Executives in upmarket companies such as L'Oréal and Estée Lauder have tended to perceive themselves as being more involved in the 'real' beauty business and through their creativity and flair, able to better fulfil women's aspirations over sustaining a youthful appearance. They appear to consider companies such as Colgate Palmolive as the elephants of the Health and Beauty Aid (HbA) industry, slowly plodding along, fighting battles for market share with other supermarket brands. The more glamorous corporations in the beauty industry apparently ignored the possibility that one or more of these major elephants might one day launch anti-ageing products. For example the major cosmetics companies initially seemed completely unconcerned by Proctor & Gamble's acquisition of the Olay brand, a well established skin care range offering 'younger looking skin'.

By the mid-1990s, it was apparent that the older person market had become the new battle ground for generating higher brand shares (Anon 1994). Alarm bells began to ring in the upmarket French beauty industry firms when the somewhat middle of the road company, Nivea, enjoyed a significant increase in sales from launching their Visage Intensive Moisturizing Gel containing thalaspheres and other moisturizing agents. The major cosmetic companies realized that ultimately the battle for market domination would be won by the brands offering the best anti-ageing products. Estée Lauder entered the fray with products such as Advanced Stop Signs by Clinique. L'Oréal's Lancôme brand was the platform upon which their Resolution Facial Skincare product was launched (Key Note Studies 2003).

One of the first major branded goods companies which awakened to the huge revenue opportunities with offering anti-ageing products was Proctor & Gamble (Anon 2005). The company used their vast R&D resources to formulate complex amino-peptides which are believed to stimulate regeneration of cells in the skin's outer layers. Incorporation of these compounds into the Olay brand range has permitted the delivery of a product superiority claim in the anti-ageing market. Leading Proctor & Gamble's battle for market share has been their Regenerist cream product. The company claims the product contain the vitamins and minerals capable of fighting the 'seven signs of ageing'.

Beauty and the bacteria

Case Aims: To describe the path of discovery for a medical treatment originally developed to solve one healthcare problem which was subsequently evolved into a globally successful anti-ageing, beauty treatment.

In the USA, events such as the tragic impact of the drug thalidomide and Ralph Nader's crusade against the failure of the car manufacturers to put safety ahead of profits, led to closer oversight of industry by organizations such as the Food and Drug Administration (FDA). Although the FDA regulations have reduced the chances of another thalidomide tragedy, their stringent requirement for extensive proof that new chemical compounds are safe has added huge costs to the process of developing new medical treatments. It is now virtually impossible for an individual entrepreneur or small firm to succeed as a leading edge innovator in the pharmaceutical industry because they lack the financial resources required to gain FDA approval for their new discovery. Where a medical breakthrough occurs in the SME sector, the inventor will usually licence or sell their idea to a multinational corporation. This was the case for the world's most popular non-surgical anti-ageing procedure, Botox (Anon 2006d). Since Victorian times, the bacterium *Clostridium botulinum* has been known to produce a toxin which causes food poisoning. Ingestion of the toxin can lead to a death-inducing paralysis. This bacteria was used in the assassination of the German SS General Reinhard Heydrich during the Second World War and, even more infamously, injected into cigars intended for Fidel Castro. In the late 1960s, researchers began to examine the ability of botulinum toxins to treat various neurological disorders. The chemicals interfere with muscle spasms by blocking nerve impulses, thereby temporarily relaxing muscles. In the 1980s, the San Francisco ophthalmologist Alan Scott, discovered that a tiny amount of the toxin injected into the eyelid could stop uncon-trolled blinking. Scott patented his discovery, but because he lacked the resources to gain the FDA approval for his new idea, he sold the patent to the

American pharmaceutical company, Allergan. This company, based in Irvine, California, specializes in the commercialization of therapeutic agents for treating conditions and diseases of the eye. They worked on commercializing Scott's patent as the basis for treating eye muscle disorders. In 1989, the company received FDA approval for their new drug Botox to be used in the treatment of uncontrollable blinking and crossed eyes. Allergan's scientists observed that when Botox was used to treat eye disorders, an injection of the drug led to softening of the frown lines between the eyebrows. The company filed an application with the FDA to approve Botox as a non-surgical cosmetic treatment on the basis that the product reduced severe brow furrows, horizontal forehead wrinkles and 'crows feet'. The procedure for using Botox is to inject the product into facial areas using a very fine needle. Between 24 hours and 10 days, Botox causes the muscles in the treated area to relax. The peak impact on wrinkle reduction typically occurs 2–3 weeks after the injection and the effect lasts for 3–6 months. In 1997, Allergan appointed a European, David Pyott, then running the Novaris company, to re-invigorate the company's operations by creating a leaner corporate structure and improving product commercialization capability. Pyott's claim to fame is being the driving force behind launching Botox as a non-surgical cosmetic treatment. The level of validity that lies behind this claim might be questioned by some, but is true is he was the chairman when in April 2002, the FDA approved Botox as cosmetic treatment. The speed with which Botox penetrated the skin care market has been amazing. For example, within a year after FDA approval, over 2 million Botox injections had been given. Initially Botox was used by plastic surgeons and dermatologists. Subsequently, other providers such as dentists have entered the market. Allergan retains control over approximately 90 per cent of the world Botox market. Recognizing cosmetics represent a greater opportunity than ophthalmic pharmaceuticals, Pyott has sought to acquire new products to compliment the Botox range. At the end of 2005, he outbid Arizona-based Medicis Pharmaceutical, and bought the French collagen producer, Inamed. This acquisition has provided access to the market for fillers used to thicken lips and, perhaps more controversially, the silicon breast implant business. Inamed is also a player in the lucrative weight loss market by offering a rubber 'lap band' product. This medical device, similar to stomach staples, is used to create a small pouch above the stomach; thereby tricking the body into thinking it has just been fed. The Allergen Corporation may soon be facing competition from new firms entering the market exploiting breakthroughs in gene therapy. One example is provided by GeneLink Incorporated (www.dermagenetics.com). This organization, created in 1994, developed the world's first Family DNA Bank and Hereditary Genetic Information Service. The company is using this knowledge to pioneer DNA tests that can facilitate the creation of 'genetically guided' health, beauty and wellness products. The company markets and licenses its proprietary tests to the $1.4 trillion cosmetics, nutritional supplement and healthcare industries.

A new exploitation of DNA testing technology is being undertaken via the company's subsidiary, Dermagenetics. Skin care professionals can mail a mouth swab of a client's DNA to the Dermagenetics laboratory where a selected panel of single nucleotide polymorphisms (or 'SNPs') are analysed. The SNP panel incorporates an analysis of key skin health genes which contain the codes for enzymes that are part of the natural skin cell repair and defence mechanisms. The data permit measurement of a client's genetic propensity for collagen breakdown; photo ageing; wrinkling; skin ageing; the skin's ability to tolerate environment pollutants and overall skin health. Client specific skin enhancing anti-ageing products are then formulated by adding the individual's ideal active ingredients to a proprietary based formula. During recent clinical tests, placebo creams were compared with the Dermagenetics 'genetically guided' products. For those using the genetically guided formulations, 62 per cent reported substantial reduction in wrinkles after 14 days of treatment. After 56 days, the number of participants reporting reduction in wrinkles rose to 70 per cent.

References

Anon (2006a) 'Health tourists sign up for sun, sea and surgery', *The Independent*, London, 2 July, pp. 4–5.

Anon (2006b) 'Research has shown exercise can assist seniors make a more rapid recovery from invasive surgery', www.ScienceJournal.com.

Anon (2006c) 'The new "Arctic" skin nutrition programme that freezes ageing', *The Sunday Express*, London, 2 July, p. 46.

Anon (2006d) 'Mr Botox clears up any City worry lines', *The Sunday Times*, London, 25 June, Section 3, p. 7.

Anon (2005) 'P&G groomed for global dominance: Gillette strives for cutting-edge expertise', *Strategic Direction* Vol. 21, No. 10, pp. 12–15.

Anon (1994) 'Waking up the wider market potential: product development will be the key factor', *The Grocer*, pp. 46–8.

Brownson, R.C., Baker, E.A., Housemann, R.A., Brennan, L.K. and Bacak, S.J. (2001) 'Environmental and policy determinants of physical activity in the United States', *American Journal of Public Health*, Vol. 91, No. 12; pp. 1995–2014.

Business Insights (2004) 'New profit opportunities for health and nutrition to 2009', *Business Insight Report*, London.

Business Insights (2001) 'Growth strategies in dairy products', *Business Insight Reports*, London.

Calhoun, J.G., Banaszak-Holl, J. Hearld, L.R. and Larson, D.K. (2006) 'Current marketing practices in the nursing home market', *Journal of Healthcare Management*, Vol. 51, No. 3, pp. 185–204.

Calver, S., Wolf, V. and Phillips, J. (1993) 'Leisure in later life', *International Journal of Contemporary Hospitality Management*, Vol. 5, No. 1, pp 4–10.

Castle, N.G. (2005) 'Nursing home closures, changes in ownership and competition', *Inquiry-Excellus Health Plan*, Vol. 24, No. 3, pp. 281–93.

Center for Medicare Services. (2004) *Guide to Medicare Preventative Services*, Center for Medicare and Medicaid Services, US Department of Health and Human Services, Washington, Publication CMS-10110.

Daemmrich, A. (2004) 'Medicine, science, and Merck', *Business History Review*, Vol. 78, No. 4, pp. 770–83.

DeVaney, S. A. and Haejeoing, K. (2003) 'Older self-employed workers and planning for the future', *Journal of Consumer Affairs*, Vol. 37, No. 1, pp. 123–31.

Dilworth, J.E.L. and Kingsbury, N. (2005) 'Home-to-job spill over for generation X, boomers, and matures: a comparison', *Journal of Family and Economic Issues*, Vol. 26, No. 2, pp. 267–78.

Donelan, K., Blendon, R.J., Schoen, C. and Binns, K. (2000) 'The elderly in five nations: the importance of universal coverage', *Health Affairs*, Vol. 19, No. 3, pp. 226–36.

Gardener, K. (2002) 'Cosmetic surgery: the cutting edge of commercial medicine in America', *Enterprise & Society*, Vol. 3, No. pp. 183–94.

Guadilliere, J. and Lowy, I. (1998) *The Invisible Industrialist: Manufacturers and the Production of Scientific Knowledge*, (Science, Technology and Medicine in Modern History Series) New York: St Martin's Press,.

Guy, B.S., Rittenberg, T.L. and Hawes, D.K. (1994) 'Dimensions and characteristics of time perceptions and perspectives among older consumers', *Psychology & Marketing*, Vol. 11, No. 1, pp. 35–56.

Hanson, F. (2008) 'A revolution in healthcare', *Review Institute of Public Affairs*, Vol. 59, No. 4, pp. 43–6.

Harmon, S. and Ward, C.B. (2007) 'Complementary and alternative medicines: awareness and attitudes', *Academy of Health Care Management Journal*, Vol. 3, No. 1/2, pp. 1–17.

Herne, S. (1995) 'Research on food choice and nutritional status in elderly people: a review', *British Food Journal*, Vol. 97, No. 9, pp. 12–30.

Horowitz, M.D. and Rosensweig, J.A. (2007) Medical tourism – health care in the global economy. *Physician Executive,* Vol. 33, No. 6, pp. 24–30.

Key Note Studies (2003) 'Women over 45', *Key Note Market Assessment Report*, London: Key Note.

Mathur, A. and Moschis, G.P. (1999) 'Socialization influences on preparation for later life', *Journal of Marketing Practice*, Vol. 5, No. 6/7/8, pp. 163–72.

Minda, J. (2004) 'Help wanted: life experience preferred', *Management Review*, Vol. 78, No. 1, pp. 51–6.

McCune, J. (1995) 'The face of tomorrow', *Journal of Business Strategy*, Vol. 16, No. 3, pp. 50–6.

McDermott, S., Moran, R., Platt, T. and Isaac, T. (2005) 'Heart disease, schizophrenia, and affective psychoses: epidemiology of risk in primary care', *Community Mental Health Journal*, Vol. 41, No. 6, pp. 747–58.

McNeill, K.R. and Ragins, E.J. (2005) 'Staying in the spa marketing game: trends, challenges, strategies and techniques', *Journal of Vacation Marketing*, Vol. 11, No. 1, pp. 31–40.

Merlis, M. (2000) 'Caring for the frail elderly: an international review', *Health Affairs*, Vol. 19, No. 3, pp. 141–50.

Miller, N.J. and Kim, S. (1999) 'The importance of older consumers to small business survival: evidence from rural Iowa', *Journal of Small Business Management*, Vol. 37, No. 4, pp. 1–15.

Powell, J.L. and Wahidin, A. (2008) 'Understanding old age and victimization: a critical exploration', *International Journal of Sociology and Social Policy*, Vol. 28, No. 3/4, pp. 90–103.

Rose, J.S. (2002) 'Beauty and business: commerce, gender, and culture in modern America', *Business History Review*, Vol. 76, No. 2, pp. 393–6.

Schindler, R.M. and Holbrook, M.B. (1993) 'Critical periods in the development of men's and women's tastes in personal appearance', *Psychology & Marketing*, Vol. 10, No. 6, pp. 549–65.

Smith, P. (2006) 'Looking for a lift to take business higher', *The Daily Telegraph*, London, 13 June, p. B9.

Yu, H., Fairhurst, A.E. and Lennon, S.J. (1996) 'Small retail store buyers' response to apparel markets', *Journal of Small Business Management*, Vol. 34, No. 4, pp. 14–23.

11 B2B marketing

Generic principles of marketing to financially attractive consumers (FACs)

The coverage of issues in Chapter 11 is designed to illustrate the generic principles of marketing to FACs in relation to:

1   As revenue in B2B markets comes from derived demand which ultimately is based upon the level of sales in consumer markets, it is advisable that B2B marketers should focus on meeting the needs of members of supply chains which sell to FACs. This guidance is based upon the fact that these consumers' markets are likely to be the greatest source of future derived demand.
2   The diversity of B2B market systems requires that the marketer will need to analyse market system structures to determine which provides the largest potential for exploiting the derived demand that will be generated by FACs.
3   Higher profitability in B2B markets will come from developing close relationships with those downstream members of a supply chain whose strategy is based upon providing high quality goods to FACs.
4   In those cases where a B2B company's existing industrial customers are not interested, or alternatively not capable, of operating in FAC markets, then the B2B may need to consider attempting to become a member of a different supply chain.
5   In those cases where a B2B company's existing products or services are not relevant to meeting the needs supply chain customers who are serving FAC markets, then innovation activities should be implemented to overcome this weakness.
6   Successful innovation will usually require understanding the needs of FACs. This knowledge may be available from the company's B2B

downstream customers in a supply chain or, in some cases, may require the firm to become involved in their own research with FACs.

7   In terms of prioritizing which FAC markets should be of interest, the B2B marketer will need to undertake a concurrent assessment of which markets offer the greatest opportunity to be a source of derived demand and which of these markets are best served by the B2B's internal organizational capabilities.

8   Where the B2B firm lacks the resources to implement a successful innovation programme to exploit FAC markets, the most effective solution is for the firm to become a member of a horizontal or vertical business innovation network.

Market opportunities

Most theories and case materials concerning the world of marketing are concerned with the practices and processes within consumer markets. This is despite the fact that there are many more companies involved in business-to-business (or 'B2B') marketing. One possible explanation for this situation is that individuals who work in marketing perceive consumer markets as being more glamorous. This perception is caused by being involved in products and services known to the general public and the opportunity for being responsible for promotional budgets much greater than those typically encountered in industrial markets.

The ultimate destiny of all firms is determined by customer demand. In the case of B2B operations, forecasting future demand is complicated by the existence of what is known as 'derived demand'. This concept is based upon the fact that ultimately B2B company sales are determined not by the purchase behaviour of the firm's customers, but by the activities of firms further downstream in the supply chain. The performance of these latter organizations is in turn controlled by the prevailing trend in consumer purchasing behaviour. Thus, for example, an electronics company might develop a new, low energy microchip which is used as a component by a company manufacturing security alarms which are marketed by distributors who provide security services to owners of upmarket houses. In this case, the derived demand for the new microchip is determined by the number of financially attractive consumers that decide to have their home security systems upgraded.

Understanding maturing boomer demand

Case Aims: These are intended to illustrate how data in the public domain concerning consumer market demand can be utilized by firms upstream in a B2B supply chain to assess the probable nature of derived demand.

A characteristic of some B2B markets is that downstream members in the supply chain may not have an accurate understanding of consumer demand in their market sector. In other sectors, major downstream supply chain members may have acquired such data through market research, but are unwilling to share what they perceive as confidential information with their suppliers. Under these circumstances, another option available to the B2B organization seeking to understand possible consumer sales trends in the market sector which they supply is to review data that are available on consumer expenditure or consumption patterns by age group within a nation. An example of how such data can be useful is provided by an analysis undertaken using US Department of Labour Statistics to determine annual expenditure by employed and retired individuals aged 50+ (Anon 1995).

Married couple		Single male		Single woman	
Working	Retired	Working	Retired	Working	Retired
$24,340	$17,540	$18,562	$11,340	$14,048	$9,369

Another study undertaken by Abdel-Ghany and Sharpe (1997) utilized data from the US Department of Labour Consumer Expenditure Survey to develop further understanding of the expenditure patterns of 'young-olds' (age 65–74) and 'old-olds' in the USA. From their analysis, they generated the following data on annual expenditure by household:

Expenditure Category*	Young-old	Old-old
Food at home	2,982	2,290
Food away from home	953	646
Alcohol and tobacco	366	204
Housing	6,310	5,562
Apparel and apparel services	825	524
Transportation	4,117	2,240
Healthcare	2,263	2,571
Entertainment	996	481
Personal care	274	217
Reading materials and education	232	213
Cash contributions	303	381
Personal insurance	1,314	341
Miscellaneous	398	315
Total average expenditure/household	21,333	15,989

*Source: Abdel-Ghany and Sharpe (1997)

These researchers also utilized the data to develop regression equations for each expenditure category that would permit data to be broken down by variables such as geographic region, education level of head of household, household size, ethnicity and family type.

Another feature of B2B markets is that the number of customers is usually much lower than in a consumer market and, furthermore, each of these customers usually purchases a significant proportion of the firm's total sales. In many cases, the B2B firm is engaged in supplying components or services which are utilized by a larger company for incorporation into the products that they manufacture. This output may be sold to another B2B customer (e.g. vehicles sold to truck fleet operators) or via an intermediary into a consumer market (e.g. vehicles sold to the general public). In other cases, the B2B firm may be supplying products or services to organizations in either the public or private sector which are directly involved in the provision of services to consumers (e.g. a drugs company supplying hospitals).

Meeting needs of customers and the marketing processes undertaken by the B2B usually occur within one of the supply chain types summarized in Figure 11.1. One supply chain type is where the B2B supplier is involved in delivering products to a manufacturer. This latter company is then responsible for the production and distribution of consumer goods such as food, home electronics or clothing. Another type of supply chain in which the B2B marketer may be involved is where the main providers are public sector organizations delivering

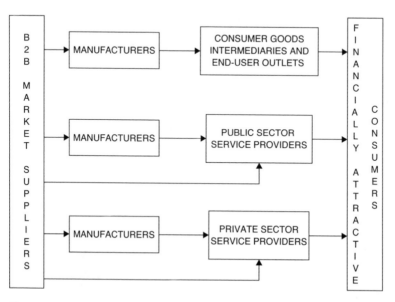

Figure 11.1 Examples of alternative B2B supply chains.

services such as healthcare. A third type of supply chain is where private sector organizations are engaged in the provision of services.

Given the future impact of population ageing on consumer expenditure, the B2B firm should determine the plans of their supply chain members in relation to their future intentions concerning the exploitation of markets containing financially attractive consumers. As downstream supply chain members may be unwilling to share their confidential plans for their future with suppliers, the B2B supplier may be advised to gain greater understanding of undertaking research to acquire knowledge about the value added processes of these customers (Crain and Abraham 2008). The data sources that can be used in this research may include face-to-face discussions with customers, discussions with distributors or inter-mediaries, customer companies' annual reports, financial community reports, and materials issued by companies as an element of their public relations activities. The aim in utilizing acquired data is to identify the core competences of downstream supply chain members. Most companies can be expected to rely on the same core competences in the implementation of any new future strategy. Hence, the analysis of their current operations can usually provide an invaluable indicator of a downstream supply chain company's probable future business plans.

An example of this type of analysis is provided by the data one would acquire about the global athletic shoe company, Nike. Available data would reveal the company strategy has been radically revised following their recognition that shoe manufacturing is now a commodity business. In response to this situation, Nike has focused on further developing core competences in product development and the marketing of branded goods. To provide added support for their branded goods operation, the company has opened their own retail outlets. In addition to pro-viding greater control over end-user markets, these outlets are invaluable sources of real-time data on changing consumer attitudes and purchase behaviour. As Nike in recent years has already moved into the supply of upmarket branded athletic shoes to health-orientated financially attractive consumers, a B2B marketer in this industry seeking to expand sales to Nike would be advised to concentrate on developing a plan based upon supplying products or services which could assist this customer to develop new innovations suited to meeting the needs of the 50+ consumer.

B2B market opportunities

Case Aims: To identify sectors where increased demand from maturing boomer markets offer revenue growth opportunities for B2B companies supplying products or services to other companies further downstream in a supply chain.

Virtually every B2B market offers opportunities for companies to exploit the growth of demand from the customers downstream in their sector's supply chain where future revenue is expected to come from sales to 50+

consumers (Doka 1992). Some of the key market sectors where one can expect the downstream customers of B2B companies to be marketing more products and services include:

1   *Home products.* These include security systems, home entertainment systems, comfort items such as air conditioning, and housekeeping, repair and maintenance services.
2   *Healthcare.* Older consumers will need prescription and over-the-counter drugs, corrective devices such as hearing aids, and a variety of health-related services such as home healthcare, adult day care, respite care and nursing home care.
3   *Wellness and youth-enhancing products.* Many older consumers want to look and feel as young as possible. Products and services that will be in demand include exercise equipment, health-club memberships and weight-control products; foods low in cholesterol or salt; vitamins; and products that mask or retard ageing such as cosmetics, hair colouring and skin moisturizers.
4   *Recreational and leisure services.* While some mature consumers are home centred, many enjoy travel and entertainment away from home. There will be great opportunities for hotels, travel services, restaurants and entertainment and hospitality services in general.
5   *Educational services.* The need to learn and grow never stops, and older consumers have the time to indulge intellectual interests. A range of educational services will prove appealing, from educational travel such as Elderhostel (an international organization that provides low-cost housing and 'mini courses' at college campuses) to community education to credit-bearing programmes aimed at preparing older people for second careers.

Strategies and priorities

As summarized in Figure 11.2, there are four different strategic implications confronting the B2B firm. The applicability of each strategy is dependent upon the degree of interest either the firm or their downstream supply chain members have in the future opportunities presented by the provision of goods and services to financially attractive consumers.

Where neither the B2B firm nor members of their supply chain are interested in financially attractive consumers, then a *status quo* strategy will probably remain in effect. Should the B2B firm have no interest in financially attractive consumer markets even though supply chain members perceive significant opportunities, there is the possibility these latter organizations will go elsewhere for some of their future supplies. This could reduce the B2B firm's revenue. Hence, B2B firms facing this potential scenario would be well advised to locate new opportunities to

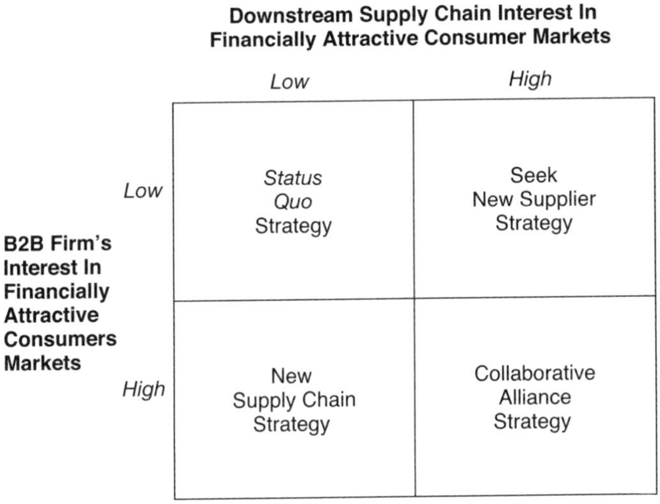

Downstream Supply Chain Interest In
Financially Attractive Consumer Markets

	Low	High
Low	Status Quo Strategy	Seek New Supplier Strategy
High	New Supply Chain Strategy	Collaborative Alliance Strategy

B2B Firm's Interest In Financially Attractive Consumers Markets

Figure 11.2 Supply chain interest assessment matrix.

compensate for a possible decline in future sales from their current industrial market customers.

Where the B2B firm perceives opportunity in financially attractive consumer markets, but this viewpoint is not shared by members of the existing supply, the firm may be forced to identify alternative channels through which to gain access to these increasingly important consumers. In this instance, there may be two options available to the B2B firm. One is to identify another supply chain company engaged in servicing financially attractive consumers. The other option is for the B2B firm to consider the feasibility of direct marketing to this consumer target within either their existing or a completely new market sector. Possibly the most attractive proposition is where a mutual interest in financially attractive consumers exists across all members of the supply chain. This will permit collaborative alliances to be created. These alliances will have the common objective of permitting supply chain members to jointly evolve suitable strategies for exploiting opportunities for revenue growth which may emerge as the result of population ageing.

In B2B markets, a firm may identify more than one opportunity to work with a supply chain customer to service financially attractive consumers' needs. Under these circumstances it would probably be advisable to determine which market sector should be given priority and, where possible, determine an optimal market entry strategy. There are two dimensions influencing such decisions: market attractiveness and the firm's capability to exploit the sector. A market attractiveness assessment can be undertaken by determining which factors are crucial to success. These will vary by industrial sector, but common attributes often include variables such as ease of market entry, strength of customer demand, market growth rate, intensity of competition, ability to access potential customers, financial resources required to service the market sector and the power customers exert over suppliers. For each factor the firm can allocate a score on a scale of 1–10. A score of <5 would indicate a low attractiveness and a score of ≥5, a high level of attractiveness. By summing the scores and dividing by the number of variables used in the analysis, a mean overall score is generated for market attractiveness.

In the case of internal company capability, again the variables selected will vary by industrial sector. Some of the more generic variables that may apply in most situations include financial resources, marketing competence, innovation competence, product/service performance, quality, location, modernity of process systems and the age of fixed assets. The firm can allocate a score on a scale of 1–10 for each capability variable. Then by summing these scores and dividing by the number of variables used, this generates a mean score for the firm's overall internal capability. The implications of the two scores can be assessed by using a decision matrix of the type shown in Figure 11.3. This matrix presents the B2B firm with four different strategic options.

Opportunities which fall into the high attractiveness/high capability cell usually provide the greatest opportunity because they will probably permit the B2B firm to attain a leadership position in the supply of products and services to downstream members in the supply chain. The second cell, which is slightly less attractive, is that of low capability/high sector attractiveness. This sector exhibits the characteristics of offering high revenue generation, but success in this cell does demand capability improvement by the B2B firm. Hence, in most cases implementation of this strategy will be dependent upon the firm having the necessary organizational skills and being able to access the financial resources needed to fund the capability upgrade programme.

Opportunities which fall in the low capability/low market attractiveness cell provide minimal revenue potential and hence should usually be ignored. Where

Market Sector Attractiveness

		Low	High
B2B Firm Capability	Low	Financially Attractive Consumer Market Avoidance Strategy	Financially Attractive Consumer Capability Development Strategy
	High	Financially Attractive Consumer Sub-contractor Role Strategy	Financially Attractive Consumer Supplier Leadership Strategy

Figure 11.3 A market sector decision matrix.

the market sector is not very attractive, but the firm has high internal capabilities, then one solution is to share these competencies with another firm. Usually this latter firm will be a lead supplier in the sector supplying financially attractive consumers. This solution will permit the B2B firm to adopt the role of sub-contractor, leaving the other organization to remain responsible for managing market entry activities.

Opportunities for B2B companies

Case Aims: To illustrate how B2B electronics companies can exploit maturing boomer markets by acting as a sub-contractor for a large company engaged in the construction of new upmarket homes.

A key advantage for firms in B2B markets, by supplying their products to other B2B organizations further down the supply chain, is that one or more of these latter organizations will assume the more expensive responsibility of marketing products or services to consumers. One example of this effect is provided in the US electronics industry where some firms developing or manufacturing electronic devices are supplying these to the developers and construction firms involved in the creation of new, assisted accommodation and gated communities which are increasingly popular among maturing boomers (Anon 2005). For example SunRiver St George, a 55-plus retirement community just south of St George, Utah has been built with the latest home monitoring and communications technology. Among the innovations are fibreoptic cable to each house installed by a sub-contractor in the communications business that enable residents to receive cable television and achieve simultaneous speeds of 1 gigabyte per second access to the internet. As well as providing access to the internet and multi-channel television programmes, the system provides information on community events and association news, which helps residents when scheduling their social events on the on-screen electronic diaries. Linked into the network is an integrated security, HVAC and lighting control, which permits the community's security company to monitor residents' homes, which increases the residents' feelings of personal safety. Another aspect of the fibreoptic system is an interactive online communications network which permits residents to participate in events such as the homeowners association meetings while remaining seated in their own living rooms. The advent of internet links when coupled with video-camera systems are now becoming increasingly popular among maturing boomers when purchasing a new house where they wish to relocate upon retirement (Zalud 2002). For example Cenuco Security of Boca Raton, Florida has developed the system that includes two home-based colour cameras, a carrier service, gateway server access and software to run the webcam system on a home computer. Homeowners on a centralized home security service can take advantage of

48 hours of image archiving to look backwards in time. These types of system also allow homeowners to monitor their homes from another location when they are away from home. One electronics company has gone even further and developed their remote monitoring iRobot-C product which is an internet-controlled 'physical avatar' (Lewis 2001). The iRobot-C is able to prowl the house or garden and can even climb stairs. The machine transmits over the internet real-time pictures from a nose-mounted videocam, with sound picked up by the machine's microphone array. The user controls the robot remotely through simple mouse clicks on a browser screen.

Major consumer goods brands have also needed to forge closer links with suppliers in order to respond to rising demand among consumers, especially those in the financially attractive consumer category, for more products formulated from more natural, preferably organic, ingredients (Fuhrman 2008). The demand for such products is based upon a growing perception that products and drinks formulated from natural, organic ingredients are much healthier. This demand for such ingredients has been beneficial both for developing nations where many of the plants are grown which are now in demand and from the companies which utilize these crops to formulate ingredients that are supplied to the major food and drink manufacturers. BI Nutraceuticals in California, for example, produces a line of natural and organic superfruit extracts, including acai, acerola, blueberry, eleuthero root, ginkgo, goji berry, grape seed, guarana seed and yerba maté. Since these are ingredients for use in the formulation of 'natural products', the use of preservatives during growing or in further processing is prohibited. As a result these organic ingredients have a shelf life less than that of a synthetic equivalent. This means that suppliers of these ingredients need to work closely with beverage and food manufacturers to develop physical processing and packaging solutions that can lead to achieving an adequate shelf life for the final product.

Market relationship management

The characteristic of B2B markets, of a few buyers each purchasing a significant quantity of goods, means that the core of the marketing process is the management of the interaction between the supplier and each of their customers. In most B2B markets this responsibility falls upon the shoulders of the company salesforce. Other promotional activities such as advertising and sales promotions which are common in consumer goods markets are used to a much lesser degree in B2B marketing.

The basic role of the salesforce has remained unchanged for decades in the sense that their primary responsibility is that of creating and maintaining revenue flows for their employers' organizations. In those cases where the customer is buying standard specification goods and there are a number of equally capable suppliers, then the sales person is essentially involved in sustaining a transactional process. In such cases, success is often dependent upon matching or beating the prices offered by other suppliers. As technology has become more complicated and the role of the B2B supplier has evolved towards more that of acting as a source of specialist expertise, their customers, who continue to exhibit a transactional orientation are probably being somewhat myopic. This is because where a customer's purchase decision is based on price, supplier profit margins will be low and the supplier can rarely afford to provide the level of augmented service required to fulfil the role of assisting the customer to enhance and improve the technical performance of products being manufactured (Good and Schultz 2005). In markets where downstream customers are seeking to retain market share through the provision of superior performance products or services, this perspective has led to the emergence of an alternative approach to B2B marketing where the supplier and customer seek to establish a mutually beneficial relationship. The costs of supporting a salesforce engaged in building closer relationships with customers in B2B markets will be high. This is because sales staff will have to be technically qualified to work with customer personnel, such as scientists and engineers. Additionally, with the sales team spending more time working in an advisory capacity, this will reduce their availability to be generating orders from other customers. Compensation for these increased costs will accrue from the fact that profit margins will be higher because customer purchase decisions are not based on the lowest available price. An additional benefit to the supplier is where a close working relationship has been established; this tends to significantly increase customer loyalty (Brennan *et al.* 2003).

The concept of organizations working more closely together has in recent years led to B2B firms learning from their counterparts in consumer service sector markets and adopting a customer relationship management (CRM) orientation. Underlying the concept of CRM is the philosophy that both parties are committed to the creation and ongoing operation of a mutually beneficial collaboration (Wilson 2006). The issue of building close relationships to provide stronger customer loyalty has become even more important as the internet began to emerge as a new source of competitive threat in B2B markets. This is because the first application of the internet was to permit price-orientated firms purchasing standard specification components to move from domestic to global sourcing when seeking to attract bids from the lowest priced suppliers. These transactional-orientated firms subsequently evolved their internet systems to permit further cost reductions in their procurement operations, by automation of the entire online order placement, logistics administration and payment cycle process (Singh *et al.* 2007).

Initially some B2B industry observers predicted that the use of the internet to assist price-based transactional activities would result in the disappearance of both relationship-orientated marketing strategies or the need for firms to employ a terrestrial salesforce. Advances in internet technology which permitted faster data transmission, transfer of visual materials and enhanced download speeds have proved these dire forecasts to be invalid (Chaston 2000). Companies such as Cisco in the USA, one of the world's largest producers of the switchers and routers which provide the physical backbone of the internet, have utilized technological advances to greatly expand and upgrade their commitment to creating even stronger downstream customer relationships. The capability of being able to create databases that can be accessed online by customers means that B2B suppliers can now offer customers much more detailed information on topics such as component specifications and applications on a 24/7, real-time basis. Those customers not requiring further data can then immediately place an order and confirm the purchase via the internet. Where the customer needs additional support, such as modifying or redesigning a component to fit a specific application, they can use the supplier's online automated design and pricing software to examine the implications of purchasing a customized component. In those cases where more detailed information is required, then via the supplier website prior to a purchase decision being reached, the customer can be automatically routed to a tele-support operation staffed by the supplier's technical specialists. Having created such systems which fulfil many of the tasks previously undertaken by the supplier's terrestrial salesforce, relationship-orientated firms have now redefined the role of their sales personnel to that of spending even more time acting in an technical advisory capacity working on a 1-to-1 basis with those customers who are facing very complex problems or are engaged in new product development projects, which will subsequently provide the B2B supplier with a new sales opportunity.

B2B suppliers who have used the internet to further develop their CRM strategy have found that creation of an interactive company website soon results in staff from a diverse range of departments in their customers' operations making contact and building relationships with their counterparts within the supplier company (Eid *et al.* 2002). As well as assisting both parties to become more knowledgeable about each other's business plans and day-to-day activities, these interactions help further cement supplier–customer loyalties. Additionally, by the transfer of routine ordering or customer problem resolution issues to the supplier's online operation, the additional freedom granted to the terrestrial salesforce is often exploited by those individuals working more closely with any of the firm's newer customers who have yet to be convinced of the benefits of forming a close relationship. As the salesforce has become more deeply involved in an advisory capacity, this has created an added benefit for their employer; namely as the salesforce acquire a deeper understanding of customer strategies and operations, this in turn can provide invaluable data for the B2B's marketers engaged in planning the firm's future market expansion and new product development strategies.

Reverse relationships

Case Aims: To illustrate the key role that expert B2B market suppliers now play in assisting major brands develop new products which assist maturing boomers feel healthier and look better.

The increasing pressure on major Western branded goods' companies to survive through innovation is causing many of these organizations to recognize that access to new technologies and solutions can often only come from working more closely with key suppliers. This is because in many cases, these B2B suppliers have a better understanding of both sourcing materials and the incorporation of new compounds into products than their customers (Berry 2008). One area where this situation is especially true is in the food and drinks industry, as major firms seek new ways of meeting the needs of maturing boomers wanting to move to a healthier diet (Scott 2006). In the UK, the retailer Marks and Spencer reported their Eat Well range will make up 40 per cent of total food sales within six months following launch. Another company which has benefited from this increased interest in healthier eating is Whole Food Market, one of the biggest retailers of natural and organic foods in the world, with 2005 sales of $5 billion. A key growth area is in the supply of ingredients to the manufacturers of healthier food products. This trend has emerged as older consumers want to increase the level of fibre in their diet because this material has been demonstrated to reduce the risks of certain cancers, diabetes, digestive disorders and heart disease. Tate & Lyle has developed a range of pre-biotic dietary fibres for use in dairy products. Cargill Corporation in America has developed new soluble fibres that are produced by further processing of barley. Grain Processing Corporation of Iowa have developed a rice maltodextrin fibre which is easier to digest that can add body and texture to frozen desserts without increasing sweetness or depressing a product's freezing point. The Beneo-Orafti company has exploited advances in the understanding of microbial ecology in the intestinal tract to develop a compound which medical tests found to delay the ageing process. The other area where the expertise of ingredient suppliers has been in demand to provide new, more natural formulations for products to be marketed to maturing boomers has been the health and beauty and cosmetics industries (Milmo 2006). Again the developing nations have benefited from this trend because they are providing the raw materials which are in demand for these new, anti-ageing care formulations. The popularity of these ingredients has also coincided with another trend, namely the ethical positioning of cosmetic products to meet the concerns of consumers about seeking to alleviate poverty in developing countries. Import data for the EU reveals that 88 per cent of imports of jasmine oil come from Egypt and India; 56 per cent of geranium oil from Egypt; 83 per cent of vetiver oil from Haiti; and 44 per cent of cocoa butter, fat and oil from Ivory Coast. Following processing, these ingredients are used by leading companies such as Procter & Gamble, Colgate-Palmolive, Nivea and Kimberley-Clark in their new formulations offering enhanced moisturizing properties. Many of the natural ingredients used in cosmetics, particularly triglycerides, waxes, fatty acids and fatty alcohols, contain impurities. Removal of these impurities has provided opportunities for B2B companies such as Croda from Japan who have developed new systems for ingredient purification. One of the new formulations created by Croda is based around purifying chemicals extracted from orange-peel skin which can be incorporated into skin care products because these ingredients are capable of boosting collagen production and enhancing the skin's own natural defence systems (Jeffries 2006). According to Croda, one of their formulations, Phytessence Stevia, is a moisturizer with three times greater skin hydration than glycerin and consequently can improve the skin's smoothness after only a much shorter period of treatment. The complexity of new skin care formulations using these new types of ingredients is demonstrated by The Estée Lauder Company's development of Fluid Motion™ Technology, which, according to the company, makes the skin appear sleeker and optimizes the flow of fluids. Ingredients used in this technology include siegesbeckia which is known from traditional Chinese medicine to reduce collagen degradation, forskolin, a plant extract from India which helps skin optimize its natural texture, and Brazilian guarana seeds that work with the body's natural enzymes to make skin look more contoured. Another B2B company, Lipo Chemicals, Inc., provides a number of spa and bath ingredients that work to exfoliate the skin and increase moisture. Liposilt® is a bio-active silt, rich in organic components and appropriate for body wraps, skin cleansing, spa products and moisturizing creams and lotions. Derived from two fresh water lakes of Eastern Europe, Liposilt Green and Liposilt Black both contain humic acid, nitrogen and fatty acids, and more than 90 per cent organic matter. Liposilt Black is claimed to improve the surface characteristics of skin, create a more even skin tone, reduce sebum content and increase moisture levels. Another marketer of skin care spa products is the Victoria's Secret Corporation. This company's spa collection features a gel-cream formulation containing marine and botanical ingredients, vitamins A, C and E, grape seed oil, white tea complex and caffeine. These new formulations are the culmination of a product development partnership between Victoria's Secret and Murad Research Laboratories.

Innovation strategies

B2B firms seeking to sustain above average sales and profitability often need to rely upon innovation to achieve this aim. Studies have suggested that only certain types of firms have the strategic skills and financial resources to permit the exploitation of new products as a route through which to achieve long-term growth (Bhaskaran 2006). Successful firms can be classified as 'prospectors' when they fit the profile of being highly innovative and tend to be pioneers in their sector of industry. In contrast, 'defenders' are very much less successful because they have a narrow product–market range and undertake virtually no new product development activity. A third group of firms who tend to also perform poorly over time are 'reactors'. These are firms who only initiate new product projects when faced with major changes in their external environment that could endanger future performance. A group of firms which perform reasonably well are the 'analysers'. Firms of this type exhibit the mixed characteristics of being both prospectors and defenders (Freeman 1974; Miles *et al.* 1978).

A B2B firm may decide the current product portfolio does not provide an appropriate base upon which to expand sales of products to supply chain members engaged in servicing the needs of financially attractive consumers. Under such circumstances, the probable solution is to identify a potential growth opportunity that can be exploited through the launch of a new product or service. Research has demonstrated the probability of new product success can usually be greatly increased by the firm drawing upon available market intelligence (Verhees and Meulenberg 2004). In the case of B2B markets, this information may be provided by downstream members of the supply chain or by making direct contact with consumers in the end-user market. As shown in Figure 11.4, some variation should be expected in the degree to which external sources can be of assistance. The situations the B2B supplier firm may encounter will influence the decision about which approach to innovation should be adopted. Where downstream supply chain member or consumers cannot provide useful information, the firm will be forced to adopt an autonomous innovation strategy. Success will depend upon there being a high level of entrepreneurial skills within the organization.

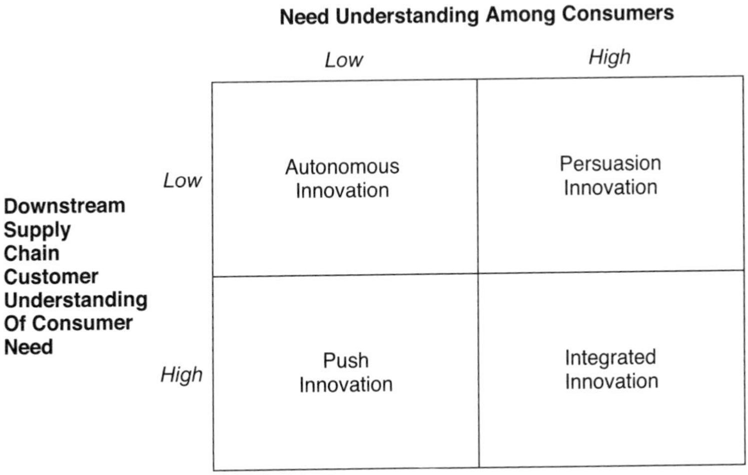

Need Understanding Among Consumers

		Low	High
Downstream Supply Chain Customer Understanding Of Consumer Need	Low	Autonomous Innovation	Persuasion Innovation
	High	Push Innovation	Integrated Innovation

Figure 11.4 B2B innovation pathways.

Should it emerge that consumers cannot provide knowledge about areas of unsatisfied needs, but the downstream supply chain members do understand end-user behaviour trends, the B2B supplier firm will need to work in partnership with the downstream supply chain members to implement an innovation push strategy. This push approach is required because consumers have a low awareness about any unsatisfied needs. Under these circumstances, once the new products have been developed, a successful launch will depend upon a market push by the downstream supply chain members building end-user market awareness and by educating the consumer, thereby stimulating new product trial.

There may be cases where the consumers' markets have been able to provide information concerning their needs for a new product, but downstream supply chain members have no desire to either seek out, understand or wish to exploit these newly identified end-user potential purchase traits. This places the B2B supplier in a difficult position of having to implement a persuasion strategy aimed at convincing downstream supply chain members that a new product opportunity exists. In some cases it may be possible for the B2B supplier to form an alliance with consumers and persuade them to communicate their unsatisfied needs to manufacturers and end-user outlet operations. Pressure from the B2B supplier, assisted in some cases by the emergence of new product demand from consumers, will hopefully persuade downstream supply chain members to begin making the new product available.

The preferred scenario shown in Figure 11.3 is that of both consumers and downstream supply chain members both being able to assist in the identification of the same areas of unsatisfied needs. The B2B supplier firm is then in a position to work with these supply chain members on an integrated innovation strategy exploiting their joint capabilities to develop a successful new product.

Exercise innovation

Case Aims: To illustrate how maturing boomers increasing interest in remaining fit and healthy offers new opportunities for exercise equipment manufacturers to use innovation to achieve further growth in a B2B market.

The fitness industry is expected to continue to benefit from favourable sociocultural and demographic trends that will ensure a steady level of growth in demand for fitness equipment. This trend for healthier lifestyles has created a need for convenient methods of exercise, which in turn has generated increased demand for home fitness equipment as well as equipment for health and fitness clubs. Much of the consumer health movement is fueled by factors such as heightened media attention, increasing healthcare costs and growing health problems such as obesity. In the USA, for example according to the US Center for Disease Control and Prevention, the rate of obesity among US adults between 1991 and 2002 increased by 74 per cent. The other key factor influencing demand is that maturing boomers are keen to postpone the effects of ageing for as long as possible. Hence, there is a high level of commitment within this consumer group to remain fit and healthy. As a consequence, maturing boomers are a key source of new members for health and fitness clubs which are being opened across the world. The prevalence of increased interest in physical activity is greatest among persons aged 50+ with higher levels of education and income (Tompkins *et al.* 2006). In the USA, for example, the number of frequent exercisers aged 45+ using health and fitness clubs increased by 47 per cent between 1987 and 1996. Their reasons for exercising are changing, with many people working out to maintain health and vitality rather than to improve their appearance. In terms of exercise machines, treadmills and stationary bicycles are especially popular with people aged 55 and older (Johnson 1998). Within the exercise equipment manufacturing industry the primary area of growth is expected to be machines that offer an increased level of interaction between the machine and the consumer. Manufacturers are focusing their efforts on the addition of TV, radio and internet access. Those firms in the forefront of these types of developments tend to supply the mid- to upper-end of the health and fitness club market. Their products are expensive, so their primary supply chain is to sell through specialty distributors to fitness gyms, spas and resorts. These distributors' end-user clients include businesses such as corporations, hospitals, health clubs, hotels/resorts, apartment complexes, YMCAs and golf club/ residential communities.

An example of how B2B component suppliers in the exercise market are utilizing technology to assist their customers develop improved exercise equipment is provided by the Lord Corporation in Cary, North Carolina (Greg 1997). The company manufactures the brakes of step machines and recumbent exercise bicycles which enables users to vary the machines' resistance to accommodate their individual levels of fitness and the desired intensity of their workout. In the past, exercise machines were equipped with eddy-current brakes, which had the weakness of not providing sufficient torque at low speeds. Lord Corporation has developed a new brake which exploits magneto rheological (MR) fluids which are dense suspensions of iron particles that are measured in microns. Under normal conditions, the materials are liquids with a viscosity similar to that of motor oil, but they stiffen within milliseconds when a DC magnetic field is applied to them. The stiffness is directly proportional to the strength of the magnetic field. The material returns to a liquid state when the field is removed. Brakes using MR fluids provide a smooth resistive torque directly proportional to the current and hence, resistance is independent of rotation speed. Another advantage of MR brakes in exercise machines is that they cost less than the eddy-current brake to manufacture and require much less electricity to operate.

Innovation networks

Most new product marketing management theories are based upon identifying the factors influencing the success achieved by multinational consumer goods firms. This has resulted in some of the authors of early academic texts on industrial marketing to assume consumer goods; mass marketing practices are utilized, without modification, in industrial markets. One aspect of branded consumer goods' marketing theory that was assumed to also be relevant to industrial marketing was the strategic need to engage in intense competition with other companies operating in the market. Acceptance of the universal validity of this concept was challenged in the 1980s when Nordic academics researching industrial markets identified firms who were more likely to collaborate than compete with each other. Initially these observations were dismissed as aberrations, especially among the American academic community. Through their persistence, coupled with similar research results being published by other European academics confirming the existence of collaboration in other industrial markets, most marketing theorists have come to accept that collaboration, not intense competition, is a common feature within many B2B markets around the world.

A common problem among smaller firms is the scenario of limited resources constraining the scale of business performance. Successful new product development is critically dependent upon access to adequate resources in key areas such as market information, knowledge of new technologies, employee R&D skills, finance and access to specialist equipment. One way to overcome this problem is to collaborate with other organizations either at the same level or with firms further downstream in the supply chain in the development of new products through the creation of a business innovation network (Rogers 2004). One of the catalysts in terms of creating interest in the potential benefits associated with the formation of business networks was the research undertaken by Piore and Sabel (1984). A large part of their study focused on certain industrial districts in Northern Italy to provide evidence about the benefits of networks for sustaining economic growth. The subsequent widespread acceptance of their views concerning the superiority of small firm networks to support innovation was seen as highly relevant in what they described as 'post-Fordist economies'. These are Western economies where economic output is no longer dominated by the activities of large corporations engaged in mass production and mass marketing.

The theory of using collaborative relationships to stimulate sectoral growth was assisted in gaining academic respectability when the Harvard University Professor Michael Porter (1990, 1996, 1998) published his findings which supported the view that co-operation is as equally important as competition in the management of successful companies. He helped extend collaboration theory by supporting the view that co-operation between groups of companies, or 'clusters', was an important model which can assist regional-level industrial economic regeneration. Observations of clusters such as the IT cluster in Silicon Valley and the fashion goods industry in Italy have subsequently led some Governments to fund major programmes aimed at attempting to stimulate the formation of new clusters within their countries. This led the Danish Technological Institute, for example, to use the concept as the basis of a programme to assist network formation and thereby stimulate economic regeneration. Initially used in Denmark, the Institute's networking model was also adopted by Government support agencies in Australia, Canada, New Zealand, Norway, Spain, South Africa, Sweden, UK and USA. In Denmark, the Danish Technology Institute led a scheme promoting network formation which for a period utilized virtually the entire Danish Government's small business support budget (Chaston 1996).

Although other researchers have demonstrated the benefits in using business networks to assist innovation to achieve economic regeneration in industrial districts, subsequent studies have concluded that the interpretation of available data by Piore and Sabel may have not been totally accurate. Lazerson and Lorenzoni (1999), for example, raised doubts about the validity of the concept and conclusions which had been drawn by undertaking a longitudinal analysis of economic events in certain industrial districts in Italy. They noted that the concept of a post-Fordist industrial model was not necessarily relevant because many of the artisan networks in Italy existed well before the twentieth century moved to exploit mass production. Furthermore, they also pointed out that the destiny of many B2B firms within business networks may be under the complete control of a very large firm who is their only customer. Unfortunately, some of these large firms, by continuing to operate a non-innovative, myopic strategy apparently ignoring changes in world markets, have actually acted as an obstacle in terms of innovation being a primary business philosophy within some industrial regions. The adverse influence of local large firms is described by Lazerson and Lorenzoni as 'over embeddedness'. This trait reflects an excessively inward looking orientation among influential members of a business network. In the opinion of these researchers, the only reason growth through innovation has occurred in these circumstances is because the influence of myopic large local firms has been negated by the arrival of what they describe as 'external pollinators'. These latter sources have in many cases been intermediaries from overseas markets such as major upmarket US retailers. These firms are keen to purchase Italian fashion goods, but first have to persuade network members that their current products are not those being sought by customers in other countries.

With other researchers now also concluding that not all firms wish, or alternatively are able, to participate in business networks, a more balanced view has begun to emerge about how these organizational structures can play a role in assisting the expansion of entrepreneurial effort within a sector (Kingsley and Malecki 2004). For example evidence has emerged concerning the different ways in which firms utilize networks to assist their new product development and how these activities will be influenced by the nature of their relationship with other network members (Elfring and Hulsink 2003). Network relationships are usually described in terms of 'weak' and 'strong' ties. Weak ties tend to be somewhat more informal and the level of inter-firm interaction tends to vary significantly over time. Weak ties are typically used when a firm is seeking to access new or novel information. Such knowledge often exists in a tacit form in organizations such as research laboratories or universities. Thus, the firm will be required to extend their contacts outside of other network members with whom they are in regular contact in order to undertake a broader than usual search to acquire information on 'leading edge' knowledge or technologies. The outcome is that weak ties tend to be exploited by firms during the idea search stage or in the resolution of a highly complex problem about which other network members with whom the business usually works are unable to help.

Strong ties are usually associated with frequent interchange of information between network members with whom the firm has established a relationship based upon mutual trust and commitment. The nature of the relationship is critical because innovation often involves the exchange of confidential or commercially sensitive data. This type of information is something which firms would be inclined not to share with organizations about which their management have minimal prior experience. Hence, the majority of collaborative new product development activities are associated with drawing upon strong ties with existing network members to progress the project from idea identification through to market launch.

The potential benefits of collaboration are now being increasingly recognized by large firms who traditionally have exhibited an adversarial attitude towards both their competitors and other members of their supply chain. This move towards a collaboration philosophy is reflected in B2B alliances between firms such as Nokia and Sony, IBM and Apple, Home Depot and ServiceMaster. Nevertheless, it should be recognized that the degree to which firms collaborate with each other will vary between industrial sectors and between countries. Collaboration tends to be more common in new industrial sectors such as IT and telecommunications. In relation to geographic variation, firms in the Nordic countries tend to work more closely together than their counterparts elsewhere in Europe.

Although there is widespread evidence that networking can be a positive influence in sustaining the performance of B2B firms, the actual benefits and processes of networking are less well understood. Where firms are committed to continuous improvement through lifelong learning, some experts feel informal networking provides the most effective basis for knowledge acquisition and exchange. In formalized networks, firms' agreements to collaborate are usually associated with the aim of achieving a specific business purpose. Very frequently, network formation occurs because it permits the sharing of resources, leading to the creation of larger scale trading entities. Additionally, once a synergy based upon the sharing of resources has been identified, this will frequently permit small firms into new markets and, in some cases, successfully enter industrial sectors usually dominated by larger firms (Coviello and Munro 1995).

In recent years, it has become apparent that small firm international B2B market entry is more likely to succeed by joining a formalized, export network. Early theories about SME sector export networks suggested that networks should be permanent entities. Subsequent observations of actual networks has revealed, however, that firms exhibit a pragmatic view that a network should only exist for as long as members are obtaining benefits from their participation. This is validated by case data about how most formal networks, once formed, only exist for a few years and then are dissolved. This final outcome occurs because members' strategic aims have been achieved and the network is no longer perceived as advantageous by the majority of the participants. In many export situations, for example, a group of firms will establish a network to enter a new overseas market. Once individual firms have developed their own marketing and service capabilities in the new market, the tendency is for the network to be closed down unless there is agreement to launch a new initiative in another country elsewhere in the world.

In some cases, the network will be a horizontal format with collaboration between firms at the same level within the supply chain. An example of this structure are small Danish firms manufacturing industrial clothing who collaborated in both developing new products and in the joint exploitation of the German corporate clothing market. Other networks are of a vertical nature where suppliers, intermediaries or end-users are seen as having a critical role in the provision of knowledge or resources. Mosey's (2005) examination of small Australian B2B networks in a vertical bio-technology cluster, for example, revealed that these operations relied heavily on strong links with universities, public sector research laboratories, large pharmaceutical firms and specialist medical staff working in hospitals. This latter group were perceived as a critical source of information because they provided information that led to new idea generation within the small firms and also guidance over product performance or specification during the prototype development phase of product development project. This researcher also concluded that a common view of small high technology firms reliant upon networks to achieve innovation may not always be a valid conclusion. An illustration of this perspective was provided by a study of Melbourne firms working in the same area of the Australian information technology B2B market. Although these firms faced severe challenges in the development of new products or services, most of these firms considered in-house R&D and other knowledge sources within the firm as the crucial components for successful innovation. Very few of these firms used collaborative links with other firms located at the same level in the supply chain as a source of assistance or to provide access to scarce resources.

References

Abdel-Ghany, M. and Sharpe, D.L. (1997) 'Consumption patterns among the young-old and old-old', *Journal of Consumer Affairs*, Vol. 31, No. 1, pp. 90–112.

Anon (2005) 'Nothing retiring about this community's technology', *SDM*, Vol. 35, No. 11, pp. 11–13.

Anon (1995) 'Expenditure patterns of retired and non-retired people', *Family Economics Review*, Vol. 8, No. 3, pp. 46–8.

Berry, D. (2008) 'Fiber update', *Dairy Foods*, Vol. 109, No. 8, pp. 68–70.

Bhaskaran, S. (2006) 'Incremental innovation and business performance: small and medium-sized enterprises in a concentrated industry environment', *Journal of Small Business Management*, Vol. 44, No. 1, pp. 64–91.

Brennan, D.R., Turnbull, P.W. and Wilson, D.T. (2003) 'Dyadic adaptation in business-to-business markets', *European Journal of Marketing*, Vol. 37, No. 11/12, pp. 1638–65.

Chaston, I. (2000) *E-Commerce Marketing Management*, London: McGraw-Hill.

Chaston, I. (1996) 'Critical events and process gaps in the Danish Technological Institute structured networking model', *International Small Business Journal*, Vol. 14, No. 3, pp. 31–42.

Coviello, N.E. and Munro, H.J. (1995) 'Growing the entrepreneurial firm: networking for international markets', *European Journal of Marketing*, Vol. 29, No. 7, pp. 49–62.

Crain, D.W. and Abraham, S. (2008) 'Using value-chain analysis to discover customers' strategic needs', *Strategy & Leadership*, Vol. 36, No. 4, pp. 29–36.

Doka, K.J. (1992) 'When gray is golden: business in an aging America', *The Futurist*, Vol. 26, No. 4, pp. 16–21.

Eid, R., Trueman, M. and Ahmed, A.M. (2002) 'A cross-industry review of B2B critical factors', *Internet Research*, Vol. 12, No. 2, pp. 110–24.

Elfring, T. and Hulsink, W. (2003) 'Networks in entrepreneurship: the case of high-technology firms', *Small Business Economics*, Vol. 21, No. 4, pp. 409–20.

Freeman, C. (1974) *The Economics of Innovation*, London: Penguin.

Fuhrman, E. (2008) 'Organic, natural ingredients grow', *Beverage Industry*, Vol. 99, No. 4, pp. 39–43.

Good, D.J. and Schultz, R.J. (2005) 'The emerging role of the sales technologist', *Southern Business Review*, Vol. 30, No. 2, pp. 11–20.

Greg, P. (1997) 'Exercise equipment puts on magnetorheological brakes', *Mechanical Engineering*, Vol. 119, No. 5, p. 124.

Jeffries, N. (2006) 'Integrating science and nature', *Global Cosmetic Industry*, New York, June, pp. 34–8.

Johnson, D. (1998) 'Tracking fitness: from fashion fad to health trend', *The Futurist*, Vol. 32, p. 8.

Kingsley, G. and Malecki, E. (2004) 'Networking for competitiveness', *Small Business Economics*, Vol. 23, No.1, pp. 71–82.

Lazerson, M. and Lorenzoni, G. (1999) 'Resisting organizational inertia: the evolution of industrial districts', *Journal of Management and Governance*, Vol. 3, pp. 361–77.

Lewis, P.H. (2001) 'Remotely interesting', *Fortune*, New York, 2 April, pp. 191–93.

Miles, R.E., Snow, C.C., Meyer, A.D. and Coleman, H.J. (1978) 'Organizational strategy, structure, and process', *Academy of Management Review*, Vol. 3, No. 3, pp. 546–63.

Milmo, S. (2006) 'Naturals, organics, ecology', *Clinical Market Reporter*, New York, 15 May, pp. 24–6.

Mosey, S. (2005) 'Understanding new-to-market product development in SMEs', *International Journal of Operations and Production Management*, Vol. 25, No. 2, pp. 114–30.

Piore, M. and Sabel, C. (1984) *The Second Industrial Divide*, New York: Basic Books.

Porter, M.E. (1998) 'Clusters and the new economics of competition', *Harvard Business Review*, Vol. 76, No. 6, pp.77–90.

Porter, M.E. (1996) 'What is strategy?', *Harvard Business Review*, Vol. 74, No. 6, pp. 61–78.

Porter, M.E. (1990) *The Competitive Advantage of Nations*, New York: The Free Press.

Rogers, M. (2004) 'Networks, firm size and innovation', *Small Business Economics*, Vol. 22, No. 2, pp. 141–56.

Scott, M. (2006) 'The world is getting older but wants to stay fit , exercise and diet', *Financial Times*, London, 9 October, p. 7.

Singh, T., Gordon, G. and Purchase, S. (2007) 'B2B e-marketing strategies of multinational corporations: empirical evidence from the United States and Australia', *Mid-American Journal of Business*, Vol. 22, No. 1, pp. 31–45.

Tompkins, L.T., Kent, R. and McDonald, M. (2006) 'Fitness Pro: managing a growing business', Vol. 12, No. 1, pp. 27–42.

Verhees, F.J.H. and Meulenberg, M.T. (2004) 'Market orientation, product innovation and performance of small firms', *Journal of Small Business Management*, Vol. 42, No. 2, pp. 134–55.

Wilson, R.D. (2006) 'Developing new business strategies in B2B markets by combining CRM concepts and online databases', *Competitiveness Review*, Vol. 16, No. 1, pp. 38–44.

Zalud, B. (2002) 'Home, sweet camera-equipped home', *SDM*, Vol. 32, pp. 54–7.

12 Twenty-first century 'Es'

Generic principles of marketing to financially attractive consumers (FACs)

The coverage of issues in Chapter 12 is designed to illustrate the generic principles of marketing to FACs in relation to:

1   Based on most major world events in the twentieth century not being forecasted before their occurrence, it seems probable that the same inability to make long-term forecasts will also apply in relation to many major events that may occur over the balance of the twenty-first century.

2   Based upon the rising level of debt over the last 10 years among the 18–49 year age group, when coupled with the impact of a major economic downturn, it is proposed that FACs will offer greater potential to sustain a firm's sales revenue and profitability for existing or new products and services for the foreseeable future.

3   The medium-term prospects for increasingly constrained supplies of non-renewable energy leading to higher prices means opportunities exist for entrepreneurs to develop solutions that can assist in alleviating the impact of higher energy costs which consumers will inevitably have to face.

4   Even among firms operating in conventional energy industry sectors, greater focus on marketing to the less price-sensitive FACs is advisable for existing and new products.

5   As the cost of renewable energy is usually higher than energy generated from conventional sources, firms in the renewable energy sector would be advised to focus marketing efforts on FACs.

6   Significant growth for many firms over the next 10 years will often be reliant upon the development of new products or services. In order to optimize profitability generated from investing innovation, many firms should consider giving priority to innovation capable of meeting the needs of FACs.

Forecasting futures

At the beginning of the twentieth century, three empires, the British, the Austro-Hungarian and Ottoman, controlled the day-to-day lives of millions of people across the globe. Royalty ruled over further millions of impoverished peasants in Russia and China (Fenby 2008). The USA was only just beginning to emerge as the new major source of industrial innovation. Across the world from Ireland to India, individuals were emerging who would eventually achieve political independence from the British Empire (Brendon 2007). Similarly in Russia and China, political dissidents were building a power base among the population which would eventually lead to the overthrow of their nation's rulers.

The impossibility of accurately forecasting world events is demonstrated by the political map: the world's three largest empires have disappeared forever; communism's control over Europe collapsed as Russia evolved into a less powerful, but still authoritarian state; China's politicians modified their communist principles in order to create economic growth; the USA's self-defined role as the protector of democracy is engaged in an expensive war on religiously inspired terrorism which currently involves having thousands of troops operating in Iraq and Afghanistan; and the advent of new technologies, such as atomic power and computers, which nobody had predicted at the beginning of the twentieth century.

The twenty-first century was welcomed in around the world with firework displays and many consumers exhibiting a high level of the 'feel good factor'. Less than 10 years later, however, the world is facing what possibly may still prove to be a financial crisis at least equal to that which occurred during the Great Depression. Similar to the beginning of the previous century when none of the century's subsequent major political or economic events which shaped world history were accurately forecasted, it is very unlikely politicians and economists will be able to accurately forecast the impact of current events on the world economy over even the next 10–25 years, let alone the balance of the century. The only thing which appears certain about current economic events is a general consensus of opinion that the crisis was created by excessive lending to both individual consumers and to nations. This error was then compounded by the decision of the financial community to sustain profitability by creating complex instruments which by shifting liabilities out of their balance sheets, created the mirage that Government regulations over asset/lending coverage ratios had not been breached. In terms of forecasting the final outcome of this century's first economic downturn, the experts' views range from a mild recession to a massive and prolonged depression. A fundamental issue influencing doubts about the accuracy of any of these forecasts is that the world has no previous experience of handling a financial crisis on the scale of that which emerged in 2008 (Aldrick and Conway 2008).

Even those who supposedly are nearest to the financial statistics, such as the Federal Reserve in the USA and the Bank of England, have been forced over the last 12 months to repeatedly revise their estimates of the toxic debt held by the world's financial institutions. For example in April 2008, the Bank of England forecasted 'market-to-market' losses of £63 billion. By October 2008, the Bank was forced to revise this estimate to upwards of £123 billion. In the USA over the same period, estimated losses have risen from $793 billion to $1,577 billion. Even though the accuracy of such forecasts appears to be approaching a more realistic appreciation of the real scale of the banking crisis, there still remains the issue of how many further financial losses exist inside other sectors of the financial community such as the hedge funds and the insurance companies.

To this black scenario now has to be added the problems facing some of the world's weaker countries such as Iceland and former Warsaw Bloc countries whose economies are liable to go into meltdown unless they are able to be rescued by the richer nations or the IMF. What is certain, however, when the bottom of this current recession or depression is finally reached, the average consumer in most Western nations will much poorer and will be forced to drastically revise their spending patterns for at least one, or possibly even two decades. Hence one 'E factor' which can be accurately predicted to prevail during the first half of the twenty-first century will be that of many of the world's consumers being forced to economize.

Economizing

As children, teenagers, adults and finally parents, maturing boomers have been the first generation in the world's developed economies where a large proportion of the population could afford to participate in conspicuous consumption. People living in Western nations were able to purchase one or more cars, home appliances, electronic goods while concurrently being able to afford activities such as vacations, a diverse choice of entertainment and a wide range of sporting activities. Key factors which supported high discretionary spending by this group included rising incomes, a long period of secure employment and a welfare state providing either subsidized or free care from 'the cradle to grave'.

Even though maturing boomers will clearly have been impacted by the 2008 world financial crisis, on average the majority of this consumer group will remain reasonably financially secure and able to sustain their lifestyle without having to make significant adjustments to their personal spending level. The same cannot be said for their children and grandchildren. This is because there is a whole set of interacting factors that will significantly reduce younger peoples' spending power and force them to adopt a more economic lifestyle (Malehorn 2008).

The downturn in the purchasing power of younger people in the Western world was already evident by the late 1980s. This was because of the emergence of the combined influence of declining national economic performance, population ageing and rising healthcare costs. Western Governments could no longer depend upon an expanding tax base to sustain the welfare policies that emerged after the Second World War. In relation to retirement even consumers in the nations with extremely liberal social welfare schemes have now begun to realize that the absolute value of their state retirement benefits will continue to fall and that the age at which individuals qualify for such benefits will continue to be extended. Furthermore, in the private sector, employers can no longer afford to fund final salary pension schemes. Hence, such schemes are already being scrapped for younger workers. Furthermore, it is highly probable that the public sector will soon be forced to follow this trend.

The implications for the average Western nation consumer in the 18–49 year age group of a shrinking welfare system, lack of growth in the value of real wages, higher unemployment and the need to self-fund college education means that these younger consumers are being forced to live a much more economical lifestyle than their parents. This is because their discretionary income will continue to be eroded as they are forced to accept a greater proportion of the responsibility for funding their own education, healthcare and pension provision (Schooley and Worden 2008). To this burden has to now be added repayment of the huge debts which the average younger consumers have accumulated over the last 10 years (Christen and Morgan 2005). Many people took on a higher level of debt on the assumption that repayments could be funded by an increase in personal net asset value created by the apparently exponential, never ending increase in the value of their homes. The collapse in house prices which started in 2007 and the resultant creation of negative equity now means for the foreseeable future, the average Western consumer's discretionary spending will be reduced as they struggle to discharge existing liabilities by only being able to rely upon earned income (Betti *et al.* 2007). Additionally, the action of some Governments to increase their level of public borrowing to support increased public sector spending as a Keynesian strategy to reduce the impact of the global economic downturn will eventually be followed by consumers facing higher tax bills as they are forced to repay their nation's public sector debt. This scenario provides very concrete reasons for firms to revise their marketing strategies by de-emphasizing the importance of the 18–49 year age group and instead seek to build market share among financially attractive consumer markets.

Some of the more optimistic marketers within the Western multinationals and global corporations will perceive that sales revenue compensation in the face of lower spending by Western consumers can be achieved by achieving greater market share within the BRIC nations (Brazil, Russia, India, China). Unfortunately, such thinking could prove somewhat illusory because it ignores both economic and political reality. The sociodemographics of the BRIC nations are still very similar to that of the Western nations early in the Industrial Revolution; namely there are a high number of poor impoverished individuals living in small villages engaged in subsistence farming; a high number of poorly paid urban workers employed in industry and a relatively small middle-class population. Hence, similar to the economic history of the Western nations, it will be many years before sustained economic growth within the BRICs will create the number of middle-class and skilled blue-collar workers that are needed to create a consumer society of the type which emerged in the USA and Europe after the Second World War.

Even more importantly, especially in China and India, the two most densely populated BRIC nations, there remains a huge historical memory which has not forgiven the disruptive activities of the European and American nations over the last 300 years. Inside these countries, Westerners are still remembered as oppressors. Hence, wherever possible, the national ethos is to become economically independent of any foreign industrial assistance. China, for example, is a country which has frequently demonstrated a behaviour trait of tolerating foreigners for a short period of time while their presence is perceived as economically beneficial and then evicting these visitors when their usefulness is seen as having come to an end (Fenby 2008). Even a superficial assessment of China and India reveals they have already acquired the domestic expertise to operate across a diversity of industries such as steel, car production, manufacturing electronic goods, computing and pharmaceuticals. In some of these sectors, the BRICs have already achieved self sufficiency. Hence, based on their current rate of progress, their need for the ongoing involvement of the Western multinational corporations operating inside their borders will be virtually minimal within 15–20 years.

A successful BRIC challenge to the Western corporates*

Case Aims: To illustrate how companies from the BRIC nations are acquiring a level of scientific and technical expertise that is permitting them to successfully challenge the Western corporate giants' domination of technology-based sectors of world markets.

The huge costs associated with the development and approval of new drugs has been reflected in the ever increasing rise in the prices being charged by the global pharmaceutical companies. In recent years, one way in which Governments and healthcare insurers have sought to reverse this trend has been to approve the much greater use of lower cost, generic drugs. India has been the leading source of new entrepreneurs that have benefited from the trend towards the increased use of generics. The turning point in the country's pharmaceutical industry came when the Indian Government repealed the country's laws under which imported drugs were protected by patents. The explicit purpose of this legislation was to terminate the nation's reliance upon imports and to make the country self-reliant through expanding domestic production. To achieve this aim, the Indian companies exploited the time lag until international patent law will again apply to utilize reverse engineering to discover the formulations of leading patented drugs produced elsewhere in the world. Many of the major companies in the Indian drugs industry share the same development pattern of starting life as a small family business which gradually evolved over time into a global player. India's largest company Ranbaxy was founded in 1962 by Ranjit Singh to market pharmaceuticals in Amritsar. Unable to repay funds borrowed from Bhai Mohan Singh, this latter individual took over the company in lieu of the loan repayment and he appointed his son Dr Parvinder Singh to run the business. In 1969 the company began manufacturing Calmpose, a generic version of Valium. As the company product line began to broaden, the company entered key overseas markets in North America and Europe. Now run by Dr Pavinder's son, Malvinder Mohan Singh, in mid-2008, the Singh family announced their intention of accepting a take-over offer in the region of $4 billion from the Japanese corporation Daiichi Sankyo. The Indian drugs industry achieved worldwide recognition for innovative achievement when the firm Cipla offered to supply a triple combination drugs treatment for AIDS to countries in Africa for $350, against the American patent holder's price of $12,000. This company, now India's second largest pharmaceutical company, started life as a small entrepreneurial family business when in 1935, Dr Khwaja Abdul Hamied set up the business in a rented bungalow in Bombay. After the Second World War, the company began manufacturing products under licence and also developed their own products such as Rotahaler, the world's first such dry powder inhaler device, the anti-cancer drugs, vinblastine and vincristine, developed in collaboration with the National Chemical Laboratory and the antiretroviral drug, zidovudine The expertise acquired in manufacturing drugs under licence and the development of their own products provided the basis for Cipla to successfully enter the global market supplying generic products. Upon the death of his father, the son Dr Yusuf Hamied, who joined the company in 1960, has subsequently led the company's continued expansion taking the business into over 170 overseas markets. Dr Reddy's Laboratories was founded in 1984, with a $120,000 bank loan, by Dr Anji Reddy, the son of a wealthy tumeric farmer. Within only a few years, the company enjoyed success with copies of Bayer's antibiotic ciprofloxacin and AstraZeneca's omeprazole. This latter product, under the trade name Losec, became one of the world's largest selling drugs. In the 1990s the company moved into development of new drugs, but lacking the funds to support clinical testing, the company licensed their first product, an insulin sensitizer, to Novo Nordisk in 1997. This was the first ever licensing of an Indian-developed drug to a multinational pharmaceuticals company. Rapid growth through expansion into numerous overseas markets, a series of acquisitions in America and a merger with Cheminor Drugs made Dr Reddy's India's third largest drugs company in 2001. In the same year, the company became the first non-Japanese Asian company to be listed on the New York Stock Exchange.

*Sources: Malhotra and Lofgren 2004;
www.cipla.com; www.drreddys.com; www.ranbaxy.com.*

Energy

One of the fundamental reasons that so many maturing boomers have been able to participate in conspicuous consumption during the twentieth century was the extremely low cost of energy. Even after the 1970s OPEC oil crisis finally caused the Western nations to recognize the price of oil could no longer continue to remain below $10 a barrel, energy prices when assessed in relation to rising incomes and discounting for the influence of inflation, remained extremely low throughout all of the twentieth century.

At the beginning of the twenty-first century, prices for oil and other commodities began to rise dramatically. To a large degree this was fuelled by the rapid growth in the Chinese and Indian economies (Rees 2008). By the end of 2007, as oil prices hit over $150 a barrel, some forecasters were predicting a price of $200 by mid-2008. Even in the twentieth century politicians and scientists had been urging Western consumers to reduce their consumption of petrol. But such recommendations did not achieve any marked impact on changing peoples' behaviour. Sales of cars continued to rise accompanied by consumers' increasing desire to drive high petrol consumption vehicles such as SUVs. Rapidly rising oil prices in the twenty-first century, however, had the impact which politicians had been failing to achieve for years. People have started to drive less, increase their use of public transport and are seeking to dispose of their 4 × 4 gas guzzlers.

The market interaction between oil and other natural energy resources also led, in 2007, to consumers facing huge rises in the costs of gas and electricity. Prices of these alternative energy sources were further impacted by the Western nations' determination to cut back on the use of coal in order to reduce greenhouse gas emissions. However, as the implications of the global downturn began to register on speculators within the world's futures markets and companies within the BRICs began to experience a rapid fall in export sales, oil along with other commodity prices rapidly declined to well below $100 a barrel, which in time can be expected to cause a fall in consumers' utility bills. Unfortunately, these abrupt declines in energy prices are likely to be relatively short lived. Similar to Western nation consumers in the twentieth century, as average incomes rise in the BRIC nations this will be accompanied by an increase in car ownership. Oil is a non-renewable resource and as the number of cars on the road continues to rise in these emerging economies, the increasing demand for petrol will lead to a return to higher oil prices (Moeller 2008). This event will again trigger an upward climb in the price of other natural energy resources such as coal and gas which in turn will place upward pressures on global electricity prices (Hartley *et al.* 2008).

Western Governments, in recognition of the finite availability of oil and the need to reduce greenhouse gas emissions, are promoting a return to atomic energy accompanied by a switch to renewable energy such as wind and wave power. Despite this trend, the medium term prospects are that the average consumer can never ever expect a return to the level of energy prices which had such a major influence on the lives of their parents, the maturing boomers. This group were the first and possibly the last generation in history to live in a world where very low cost energy permitted a large proportion of Western nation populations to participate in conspicuous consumption. Given, however, that many financially attractive consumers are continuing to enjoy higher than average incomes, companies operating in the conventional energy market such as manufacturers of conventional central heating systems would be well advised to focus on this market sector which will be in a much better position to afford to purchase new and replacement products.

Environmentalism

In the 30-year period 1950–1980, only a minority of individuals in the Western nations were concerned about the potential adverse impact of uncontrolled consumption on Planet Earth in relation to either environmental damage or the exhaustion of natural resources. Even the advent of the OPEC oil crisis in the 1970s, which signalled an end of the era of low-cost energy, had minimal impact on consumers wishing to conserve their use of energy. In the 1980s, however, higher oil prices and the impact of events such as acid rain, Chernobyl and Three Mile Island did cause consumers to revise their opinions about the need to start protecting the environment and to be concerned about the declining availability of key, non-renewable, natural resources.

The degree to which there was an increase in environmental awareness varied by both industry and countries (Mitchell and Dupre 1994). Firms in industries with a poor track record in areas such as dumping industrial effluent into lakes and rivers were forced by public opinion and Government legislation to take action to reduce the impact of their operations on the environment. In Western countries, some consumers began to reflect their concerns about the environment by modifying their purchasing patterns and lifestyles (Kilbourne 1995). Within mainland Europe, the level of response was much greater than, for example, in the UK or USA. Within some EU countries, heightened awareness over environmental issues led to the election of the world's first ever 'green' parties. These new political parties adopted a manifesto about the need for greater environmental responsibility. Their primary message was aimed at persuading both industry and consumers of the urgent need to accept the '3Rs' of reduce, re-use and recycle.

Firms required by legislation to modify their manufacturing operations in order to reduce their impact on the environment found that implementing these actions was usually accompanied by operating rising costs. These operational changes were also often accompanied by a decline in the quality of the firm's output. Hence, the dilemma facing firms located in countries that had introduced new, tighter environmental regulations was how to compete against firms located in developing economies where looser industrial regulations permitted these companies to compete on the basis of lower prices (Fisk 1974). The solution adopted by many Western firms was to use 'green' marketing strategies to convince their customers that paying a premium price, in some cases to purchase inferior quality goods, was an appropriate behaviour shift because they would be reflecting a greater sense of personal environmental responsibility. In some cases, these firms engaged in what has subsequently become known as 'greenwashing'. This activity involves companies advertising invalid claims about their green credentials. An example of greenwashing is a firm which communicates it was their decision to remove harmful chemicals such as CFCs from their products when in fact they had only taken such actions in the face of changes in Government legislation (Bonini and Oppenheim 2008).

The American marketing agency that specializes in environmental issues, TerraChoice, has proposed that greenwashing by firms involves committing one or more of the following 'Six Sins of Greenwashing' (www.terrachoice.com):

1   *The Sin of the Hidden Trade-off* where the company may claim use of a sustainable raw material but fails to mention other non-green practices that are necessary in order to incorporate the material into their final product.
2   *The Sin of No Proof* where a claim of the product being environmentally friendly is made but no proof is provided about the validity of the claim.
3   *The Sin of Vagueness* where the firm uses meaningless phrases such as 'toxin-free' in an attempt to establish green credentials.
4   *The Sin of Irrelevance* where a claim is made which in fact would apply to any manufacturer's products within an industrial sector.
5   *The Sin of Fibbing* where a claim is made such as a product having been certified as green when in fact no such action has even been undertaken by the company.
6   *The Sin of Lesser of Two Evils* where a claim is made about a product within a category being less harmful than an alternative product, when in reality the preferable solution would be for consumers to cease using all products within the category.

Except in those cases where firms had been forced to respond to Government legislation, many of the large multinationals were slow to respond to the emergence of the green consumer. Such opportunities left them vulnerable to the actions of smaller, more entrepreneurial companies. These latter organizations were not slow in filling the growing void for environmentally responsible products and services which emerged in Western nation consumer markets. For example small organic food producers were able to recover their higher operating costs through charging premium prices. This was because consumers accepted their claims about the higher costs associated with activities such as needing to avoid the use of fertilizers or manufacturing food products containing no artificial additives.

Eventually, even the major brands were forced to recognize the threat of lost sales. For many, this recognition was caused by the increasing market share being enjoyed by their new, smaller competitors. In some cases, such as McDonald's, added stimulus to recognize the threat of not being perceived as green came from being the target of mass demonstrations about the organization's failing to exhibit an adequate level of environmental responsibility (Karna et al. 2003).

Having determined the existence of a shift in consumer opinion in relation to environmentally responsible behaviour, some major companies took the decision to implement a 'green repositioning' across their product line. This strategic decision appears to be based upon the assumption that green issues were now a key factor influencing the purchase decision of the majority of their customers. Hence, during the 1990s many large companies made revisions to their products and services. These actions were usually followed by increased promotional spending to re-establish their environmental credentials among consumers. Unfortunately, what such organizations possibly failed to appreciate is that in an economic downturn, as consumers begin to feel financially threatened, the majority will return to a purchasing behaviour based upon choosing goods which they perceive as offering the greatest value, either because the price is lower or the quality demonstrably superior (Dolliver 2008). Hence, what possibly may have come as a surprise to some major firms who went green in the late twentieth century, was to discover in 2007 that as the economic downturn started and consumer confidence began to decline, many consumers' concerns about protecting the environment virtually disappeared. Instead, individuals began to worry about personal financial security and ceased to perceive being green as having any relevance to their current lifestyle.

One outcome of this behaviour shift, for example, is that sales of organic meats and vegetables have plummeted dramatically in many Western nations as the 18–49 year age group have returned to buying lower priced, non-organic foods. The only consumer group where the purchasing of environmentally friendly products appears to have remained relatively unchanged is among financially attractive consumers such as the maturing boomers. This probably reflects their perception that their personal wealth is less at risk during an economic downturn and hence they feel able to sustain their existing commitment to remaining environmentally responsible.

Those firms who are now finding green is no longer a viable marketing strategy have clearly failed to comprehend this is a highly segmented market containing a diversity of consumers exhibiting varying degrees of commitment to the concept of being environmentally responsible. In their study of the US market, Schwartz and Miller (1991), for example, determined that consumers could be classified into the following five groups:

1 *True-Blue Greens* who are dedicated members of the environmental movement, who are a small but highly vocal, active group within society.
2 *Greenback Greens* who are environmentally concerned, unwilling to allocate much time or money to the issue, but are willing to pay more for green products or packaging.
3 *The Sprouts* who are uncertain about the trade-off between environmental protection and the impact on the economic wellbeing of both their nation and themselves as consumers.
4 *The Grousers* who are environmentally indifferent and only purchase environmentally friendly products where there is a clear price or quality advantage.
5 *The Basic Browns* who believe environmental protection is not their problem and any contribution they might make will have an insignificant impact on the situation.

Even before the current economic downturn, Peattie (2001) had posited that the green market is one where customer behaviour can shift abruptly. Hence, great caution is needed should a firm decide being green will be a foundation stone upon which the organization's future marketing strategy will be built. Peattie also proposed that ongoing market success will only occur where the firm continues to invest in innovation to create new generations of products or services that differentiate the organization from competition.

In terms of maximizing the potential success of a green marketing strategy, there is a need to take two factors into consideration; namely the degree to which the green product offers superior performance and the degree to which purchase or usage will require a significant change in personal behaviour. As summarized in Figure 12.1, combining these two variables generates four possible outcomes. In the two cases where green product performance is equal or poorer than alternative goods, the long-term potential for success, especially during an economic downturn occur, is low. Hence, the firm should probably avoid implementing a green marketing strategy under these circumstances.

In the case where the green product offers superior performance, but would require a change in purchase or usage behaviour, the primary benefit to the consumer is the personal self satisfaction of feeling or being seen to be socially responsible. As the customers in this target group will be those who enjoy an above average income and who do no expect to be adversely impacted by adverse economic conditions, this is a relatively safe strategic proposition as long as the product proposition is of appeal to financially attractive consumers. This is because these consumers feel sufficiently confident about their personal future; that they feel able to retain their views about making a personal moral decision to try to protect the environment when making purchasing products and services.

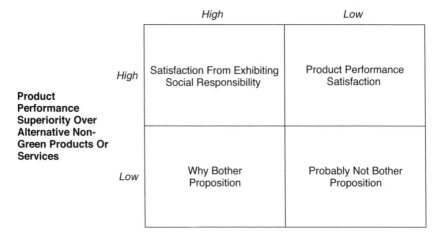

Figure 12.1 Green strategy options.

The other strategic option is where the performance of the green product is superior and the consumer is not required to make any revision in either purchase of usage behaviour. Companies who perceive a long-term opportunity exists for green marketing should, where feasible, seek to be in a position to implement this option. This is because the firm does not have to rely on customers retaining the same moral or social responsibility values in the face of changing economic conditions when justifying their purchase decision. Instead, the firm is able to exploit the more certain motivation of consumers selecting a product which offers the greatest satisfaction in terms of the superiority of performance over alternative less environmentally friendly offerings.

Emissions

The idea that burning ever larger amounts of fossil fuels could increase the level of carbon dioxide (or greenhouse gases) in the earth's atmosphere, which in turn would lead to climate change, was first proposed in the late nineteenth century (Dyson 2005). For most of the twentieth century, the theory was ignored until growing concerns about the impact of rising greenhouse gases on global warming led to the formation of the international body known the Intergovernmental Panel on Climate Change (IPCC) in 1988. Successive reports by the panel provided increasingly strong evidence that during the final decades of the twentieth century about 75 per cent of the carbon dioxide being released into the atmosphere came from the burning of fossil fuels. This in turn was causing a rapid increase in the rate of global warming. Obtaining acceptance for their ideas initially proved extremely difficult for the IPCC. Eventually under the auspices of the United Nations, in 1997 the world leaders met in Kyoto, Japan to discuss proposals about limiting carbon dioxide emissions.

Global warming offers for the entrepreneur some very new significant business opportunities. For example with oil perceived as a finite resource and a source of greenhouse gases, entrepreneurs and some large corporations have turned their attention to renewable resources such as the use of solar, wind and wave power. It should be recognized, however, that in many cases the cost of energy generated from these sources for some years can be expected to be higher than that generated by existing conventional sources such as a gas fired power station. In view of this scenario, some firms in the renewable energy sector might find their best option for the next few years is to focus on marketing their products or services to financially attractive consumers. This is because this group of consumers are in a better financial position to accept higher prices as being the cost of making a personal sacrifice that can contribute to reducing the rate of global warming in the world (Martinot 2006).

In part, due to advances achieved by NASA during the development of power sources for space vehicles, the first area of potentially cost-effective renewable energy new technology which has attracted wide attention is solar power (Caldwell 1994). This technology uses a photovoltaic device to convert sunlight into energy. As well as the benefit that sunlight is a free energy source, the technology has the added attraction that it can be used in remote locations far from utility power grids and as standalone systems in consumer products, such as outdoor lighting, personal electronics, battery chargers and solar roof panels. Like so many new technologies, the initial development of solar power industry was led by university scientists and individual entrepreneurs because major corporations remained unconvinced about the commercial potential for the technology. From these small players have emerged some of the first generation giants within the renewable energy sector.

Solar entrepreneur

Case Aims: To illustrate how one individual has spent a life committed to seeking ways of creating a commercially viable solar energy industry.

One of the pioneers in the field of solar energy is the American Stanford R. Ovshinsky. Born into a poor family in Akron, Ohio in 1923, he was a self taught scientist who led the development of the new science of amorphous and disordered materials. In 1960, along with wife and collaborator, Iris, he founded Energy Conversion Devices, Inc. to exploit science as way of solving serious societal problems in the fields of energy and information. He recognized that the key to successful solar power was to minimize the costs of producing photovoltaic devices. Currently, there are two primary types of device, crystalline systems where a light sensitive film is laid on a clear substrate such as glass and the potentially more complex product in terms of ease of manufacturing, thin film photovoltaic material. Initially crystal-line systems were more popular because they offered lower manufacturing costs and greater durability upon installation. Ovshinsky was attracted to the idea that thin film technology would eventually offer the benefit of being able to manufacture solar cells like rolls of paper which would dramatically reduce production costs and make installation a much easier process. Eventually, he developed the needed advances in materials that permitted him to launch ECD Ovonics to manufacture a low-cost thin film product. Having demonstrated the benefits of the material, other leading players in the industry are moving away from manufacturing crystalline systems and building thin film manufacturing plants.

Exploiting the power of the wind as an energy source is not a new idea. Windmills have existed for hundreds of years for use in tasks such as grinding corn. Probably because of the strong heritage of windmills in Europe, EU countries have tended to favour wind power as the most effective route through which to reduce reliance upon fossil fuels. A major drawback to wind energy, however, has been peoples' adverse reaction to the visual and noise impact of having wind farms built near their homes. To overcome this criticism, plans are now in progress to curtail further development of wind farms on-shore and to build the next generation of wind farms out at sea (Von Jouanne 2006).

There has been mounting criticism over the efficiency of wind generated energy in terms of the construction and ongoing operating costs relevant to electricity generation via more conventional sources such as fossil fuels or natural gas. Hence, some experts favour the greater use of water as a more effective source of renewable energy. Water has been used for many years to power hydro-electric plants and is a critically important economic resource in countries such as Brazil, Canada, Egypt, the USA, Norway and Sweden. Unfortunately, the construction of huge dams and diverting water flow to generate hydro-electricity can be extremely damaging to the environment. Hence, given that the majority of the earth's surface is covered by ocean, there is now increasing interest in using the ocean as an energy generation source. One approach is to exploit tidal power through the construction of tidal barriers which direct the tidal flow through underwater turbines. The viability of this solution is under some doubt, however, because the idea of creating tidal barriers is now facing increasing resistance from environmentalists concerned about the impact on the marine environment of implementing such large scale alterations in the tidal flow. As a result, harnessing the power of the waves is now perceived as a lower cost and environmentally more benign approach to using the oceans as a power generation source.

Wave power entrepreneurs

Case Aims: To illustrate how entrepreneurs are developing solutions that will provide the basis for entirely new sectors within the alternative energy, wave power industry.

A leading innovator in the field of wave power is Pelamis, a Scottish company founded in 1998 by Doctors Yemm, Pizer and Retzler (Thilmany 2008). Their idea is to build a wave energy converter that generates electricity from the movement of ocean waves. Each converter is a semi-submerged, articulated structure composed of cylindrical sections linked by hinged joints. Hydraulic rams resist the wave-induced motion of these joints. The force of that resistance is used to pump high-pressure fluid through hydraulic motors via smoothing accumulators, to drive electrical generators that produce energy. Arrays of these interlinked converters are called wave farms. The electricity that they produce is available for utility and electric companies to purchase. A wave farm of 40 converters, covering a square kilometer of ocean surface, can generate enough electricity to power 20,000 homes. The company has three projects under way, two off the coast of the UK and one near Portugal. Another power generation approach is to use tethered buoys which have turbines that generate electricity as the buoys rise and fall in response to the passing waves (Von

Jouanne 2006). The buoys are connected to a central collection hub on the ocean floor from which the generated electricity is then directed on-shore via an undersea cable. A leading company in this field is US company Ocean Power Technologies. Formed by Doctors Taylor and Burns in 1994, the company has developed their own proprietary PowerBuoy™ technology which captures wave energy using large floating buoys anchored to the sea bed. Ocean trials commenced in 1997 off the coast of New Jersey and full-scale prototypes generating 40 kW of electricity have been installed off Hawaii and New Jersey. The company was floated on the London Stock Exchange's AIM market in October 2003 and completed its US Nasdaq IPO in April 2007. The company has now begun the initial phase of installation of a 1.39 MW wave farm off the northern coast of Spain. This project is a joint venture with the Spanish utility Iberdrola SA. A full size demonstration plant of up to 5 MW capacity is also being planned for installation in UK waters.

The other even more important solution to the problem of greenhouse gases is to reduce emissions from sources which are burning hydro-carbon fuels, such as coal powered power stations and of course, the ubiquitous human toy, the car. In relation to coal, the primary innovators in this area are the big mining companies because unless a solution can be found to reduce emissions, the world coal industry could face a difficult future. Although advances in power station design and the scrubbing of gases emitted from chimneys are improving air quality, there is still need for emissions from coal powered plants to be further reduced. The primary new technology which is being promoted by the energy industry is the capture and under sea storage of carbon dioxide. To-date the claims in the numerous industry PR releases have been much more positive than the actual commercial viability of the technical breakthroughs yet achieved for this new technology (Takeshita and Yamaii 2006).

In the nineteenth century, some early cars were powered by electricity. The weight and poor storage capabilities of electric batteries meant this technology was inferior to the alternative of the internal combustion engine. Although some people believe further developments over the years of the electric car have been blocked due to a conspiracy between the car and oil industry, it is only very recently that the car industry has begun to look at alternative power sources in place of strategies based upon reducing by improving engine efficiency and exhaust systems. Given the costs associated with developing a realistically priced vehicle powered by an alternative energy source that can travel a reasonable distance which can compete with the conventional car, not surprisingly most of the R&D in this field has been undertaken by the major car companies (Soble 2008).

As has frequently been the case in the past 20 years in a number of consumer goods industries, the Japanese are ahead of the Americans in this race. Their first innovative solution was to add electric power to augment a petrol powered vehicle. The first hybrid car to use this approach was the

Toyota Prius. This vehicle was an immediate marketing success in eco-orientated markets such as California. Other car manufacturers outside of Japan have since raced to regain market share which they appear to be losing to their Pacific Rim competitors (Newberry 2001). The primary focus of many firms' research efforts has been on improving the range of the electric car. This has led to a number of companies developing cars equipped with lighter batteries such as an array of lithium cells. The other path of development has been the 'plug in' electric car, which can be recharged by connecting the vehicle to a mains electricity socket. Meanwhile, within and alongside the car industry, work on developing alternative solutions such as the use of hydrogen power cells is also being progressed.

Entrepreneurship

With the world entering a massive economic downturn in 2008/2009, the issue arises of how firms should react in terms of defining a strategic response to the current extremely difficult business conditions. For those organizations with the resources and capability, the best survival option is to adopt an entrepreneurial organizational culture (Slevin and Covin 1990). This will assist firms' focus upon implementing a strategy of exploiting innovation to achieve and sustain superiority over competition.

Part of the rationale for this recommendation concerning innovation is currently that the costs of such activities are lower than at the end of the twentieth century. This has occurred because during a recession, the costs of innovation are reduced across areas such as hiring skilled staff, purchasing capital equipment and, due to reduced market demand for advertising space, implementing promotional programmes. The other dimensional advantage of innovation is that only a few competitors will also adopt this strategy. Consequently, entrepreneurial firms will tend to be unopposed in the marketplace, thereby free to launch new products and services that will attract new users and increase existing customer loyalty.

In recommending the proposed action of investing in innovation, it is also critical that the firm remembers that throughout the twentieth century there have been a number of occasions when an entrepreneurial individual had an idea which eventually led to the creation of a major corporation operating on a global scale. Then along comes another entrepreneur who successfully topples the incumbent from their leadership position. Christensen (1997) has proposed that the downfall of the incumbent is not the fault of the management, but instead the blame lies more with the firm's key customers continuing to push for improvements to existing products. As a result, the market incumbent may be aware of an emerging disruptive technology but is not really in a position to effectively counter the new threat.

There are clearly examples that exist which validate Christensen's hypothesis. Nevertheless, examination of low technology sectors such as the food industry would suggest that only a minority of major company deaths can be explained by the advent of a disruptive technology. Furthermore, the expertise which existed within these major corporations should have permitted reaction to a newly emerging market trend by counter attacking through the establishment of their own operation or alternatively, acquiring the entrepreneurial challenger before they can adversely impact the firm's market position. For example when Canon started to make inroads into the photocopier market with their lower price, desk top machine, Xerox clearly had both the technical expertise and dominant market position which would have permitted them to defeat their new enemy. Similarly, it seems inexplicable why the large multinationals in the branded foods and food service industries did not observe McDonald's early success and immediately move to open their own chain of fast-food outlets. Instead, they appear to have not only ignored the threat posed by Ray Kroc, but also continued to remain on the sidelines even when James McLamore and David Edgerton began to expand out from Miami with their Burger King operation.

Many examples of entrepreneurs defeating incumbent firms seem to be explained by the latter organizations having lost the flexibility and proactive culture upon which their global success had originally been based. There appears to be no one single explanation of why a culture shift towards becoming a conventional, passive and non-innovative organization has occurred. One reason is that senior management may become fixated on believing the strategy which has provided success in the past will continue to serve the company well in the future (Morris *et al.* 2006). This scenario is illustrated by the very common strategic decision among major branded goods companies to continue to seek ways of building market share among the 18–49 year age group in both their domestic markets and subsequently targeting the same consumer market upon their entry into newly developing economies overseas. In the case of these firms' adherence to this strategy in their domestic markets this clearly ignores the reality that for the 18–49 year age group to repay the huge personal debts they have accumulated in recent years means the spending power of this age group will be drastically reduced for the foreseeable future.

Another cause of non-entrepreneurial behaviour is that most individuals in the world of business want a secure and highly paid career. Hence, they soon learn that to progress up the corporate ladder or to be recruited for a senior position in another company, it is important to develop a reputation for being a 'safe pair of hands'. Such individuals can never be expected to exhibit risk to their personal image by being perceived as exhibiting an entrepreneurial talent. The outcome of senior managers being risk avoiders is that many major firms are overtaken, and sometimes totally disappear, because the organization's senior management lacks the leadership skills to respond to the market entry by an entrepreneurial upstart (Hill and Hansen 1991).

Business leaders whose preference is to avoid implementing change or to consider a strategy based upon innovation in the face of the first twenty-first century economic downturn would do well to reflect on Parnell *et al.*'s (2005) review of corporate failure. In this study, they observed that leaders 'should resist the notion that today's source of competitive advantage will be eternal'. Regretfully this type of leaders, as their organization moves from growth into market maturity or need to react to a period of economic adversity, also seem to believe any actions by disruptive younger managers to persuade the business to be more innovative should be discouraged. As a result, younger managers learn to accept the *status quo* to retain their jobs or alternatively, quit and join a more entrepreneurial organization (Amabile *et al.* 1996).

In part, this culture of a conventional, conservative leadership style in large corporations emerged in the late twentieth century because senior managers came to understand there was a need to avoid risk and instead build stable businesses to achieve steady sustained profit growth (Wiseman and Gomez-Mejia 1998). This trend was created because major investors within the financial community such as big pension funds wanted to enjoy ongoing dividend growth and a steady increase in the market value of the company shares which they had purchased. As is all too apparent in the business press, major entities within the financial community now enjoy sufficient power not just to express criticisms about what they perceive as a poorly managed company, but can orchestrate the removal of the incumbent CEO whose decisions they feel are damaging their investment. These financial community experts often go well beyond generating informed performance forecasts and now believe they are qualified to make recommendations on the optimal future strategic direction for the companies in which they are significant investors. This situation means there now exists the very worrying scenario that individuals from the financial community, many of whom have never actually worked in the industrial sector or managed a business, have more influence over the future of a CEO over whom they are passing judgement, than a company's board of directors.

Entrepreneurial opportunities

New technology has been a critical driver in terms of influencing the world economy during the twentieth century. There is no reason to believe that technology will not provide innumerable opportunities for the emergence of new entrepreneurial firms in the twenty-first century, even during periods of economic downturn. Furthermore, some of these technological advances can be expected to lead to the creation of entirely new industrial sectors.

For the next generation of entrepreneurs with the same competencies as a Bill Gates or a Steve Jobs, identifying new opportunities will merely require an intuitive decision about where to focus their endeavours. For less-gifted individuals, the task, however, is somewhat more difficult. Hence, where insightful intuition is lacking, one approach available to the individual or the organization is to evaluate the potential opportunities associated with a new technology by assessing the implications of the market influencing variables of the type summarized in Figure 12.2.

Given the reduced spending power of the traditional 18–49 year age group, it is proposed that the most financially rewarding innovation strategy should be one

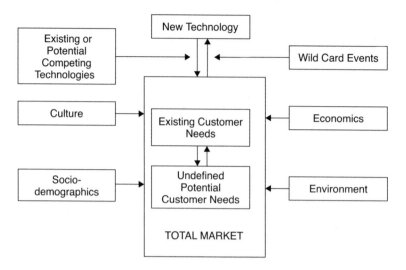

Figure 12.2 Interaction of influencing variables on market need.

based upon the opportunities that can accrue by marketing new products or services to financially attractive consumers such as maturing boomers. Another reason for proposing this orientation is the onset of population ageing that will mean maturing boomers will become the largest consumer group within many countries.

Any new technology will usually have the capability of effectively satisfying the needs of existing customers. More importantly, however, an assessment must be made of whether the new technology offers the usually even greater revenue opportunities associated with satisfying the needs of a yet unidentified group of customers. An example of this scenario is provided by the internet. This technology was initially perceived as an alternative promotional medium and system for supporting online customer purchasing. Hence, few individuals or organizations, except possibly some of the more perceptive futurists, could have predicted how the internet would have such as widespread impact on both numerous industrial processes across various market systems and also stimulate customer culture shifts that have led to the emergence of completely new forms of social interaction and consumer buying behaviour.

To survive, most new technologies have to successfully compete with existing technologies. In most cases, these existing technologies will be utilized by major corporations who have a vested interest in ensuring the failure of the new market entrant. An example of this outcome is provided by the major pharmaceutical firms who, in the early days of biotechnology, were less than supportive towards this alternative approach to the development of new healthcare treatments. Another influencing variable is a wild card event. This is a completely unexpected scenario that acts as a catalyst for increasing the market potential for a new technology. One such example was the sudden 12-month rise in world oil prices in 2007–2008 which acted as a major stimulus concerning market acceptance of hybrid and plug-in electric cars.

Customer acceptance for a new technology will also be influenced by prevailing cultural values. One of the key reasons, for example, for the very rapid growth of the first generation of mobile phones in consumer markets was the unexpectedly strong influence of the product being perceived as a 'must have item' among young people. Market penetration rates for subsequent generations of the product were also greatly assisted by the enthusiasm with which young people then moved into texting and sending pictures.

It can be predicted with some certainty that in a garage or laboratory somewhere in the world there are as yet unrecognized individuals working on new entrepreneurial, high technology ideas which have huge commercial potential. The efforts of some of these individuals will lead to the introduction of a disruptive technology that will permit these entrepreneurs to create new global corporations and in some cases, the creation of entirely new industries. There is a high probability that some of the more market aware existing large corporations are also pursuing the same objective in their own much better resourced laboratories. Where such R&D programmes are not being progressed by the large firms, these organizations still may be able to subsequently gain control of the new technology through a subsequent acquisition of a more successful, smaller firm once this latter organization has validated market demand for their new concept.

In some sectors, the major companies do seem to be satisfied to merely observe and wait. Then should an emerging technology be proven to be commercially viable by a smaller entrepreneur, the larger firms can enter the market by exploiting their technology infrastructure and greater resources to develop an effective competitive response. At the moment, for example, Richard Branson's new enterprise, Virgin Galactic, is working with a small entrepreneurial organization, Burt Rutan's Mojave Aerospace Ventures, to create the world's first commercial system capable of taking private citizens into space. Should this venture prove viable, no doubt existing global aerospace corporations, such as Boeing or BAE, will enter the market. The larger aerospace firms' ability to compete in this market would be further enhanced should the world's military decide to start injecting development funds into the field of low-cost space travel.

New acorns

Case Aims: To illustrate that even in an industry containing successful innovative firms, opportunities still exist for single individuals to launch a highly successful new business.

Once the costs for a recently introduced new technology begin to fall and more firms gain expertise in the field, it is often the case that the leading global players in the sector fail to appreciate that for a relatively small level of incremental expenditure, new ideas can rapidly be converted into successful business concepts. Such, for example, was the case with the social network sites Facebook and YouTube. Facebook was founded by Mark Zuckerberg in 2004 while he was still a student at Harvard University. Initially, membership was limited to college students but then expanded to include anybody who wished to join. The site is free to users and generates revenue from advertising. Although there have been a number of rumours that companies such as News Corporation and Google have sought to acquire the company, to-date Zuckerberg has insisted that he wishes to remain an independent company. Retention of independence has not occurred at YouTube. This enterprise was founded by Chad Hureley, Steve Chen and Jawed Chen who gained their understanding of the dotcom industry as early employees at PayPal. Their initial idea was aimed at assisting local Californian bands and their fans to exchange visual and audio materials via the internet. It only took a few months to develop the necessary website software and the business went live in 2005. By mid-2006, YouTube had become the fifth most visited website in the world. This huge customer base was created mainly by word-of-mouth advertising and by the site providing the conventional media with numerous news stories. In just after 12 months after the launch, the founders sold the company to Google for $1.65 billion.

References

Aldrick, P. and Conway, E. (2008) 'Toxic debt, losses now £1,800 bn. says Bank', *The Daily Telegraph*, London, p. B1.

Amabile, T.M., Conti, R., Coon, H., Lazenby, J. and Herron, M. (1996) 'Assessing the work environment for creativity', *Academy of Management Journal*, Vol. 39, No, 5, pp. 1154–85.

Betti, G., Dourmaskin, N., Rossi, M. and Yin, Y.P. (2007) 'Consumer over-indebtedness in the EU: measurement and characteristics', *Journal of Economic Studies*, Vol. 34, No. 2, pp. 136–47.

Bonini, S. and Oppenheim, J. (2008) 'Cultivating the green consumer', *Stanford Innovation Review*, Vol. 6, No. 4, pp. 56–62.

Brendon, P. (2007) *The Decline And Fall Of The British Empire: 1871–1997*, London: Vintage Books.

Caldwell, J.H. (1994) 'Photovoltaic technology and markets', *Contemporary Economic Policy*, Vol. 12, No. 2, pp. 97–112.

Christen, M. and Morgan, R.M. (2005) 'Keeping up with the Joneses: analysing the effect of income inequality on consumer borrowing', *Quantitative Marketing and Economics*, Vol. 3, No. 2. pp. 145–53.

Christensen, C.M. (1997) *The Innovator's Dilemma*, Boston, MA: Harvard Business School Press.

Dolliver, M. (2008) 'Deflating the myth', *Adweek*, New York, pp. 24–6.

Dyson, T. (2005) 'On development, demography and climate change: the end of the world as we know it?', *Population and Environment*, Vol. 27, No. 2, pp. 117–32.

Fenby, J. (2008) *The Penguin Modern History of China: The Fall And Rise Of A Great Power 1850–2008*, London: Penguin.

Fisk, G. (1974) *Marketing and the Ecological Crisis*, New York: Harper & Row.

Hartley, P.R., Medlock, K.B. and Rosthal, J.E. (2008) 'The relationship of natural gas to oil prices', *Energy Journal*, Vol. 29, No. 3, pp. 47–66.

Hill, W.L. and Hansen, G.S. (1991) 'A longitudinal study of the cause and consequences of change', *Strategic Management Journal*, Vol. 12, No. 3, pp. 187–200.

Karna, J., Hansen, E. and Juslin, H. (2003) 'Social responsibility in environmental planning', *European Journal of Marketing*, Vol. 37, No. 5/6, pp. 848–73.

Kilbourne, W.E. (1995) 'Green advertising: salvation or oxymoron?', *Journal of Advertising*, Vol. 24, No. 2, pp. 7–20.

Malehorn, J. (2008) 'The nation's economic outlook', *Journal of Business Forecasting*, Vol. 27, No. 2, pp. 36–9.

Malhotra, P. and Lofgren, H. (2004) 'India's pharmaceutical industry: hype or high-tech take-off?', *Australian Health Review*, Vol. 28, No. 2, pp. 182–94.

Martinot, E. (2006) 'Renewable energy gains momentum: global markets and policies in the spotlight', *Environment*, Vol. 48, No. 6, pp. 26–45.

Mitchell, A. and Dupre, K. (1994) 'The environmental movement: a status report and implications for pricing', *SAM Advanced Management Journal*, Vol. 59, No. 2, pp. 35–43.

Moeller, J.O. (2008) 'Energy and the environment', *Regional Outlook: Southeast Asia*, Singapore, pp. 74–68.

Morris, M.H., Allen, J., Schindler, M. and Avila, R. (2006) 'Balanced management control systems as a mechanism for achieving corporate entrepreneurship', *Journal of Managerial Issues*, Vol. 18, No. 4, pp. 468–95.

Newberry, J. (2001) 'Duel fuels', *ABA Journal*, Chicago, March, pp. 80–82.

Parnell, J.A., Von Bergen, C.W. and Soper, B. (2005) 'Profiting from past triumphs and failures: harnessing history for future success', *SAM Advanced Management Journal*, Vol. 70, No. 2, pp. 36–47.

Peattie, K. (2001) 'Golden goose or wild goose: the hunt for the green consumer', *Business Strategy and the Environment*, Vol. 10, No. 4, pp. 187–98.

Rees, M. (2008) 'Just the facts', *The International Economy*, Vol. 22, No. 3, pp. 77–81.

Schooley, D.K. and Worden, D.D. (2008) 'A behavioral life-cycle approach to understanding the wealth effect', *Business Economics*, Vol. 43, No. 2, pp. 7–16.

Schwartz, J. and Miller, T. (1991) 'The earth's best friends', *American Demographics*, Vol. 13, pp. 26–35.

Slevin, D.P. and Covin, J. (1990) 'Juggling entrepreneurial style and organizational culture', *Sloan Management Review*, Vol. 31, No. 2, pp. 43–54.

Soble, J. (2008) 'Japan rivals race to catch up with Prius', *Financial Times*, London, 11 June, p. 15.

Takeshita, T. and Yamaii, K. (2006) 'Potential contribution of coal to the future global energy system', *Environmental Economics and Policy Studies*, Vol. 8, No. 1, pp. 55–88.

Thilmany, J. (2008) 'Off shore analysis', *Mechanical Engineering*, Vol. 130, No. 5, pp. 32–6.

Von Jouanne, A. (2006) 'Harvesting the waves', *Mechanical Engineering*, Vol. 128, No. 12, pp. 24–8.

Wiseman, R.N. and Gomez-Mejia, L.R. (1998) 'A behavioral agency model of managerial risk taking', *Academy of Management Review*, Vol. 23, No. 1, pp. 133–54.

Index